IARIA

AA003901

ICN 2018

The Seventeenth International Conference on Networks

SOFTNETWORKING 2018

The International Symposium on Advances in Software Defined Networking and Network Functions Virtualization

April 22 - 26, 2018

Athens, Greece

ICN 2018 Editors

Eugen Borcoci, University "Politehnica" of Bucharest (UPB), Romania
Ioannis D. Moscholios,University of Peloponnese - Tripoli, Greece
Carlo Vitucci, Ericsson, Sweden

Printed from e-media with permission by:

Curran Associates, Inc.
57 Morehouse Lane
Red Hook, NY 12571

Some format issues inherent in the e-media version may also appear in this print version.

Printed by Curran Associates, Inc. (2018)

International Academy, Research, and Industry Association (IARIA)
412 Derby Way
Wilmington, DE 19810

Phone: (408) 893-6407
Fax: (408) 527-6351

petre@iaria.org

Additional copies of this publication are available from:

Curran Associates, Inc.
57 Morehouse Lane
Red Hook, NY 12571 USA
Phone: 845-758-0400
Fax: 845-758-2633
Email: curran@proceedings.com
Web: www.proceedings.com

ICN 2018

Forward

The Seventeenth International Conference on Networks (ICN 2018), held between April 22, 2018 and April 26, 2018 in Athens, Greece, was organized by and for academic, research and industrial partners.

We solicited both academic, research, and industrial contributions. We welcomed technical papers presenting research and practical results, position papers addressing the pros and cons of specific proposals, such as those being discussed in the standard fora or in industry consortia, survey papers addressing the key problems and solutions on any of the above topics short papers on work in progress, and panel proposals.

The conference had the following tracks:

- Communication
- Wireless and Mobile
- New Internet Technologies
- Software defined networking

The conference also featured the following workshop:

- ***SOFTNETWORKING 2018,*** *The International Symposium on Advances in Software Defined Networking and Network Functions Virtualization*

We take here the opportunity to warmly thank all the members of the ICN 2018 technical program committee, as well as all the reviewers. The creation of such a high quality conference program would not have been possible without their involvement. We also kindly thank all the authors who dedicated their time and effort to contribute to ICN 2018. We truly believe that, thanks to all these efforts, the final conference program consisted of top quality contributions.

We also gratefully thank the members of the ICN 2018 organizing committee for their help in handling the logistics and for their work that made this professional meeting a success.

We hope that ICN 2018 was a successful international forum for the exchange of ideas and results between academia and industry and to promote further progress in the field of networks. We also hope that Athens, Greece, provided a pleasant environment during the conference and everyone saved some time to enjoy the historic charm of the city.

ICN 2018 Chairs

ICN Steering Committee

Pascal Lorenz, University of Haute Alsace, France
Carlos Becker Westphall, University of Santa Catarina, Brazil
Tibor Gyires, Illinois State University, USA
Iwona Pozniak-Koszalka, Wroclaw University of Technology, Poland

ICN 2018
Committee

ICN Steering Committee
Pascal Lorenz, University of Haute Alsace, France
Carlos Becker Westphall, University of Santa Catarina, Brazil
Tibor Gyires, Illinois State University, USA
Iwona Pozniak-Koszalka, Wroclaw University of Technology, Poland
Carlos T. Calafate, Technical University of Valencia, Spain
Calin Vladeanu, University Politehnica of Bucharest, Romania
Gary Weckman, Ohio University, USA
Yenumula B. Reddy, Grambling State University, USA
Eric Renault, Institut Mines-Télécom - Télécom SudParis, France
Sherali Zeadally, University of Kentucky, USA

ICN Industry/Research Advisory Committee
Marc Cheboldaeff, Deloitte Consulting GmbH, Germany
Megumi Shibuya, The University of Electro-Communications, Japan
Arslan Brömme, Vattenfall GmbH, Berlin, Germany
Cristian Anghel, Politehnica University of Bucharest, Romania / Pentalog, France
Abdelmajid Khelil, Landshut University of Applied Sciences, Germany

ICN 2018 Technical Program Committee
Alireza Abdollahpouri, University of Kurdistan, Sanandaj, Iran
Hussein Al-Zubaidy, KTH Royal Institute of Technology, Sweden
Cristian Anghel, Politehnica University of Bucharest, Romania / Pentalog, France
Imran Shafique Ansari, Texas A&M University at Qatar (TAMUQ), Qatar
Suayb S. Arslan, MEF University, Istanbul, Turkey
Jocelyn Aubert, Luxembourg Institute of Science and Technology (LIST), Luxembourg
Mehdi Bahrami, Fujitsu Laboratories of America, Sunnyvale, USA
Harald Baier, Hochschule Darmstadt / CRISP, Germany
Katherine Barabash, IBM, Israel
Alcardo Alex Barakabitze, University of Plymouth, UK
Alvaro Barradas, University of Algarve, Portugal
Carlos Becker Westphall, University of Santa Catarina, Brazil
Luis Bernardo, Universidade Nova de Lisboa, Portugal
Robert Bestak, Czech Technical University in Prague, Czech Republic
Patrick-Benjamin Bök, Weidmüller Group, Germany
Fernando Boronat Seguí, Universitat Politecnica de Valencia, Spain
Radoslav Bortel, Czech Technical University in Prague, Czech Republic
Christos Bouras, University of Patras / Computer Technology Institute & Press "Diophantus", Greece
Arslan Broemme, GI BIOSIG - GI e.V., Germany

Carlos T. Calafate, Technical University of Valencia, Spain
Otavio Augusto S. Carpinteiro, Federal University of Itajuba, Brazil
Marc Cheboldaeff, Deloitte Consulting GmbH, Germany
Luiz H. A. Correia, Federal University of Lavras, Brazil
Nivia Cruz Quental, Federal University of Pernambuco (UFPE), Brazil
Sofiane Dahmane, University of Laghouat, Algeria
Alisa Devlic, Huawei Technologies, Kista, Sweden
Fábio Diniz Rossi, Farroupilha Federal Institute of Science, Education and Technology, Brazil
Ali Ebnenasir, Michigan Technological University, USA
Gledson Elias, Federal University of Paraíba (UFPB), Brazil
Qiang Fan, New Jersey Institute of Technology, USA
Pedro Felipe do Prado, Universidade de São Paulo (USP), Brazil
Mário F. S. Ferreira, University of Aveiro, Portugal
Alexander Ferworn, Ryerson University, Canada
Edelberto Franco Silva, Universidade Federal de Juiz de Fora, UFJF, Brazil
Eva Gescheidtova, Brno University of Technology, Czech Republic
Markus Goldstein, Ulm University of Applied Sciences, Germany
Róza Goscien, Wroclaw University of Technology, Poland
Tibor Gyires, Illinois State University, USA
Hiroyuki Hatano, Utsunomiya University, Japan
Tuong Hoang Duc, INRS-EMT | University of Quebec, Canada
Markus Hofmann, Nokia Bell Labs, USA
Jakob Hoydis, Nokia Bell Labs, France
Dragos Ilie, Blekinge Institute of Technology (BTH), Sweden
Kyungtae Kang, Hanyang University, Korea
Andrzej Kasprzak, Wroclaw University of Technology, Poland
Toshihiko Kato, University of Electro-Communications, Japan
Sokratis K. Katsikas, Norwegian University of Science & Technology (NTNU), Norway
Abdelmajid Khelil, Landshut University of Applied Sciences, Germany
Sun-il Kim, North Central College, USA
Wooseong Kim, Gachon University, S. Korea
Pinar Kirci, Istanbul University, Turkey
Wojciech Kmiecik, Wroclaw University of Technology, Poland
Leszek Koszalka, Wroclaw University of Science and Technology, Poland
Francine Krief, Bordeaux INP, France
Rafael Kunst, La Salle University, Brazil
Ruidong Li, National Institute of Information and Communications Technology (NICT), Japan
Feng Lin, University at Buffalo, SUNY, USA
Pascal Lorenz, University of Haute Alsace, France
Ahmed Mahdy, Texas A&M University - Corpus Christi, USA
Zoubir Mammeri, IRIT - Paul Sabatier University, France
Christopher Mansour, Villanova University, USA
Antonio Martín-Montes, Sevilla University, Spain

Boris Miller, Institute for Information Transmission Problems - Russian Academy of Sciences, Moscow, Russia
Mario Montagud Climent, Universitat Politècnica de València (UPV), Spain
Shintaro Mori, Fukuoka University, Japan
Masayuki Murata, Osaka University, Japan
Mahshid R. Naeini, Texas Tech University, USA
Mort Naraghi-Pour, Louisiana State University, USA
Constantin Paleologu, University Politehnica of Bucharest, Romania
Agnieszka Piotrowska, Silesian University of Technology - Gliwice, Poland
Marcial Porto Fernandez, Universidade Estadual do Ceara (UECE), Brazil
Iwona Pozniak-Koszalka, Wroclaw University of Science and Technology, Poland
M. J. Shankar Raman, Indian Institute of Technology Madras, India
Yenumula B. Reddy, Grambling State University, USA
Eric Renault, Institut Mines-Télécom - Télécom SudParis, France
Karim Mohammed Rezaul, Glyndwr University, Wrexham, UK
Imed Romdhani, Edinburgh Napier University, UK
Mohand-Yazid Saidi, L2TI - University of Paris 13, France
Rodrigo Sanches Miani, Universidade Federal de Uberlândia, Brazil
Panagiotis Sarigiannidis, University of Western Macedonia, Greece
Masahiro Sasabe, Nara Institute of Science and Technology, Japan
Narasimha K. Shashidhar, Sam Houston State University, USA
Mohammad Abu Shattal, Western Michigan University, USA
Megumi Shibuya, The University of Electro-Communications, Japan
Dimitrios N. Skoutas, University of the Aegean, Greece
Andrew Snow, Ohio University, USA
Kostas Stamos, University of Patras, Greece
Cristian Stanciu, University Politehnica of Bucharest, Romania
Aaron Striegel, University of Notre Dame, USA
Karthikeyan Subramaniam, Samsung R & D Institute, Bangalore, India
Bruno Tardiole Kuehne, Federal University of Itajuba, Brazil
Manabu Tsukada, University of Tokyo, Japan
Muhammad Mahboob Ur Rahman, Information Technology University (ITU), Lahore, Pakistan
Muhammad Usman, University of Trento, Italy
Robert van der Mei, VU University, Netherlands
Vasilis Ververis, Humboldt-Universität zu Berlin, Germany
Dario Vieira, Efrei-Paris, France
Quoc-Tuan Vien, Middlesex University, UK
Calin Vladeanu, University Politehnica of Bucharest, Romania
Lukas Vojtech, CTU in Prague, Czech Republic
Jingjing Wang, Tsinghua University, China
Ting Wang, Huawei Technologies co. ltd, China
Gary Weckman, Ohio University, USA
Alexander L. Wijesinha, Towson University, USA
Maarten Wijnants, iMinds-EDM-UHasselt, Belgium

Bernd E. Wolfinger, University of Hamburg, Germany
Longfei Wu, Fayetteville State University, USA
Kaiqi Xiong, University of South Florida, USA
Qimin Yang, Harvey Mudd College, USA
Mariusz Żal, Poznan University of Technology, Poland
Sherali Zeadally, University of Kentucky, USA
Ning Zhang, Texas A&M University at Corpus Christi, USA
Yangming Zhao, State University of New York at Buffalo, USA
Bo Zhou, Shanghai Jiao Tong University, China

SOFTNETWORKING Advisory Committee

Eugen Borcoci, University Politehnica of Bucharest, Romania (Chair)
Pedro A. Aranda, Universidad Carlos III - Madrid, Spain
Nicola Ciulli, Nextworks, Italy
Wolfgang John, Ericsson Research, Sweden

SOFTNETWORKING 2018 Technical Program Committee

Pedro A. Aranda, Universidad Carlos III - Madrid, Spain
Robert Bestak, Czech Technical University in Prague, Czech Republic
Eugen Borcoci, University "Politehnica" of Bucharest (UPB), Romania
Cristina Cervelló-Pastor, Universitat Politècnica de Catalunya (UPC), Spain
Nicola Ciulli, Nextworks, Italy
Didier Colle, iMinds - Ghent University, Belgium
Paolo Comi, Italtel S.p.A. - Lecco, Italy
Christian Esteve Rothenberg, University of Campinas (UNICAMP), Brazil
Rung-Hung Gau, National Chiao Tung University, Taiwan
Zhen Jiang, West Chester University, USA
Wolfgang John, Ericsson Research, Sweden
Wolfgang Kiess, DOCOMO Euro-Labs, Germany
Diego Kreutz, University of Luxembourg, Luxembourg
Alf Larsson, Ericsson AB, Sweden
Francesco Longo, University of Messina, Italy
Farnaz Moradi, Ericsson Research, Sweden
Ioannis Moscholios, University of Peloponnese, Greece
Bertrand Pechenot, Acreo Swedish ICT, Sweden
Nicholas Race, Lancaster University, UK
David Rincón, Universitat Politecnica de Catalunya (UPC), Barcelona, Spain
Paolo Secondo Crosta, ITALTEL SPA, Italy
Yuzo Taenaka, University of Tokyo, Japan
Yutaka Takahashi, Kyoto University, Japan
Ricard Vilalta, CTTC, Spain
Carlo Vitucci, Ericsson AB, Sweden
Cong-Cong Xing, Nicholls State University, USA

Copyright Information

Table of Contents

Modeling and Analysis of 5G Full Duplex Wireless Radios

José Marcos Câmara Brito
and Miguel Sílvio André Francisco

Instituto Nacional de Telecomunicações
INATEL
Santa Rita do Sapucaí, Brasil
Email: brito@inatel.br
Email: miguelarcanjo03@gmail.com

Branislav Edgar Feijo Couceiro

Instituto Superior de Tecnologias de Informação e Comunicação
ISUTIC
Luanda, Angola
Email: branislavcouceiro@gmail.com

***Abstract*—In this paper, we propose an analytical Markovian model to compute the performance of a network composed by four radios in a line wireless multihop configuration, with data in only one way, considering four operation modes, with half duplex and full duplex communications and omnidirectional and directional antennas. This kind of network was previously presented in the literature, but its performance has been analyzed only based on simulation. We use the proposed Markovian model to compute the performance of the system considering that no buffer is available on the servers, based on the following performance metrics: throughput, capacity, block probability, drop probability, and the average number of packets in the network. We showed that in a system without buffer the performance of half duplex operation can be better than the performance of full duplex operation in terms of capacity and throughput.**

Keywords–5G; full duplex communications; performance analysis; Markovian models.

I. INTRODUCTION

With the rapid growth of traffic demand in mobile communication networks, the future fifth generation (5G) mobile network is facing considerable challenges in spectral efficiency. 5G is expected to provide 1000-fold throughput of today's 4G [1].

To deal with it, several techniques have been recently developed. Among them, In-Band Full Duplex (IBFD) communications, which enable a device to transmit and receive simultaneously at the same frequency, can potentially double the spectral efficiency [1]. Until very recently, the concept of transmission and reception at the same time and frequency domain IBFD did not seem to be very promising, because of the Self-Interference (SI), which is generated by the transmitter on its own receiver [2]. Fortunately, with the recent advances in interference cancellation techniques [3]–[7], SI can be reduced to acceptable levels.

In order to perform IBFD, a new radio design has been developed. The new radio design differs mostly in the way the SI cancellation is implemented, and also in the number and types of antennas. For example, [8] proposed a radio design with two omnidirectional antennas and [9] proposed a radio design with two directional antennas and one omnidirectional antenna. In [9], Miura and Bandai analyzed the performance of the proposed scheme based only on simulation.

In this paper, we propose a first approximate Markovian analytical model to investigate the performance of the system proposed in [9], considering the same line wireless multihop network with data in only one way.

The remainder of this paper is organized as follows. Section II describes the considered radio design and the network. Section III presents the proposed Markovian model of the network. Section IV derives the performance metrics of interest. Section V presents the numerical results. Finally, the paper concludes in Section VI.

II. NETWORK SCENARIO AND ASSUMPTIONS

We use the proposed network shown in Figure 1, reproduced from [9], to evaluate the radio design in a multihop network. In this network, each node can communicate with its neighbor node and can not do carrier sense from two separated nodes, such as Node S and Node 2 in the figure.

Half duplex nodes cannot transmit and receive simultaneously, while full duplex nodes can.

Omnidirectional antennas transmissions interfere with the anterior neighbor node; for example, Node 2 transmission interferes with Node 1 reception. In this case, only one operation is allowed for a successful transmission. Directional antennas do not have this problem.

We defined the following representations of the transmission possibilities, called operation modes:

- A[Half,Omni]: representation of a conventional node using one omnidirectional antenna to transmit and receive in a half duplex mode.
- B[Full,Omni]: representation of an IBFD node using two omnidirectional antennas, one to transmit and one to receive, as proposed in [8].
- D[Full,Direc]: representation of an IBFD node using two directional Transmission Antennas (TX), TX1 to transmit from 0 to π and TX2 from π to 2π, and one omnidirectional Reception Antenna (RX). TX1 and TX2 cannot be used simultaneously. Therefore, the node can operate in two modes: TX1-RX and TX2-RX. This mode was proposed in [9].
- C[Half,Direc]: representation of the same radio design as proposed in D[Full,Direc], but operating in a half duplex mode.

In Figure 1, we have the transmission processes in the network for each operation mode. The network operation

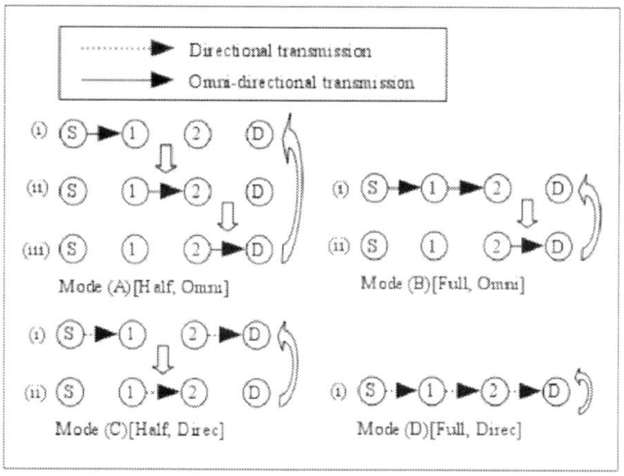

Figure 1. Transmission process for each operation mode [9].

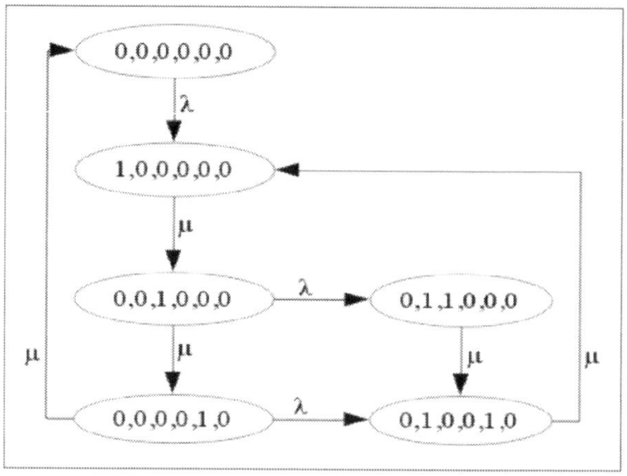

Figure 2. Mode A[Half,Omni] State Diagram.

depends on the type of nodes that it uses, so each network operates differently according to the type of nodes used.

The representation shows how each network should operate in order to achieve the maximum end-to-end throughput.

Figure 1 Mode A[Half,Omni]. In this mode, a transmission from S to D needs three steps to be completed: (i) transmission from S to 1; (ii) transmission from 1 to 2; and (iii) transmission from 2 to D. This is necessary to obtain the maximum end-to-end throughput, because only one node can transmit at a time to avoid interferences since they are not full duplex capable.

Figure 1 Mode B[Full,Omni]. In this case, nodes S and 1 can transmit simultaneously. However, the full duplex operation in node 2 can not be used, because a transmission from node 2 will interfere with the reception of node 1. Thus, in order to obtain the maximum throughput, the pattern (i) and (ii) must be repeated.

Figure 1 Mode C[Half,Direc]. Here, node 2 can transmit simultaneously with node S. However, node 1 can not transmit and receive at the same time, because of the half duplex operation. Thus, in order to obtain the maximum throughput, the pattern (i) and (ii) must be repeated.

Finally, Figure 1 Mode D[Full,Direc]. Here, nodes S, 1 and 2 can transmit simultaneously, due to the full duplex operation and the use of directional antennas.

For each one of these four operation modes, [9] has computed the maximum throughput and, based only on simulation, the throughput and the number of retransmissions as a function of the number of nodes.

The main contribution of this paper is to propose a Markovian model to investigate the performance of the system proposed in [9] in terms of throughput and other performance metrics.

III. Markovian Model

In this section, multidimensional Continuous-Time Markovian Chains (CTMCs) are used to model the system, one for each operation mode. The network consist of 4 nodes and three hops. The last node is the destination, so it does not transmit. Figure 2 shows the state diagram for mode A[Half, Omni]. The same approach is applied to the other modes in order to compute the desired performance metrics.

The transitions in the Markovian model occur due to arrival or departure of a packet in a given node. The arrival processes follow a Poisson distribution with average value λ packets/s; the service time follows an exponential distribution with mean value $1/\mu$ seconds, resulting in a maximum departure rate or service rate equal to μ packets/s.

Finding and solving a Markovian model to evaluate the performance of the presented systems is a complex task. Thus, in order to simplify the model, we considered a system without queue. This assumption could be unrealistic for most applications. However, the results and conclusions obtained using this simplified model is useful to give us some insights about the comparative performance of the systems. A new model, considering a more realistic system, is under construction.

Let $x = \{i, wi, j, wj, k, wk\}$ be the general state representation of the system, where i indicates a transmission in the first hop, wi indicates a packet waiting in the first node, j indicates a transmission in the second hop, wj indicates a packet waiting in the second node, k indicates a transmission in the third hop, and wk indicates a packet waiting in the third node. For example, $x = \{0, 0, 1, 0, 0, 0\}$ represents a state where there is a transmission in the second hop and no packets waiting in the nodes.

Only one packet can be on a server at any given moment. The packet can be in transmission in the proper hop or waiting for transmission. Thus, we have: $i + wi \leq 1; j + wj \leq 1$; and $k + wk \leq 1$. The set of generic feasible states is denoted as $S = \{x | 0 \leq i, wi, j, wj, k, wk \leq 1; 0 \leq i + wi \leq 1; 0 \leq j + wj \leq 1; 0 \leq k + wk \leq 1\}$. More specific sets of feasible states for each mode are presented in Tables I to IV.

To simplify the notation, we considered that the subset {hop, node} denotes a server, so we have three servers: server i $\{i, wi\}$, server j $\{j, wj\}$ and server k $\{k, wk\}$. Only one packet can be in a server at a moment, the packet can be in a state of being transmitted $\{1, 0\}$ or waiting for transmission $\{0, 1\}$; i.e., if $i = 1, wi = 0$ and if $wi = 1, i = 0$, meaning $i + wi$ will never be greater than 1. The same is valid for all other servers.

The stationary probabilities, $\pi(x)$ can be calculated from the global balance equations and the normalization equation, which are given as

$$\pi Q = 0, \sum_{x \in S} \pi(x) = 1. \quad (1)$$

where π is the steady state probability vector and Q denotes the transition rate matrix. The detailed transition rates and conditions for each mode can be found in Tables I to IV below.

The total transition rate from state i to state j, namely q_{ij} is the summation of transition rates from state i to state j considering all possible transitions. Once we determine the q_{ij} for all $i, j (i \neq j) \in S$, the diagonal elements in Q, i.e., q_{ii} $i \in S$ are found as

$$q_{ii} = - \sum_{j \in S, j \neq i} q_{ij}. \quad (2)$$

When the steady state probabilities are determined from (1), the performance of the system can be evaluated with respect to different parameters. The derivations of mathematical expressions for these parameters are presented in the following section.

IV. Performance Metrics

To analyze the performance of the system we considered the following metrics: blocking probability, drop probability, capacity, throughput and the average number of packets in the network.

A. Blocking Probability

The blocking probability, denoted by P, is defined as the probability of the network being in a state where there is a transmission or a packet waiting in the server i and, therefore, no packet can enter the network. This is computed by:

$$P = \sum_{x \in S} \pi(x), \ if \quad i + wi = 1. \quad (3)$$

where P is equal to the summation of all states probabilities where $i + wi = 1$; i.e., there is a packet being transmitted or waiting in the server i.

B. Capacity

The capacity, denoted by C, is defined as the average number of successful transmissions per time unit. This is computed by:

$$C = \sum_{x \in S} \pi(x) \mu, \ if \quad k = 1. \quad (4)$$

where $k = 1$ represents a transmission from server k to destination node, that is a successful transmission, and μ represents the maximum departure rate in server k.

C. Drop Probability

The drop probability, denoted by D, is defined as the probability that once a packet enters the network, it doesn't complete the transmission with success, meaning it is dropped. This is computed by:

$$D = 1 - ST. \quad (5)$$

where Successful Transmission (ST) is the probability that once a packet enters the network, it completes the transmission with success. This is computed by:

$$ST = \frac{C}{\lambda(1-P)}. \quad (6)$$

where C is the capacity, and $\lambda(1-P)$ represents the average number of packet that enter in the network.

D. Throughput

The throughput, denoted by Th, is defined as the relation between the successful transmission rate by the total arrival rate in the network and can be computed by:

$$Th = \frac{C}{\lambda}. \quad (7)$$

E. Average Number of Packets in the System

Let $N(x)$ represent the sum $i + wi + j + wj + k + wk$ in each state. The average number of packets in the system can be computed by:

$$Eq = \sum_{x \in S} \pi(x) N(x). \quad (8)$$

V. Numerical Results

In this section, we present the performance analysis of the four modes described in Section II. All computation was done in MatLab using the analytical model proposed in this paper. To compute the performance metrics, we set the arrival rate λ varying from 1 to 10 packets/s and the maximum departure rate μ equal to 10 packets/s.

The goal of this paper is to compare the performance of half and full duplex systems. Thus, the channel is considered error free. In addition, it is important to note that the performance parameters used in the paper are normalized and, therefore, depend only on the utilization factor (λ/μ) and not on the actual data rate in the channel.

Figure 3 illustrates that the mode A[Half,Omni] has the greater blocking probability because only one server can transmit at a time and also because, while a packet does not reach the end of the network, no other packet can enter the network. The mode D[Full,Direc] has the lowest block probability due to the fact that a new packet can enter into the network at any moment (if server i is empty). The B[Full,Omni] and C[Half,Direc] modes have almost the same blocking probability.

In Figure 4, we can observe that the mode A[Half,Omni] has no drop probability. This is because only one packet can be transmitted in the network at a time. The B[Full,Omni] and D[Full,Direc] modes have the greater drop probability because they use full duplex transmission, meaning a server can receive and transmit at the same time, but a packet is dropped if it is received when the server is still transmitting, due to the absence of queue positions in the servers.

Figure 5 and Figure 6 show that mode C[Half,Direc] has the best performance in terms of capacity and throughput. This result is due to the high drop probability of mode D, compared with mode C. Finally, Figure 7 shows the average number of packets in the system. Again, in this case, mode D[Full,Direc] has the best performance.

TABLE I. TRANSITION RATES AND CONDITIONS FOR MODE A[HALF, OMNI]
$S = \{x|0 \leq i, wi, j, k \leq 1; wj = 0; wk = 0; 0 \leq i + wi \leq 1; 0 \leq i + j + k \leq 1; \}$

Activity	Dest. State	Trans. Rate	Condition
Packet arrival (PA). No transmission in all network.	$i+1, wi, j, wj, k, wk$	λ	$i = 0; wi = 0; j = 0; wj = 0; k = 0; wk = 0.$
Transmission in server j or k. PA and goes to Server i waiting position.	$i, wi+1, j, wj, k, wk$	λ	$i = 0; bi = 0; j + k = 1; bj = 0; wk = 0$.
Transmission from server i to j.	$i-1, wi, j+1, wj, k, wk$	μ	$i = 1; wi = 0; j = 0; wj = 0; k = 0, wk = 0.$
Transmission from server j to k.	$i, wi, j-1, wj, k+1, wk$	μ	$i = 0; 0 \leq wi \leq 1; j = 1; wj = 0; k = 0; wk = 0$.
Transmission from server k to destination.	$i, wi, j, wj, k-1, wk$	μ	$i = 0; wi = 0; j = 0; wj = 0; k = 1; wk = 0$.
Transmission from server k to destination. Packet in server i waiting position is moved to transmission position.	$i+1, wi-1, j, wj, k-1, wk$	μ	$i = 0; wi = 1; j = 0; wj = 0; k = 1; wk = 0$.

TABLE II. TRANSITION RATES AND CONDITIONS FOR MODE B[FULL, OMNI]
$S = \{x|0 \leq i, wi, j, k, wk \leq 1; wj = 0; 0 \leq i + wi \leq 1; 0 \leq k + wk \leq 1; 0 \leq i + j + k \leq 2; 0 \leq wi + wk \leq 1\}$

Activity	Dest. State	Trans. Rate	Condition
Packet arrival (PA).	$i+1, wi, j, wj, k, wk$	λ	$i = 0; wi = 0; 0 \leq j \leq 1; wj = 0; k = 0; wk = 0$
Transmission in server k. PA and goes to Server i waiting position.	$i, wi+1, j, wj, k, wk$	λ	$i = 0; wi = 0; 0 \leq j \leq 1; wj = 0; k = 1; wk = 0$
Transmission from server i to j.	$i-1, wi, j+1, wj, k, wk$	μ	$i = 1; wi = 0; j = 0; wj = 0; k = 0; wk = 0$
Transmission from server j to k.	$i, wi, j-1, wj, k+1, wk$	μ	$i = 0; wi = 0; j = 1; wj = 0; k = 0; wk = 0$
Transmission from server k to destination.	$i, wi, j, wj, k-1, wk$	μ	$i = 0; wi = 0; 0 \leq j \leq 1; wj = 0; k = 1; wk = 0$
Transmission from server j to server k waiting position, because server i is also transmitting.	$i, wi, j-1, wj, k, wk+1$	μ	$i = 1; wi = 0; j = 1; wj = 0; k = 0; wk = 0$
Blocked transmission from server i to j, when both servers are transmitting and server i is the first to finish.	$i-1, wi, j, wj, k, wk$	μ	$i = 1; wi = 0; j = 1; wj = 0; k = 0; wk = 0$
Transmission from server k to destination. Packet in server i waiting position is moved to transmission position.	$i+1, wi-1, j, wj, k-1, wk$	μ	$i = 0; wi = 1; 0 \leq j \leq 1; wj = 0; k = 1; wk = 0$
Transmission from server i to j. Packet in server k waiting position is moved to transmission position.	$i-1, wi, j+1, wj, k+1, wk-1$	μ	$i = 1; wi = 0; j = 0; wj = 0; k = 0; wk = 1$
Blocked transmission from server j to k, when both servers are transmitting and server j is the first to finish.	$i, wi, j-1, wj, k, wk$	μ	$i = 0; 0 \leq wi \leq 1; j = 1; wj = 0; k = 1; wk = 0$

TABLE III. TRANSITION RATES AND CONDITIONS FOR MODE C[HALF, DIREC]
$S = \{x|0 \leq i, wi, j, wj, k \leq 1; wk = 0; 0 \leq i + wi \leq 1; 0 \leq j + wj \leq 1; 0 \leq i + j + k \leq 2; 0 \leq wi + wj \leq 1\}$

Activity	Dest. State	Trans. Rate	Condition
Packet arrival (PA).	$i+1, wi, j, wj, k, wk$	λ	$i = 0; wi = 0; j = 0; 0 \leq wj, k \leq 1; wk = 0$
Transmission in server j. PA and goes to Server i waiting position.	$i, wi+1, j, wj, k, wk$	λ	$i = 0; wi = 0; j = 1; wj = 0; k = 0; wk = 0$
Transmission from server i to j.	$i-1, wi, j+1, wj, k, wk$	μ	$i = 1; wi = 0; j = 0; wj = 0; k = 0; wk = 0$
Transmission from server j to k.	$i, wi, j-1, wj, k+1, wk$	μ	$i = 0; wi = 0; j = 1; wj = 0; k = 0; wk = 0$
Transmission from server j to k. Packet in server i waiting position is moved to transmission position.	$i+1, wi-1, j-1, wj, k+1, wk$	μ	$i = 0; wi = 1; j = 1; wj = 0; k = 0; wk = 0$
Blocked transmission from server i to j, because server j waiting position is occupied.	$i-1, wi, j, wj, k, wk$	μ	$i = 1; wi = 0; j = 0; wj = 1; k = 1; wk = 0$
Transmission from server k to destination.	$i, wi, j, wj, k-1, wk$	μ	$0 \leq i \leq 1; wi = 0; j = 0; wj = 0; k = 1; wk = 0$
Transmission from server k to destination. Server j has a packet waiting but can not transmit because server i is also transmitting.	$i, wi, j, wj, k-1, wk$	μ	$i = 1; wi = 0; j = 0; wj = 1; k = 1; wk = 0$
Transmission from server i to server j waiting position, because server k is also transmitting.	$i-1, wi, j, wj+1, k, wk$	μ	$i = 1; wi = 0; j = 0; wj = 0; k = 1; wk = 0$
Transmission from server k to destination. Packet in server j waiting position is moved to transmission position.	$i, wi, j+1, wj-1, k-1, wk$	μ	$i = 0; wi = 0; j = 0; wj = 1; k = 1; wk = 0$
Blocked transmission from server i to j, because server j waiting position is occupied. Packet on server j waiting position is moved to transmission position.	$i-1, wi, j+1, wj-1, k, wk$	μ	$i = 1; wi = 0; j = 0; wj = 1; k = 0; wk = 0$

TABLE IV. TRANSITION RATES AND CONDITIONS FOR MODE D[FULL, DIREC]
$S = \{x|0 \leq i, j, k \leq 1; wi = 0; wj = 0; wk = 0; 0 \leq i + j + k \leq 3\}$

Activity	Dest. State	Trans. Rate	Condition
Packet arrival (PA).	$i+1, wi, j, wj, k, wk$	λ	$i = 0; wi = 0; 0 \leq j \leq 1; wj = 0; 0 \leq k \leq 1; wk = 0$
Transmission from server i to j.	$i-1, wi, j+1, wj, k, wk$	μ	$i = 1; wi = 0; j = 0; wj = 0; 0 \leq k \leq 1; wk = 0$
Transmission from server j to k.	$i, wi, j-1, wj, k+1, wk$	μ	$0 \leq i \leq 1; wi = 0; j = 1; wj = 0; k = 0; wk = 0$
Blocked transmission from server i to j, when both servers are transmitting and server i is the first to finish.	$i-1, wi, j, wj, k, wk$	μ	$i = 1; wi = 0; j = 1; wj = 0; 0 \leq k \leq 1; wk = 0$
Transmission from server k to destination.	$i, wi, j, wj, k-1, wk$	μ	$0 \leq i \leq 1; wi = 0; 0 \leq j \leq 1; wj = 0; k = 1; wk = 0$
Blocked transmission from server j to k, when both servers are transmitting and server j is the first to finish.	$i, wi, j-1, wj, k, wk$	μ	$0 \leq i \leq 1; wi = 0; j = 1; wj = 0; k = 1; wk = 0$

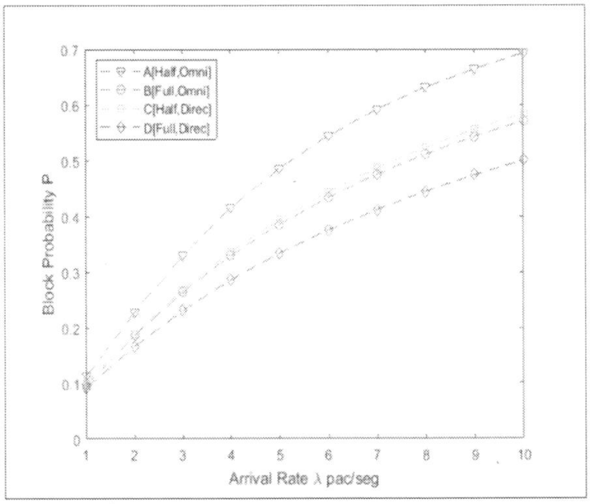

Figure 3. Blocking Probability.

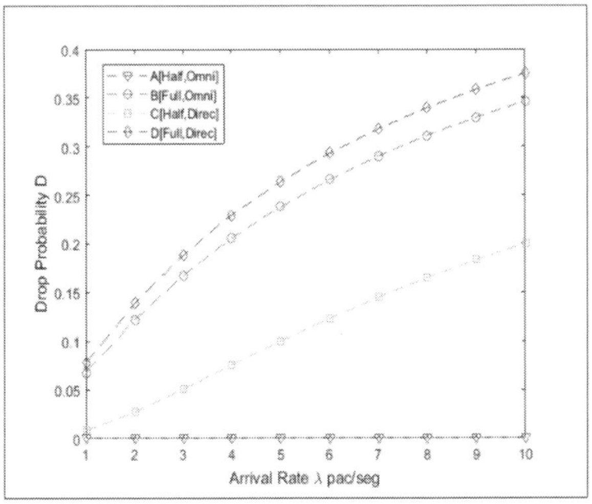

Figure 4. Drop Probability.

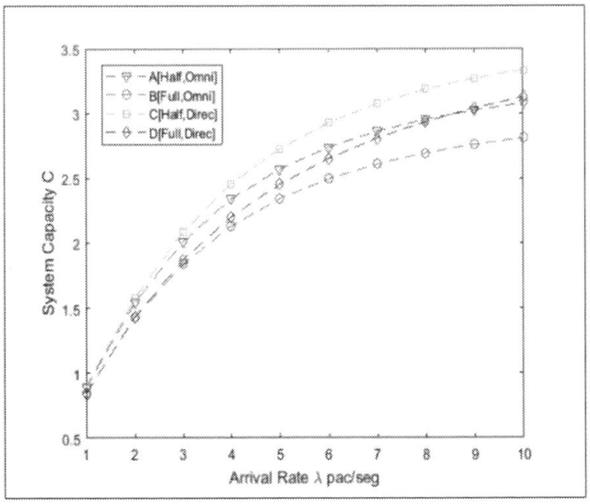

Figure 5. Capacity.

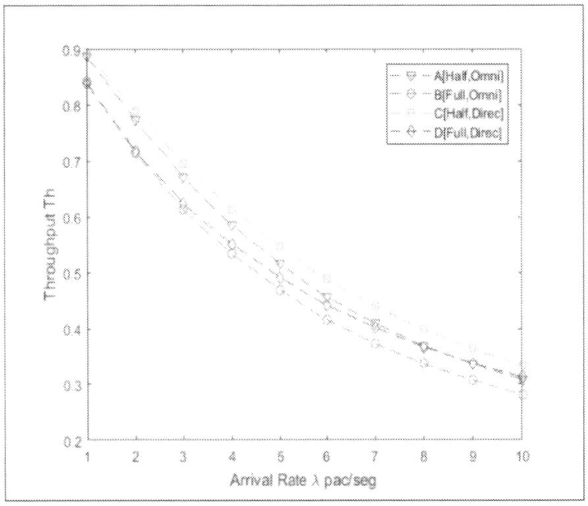

Figure 6. Throughput.

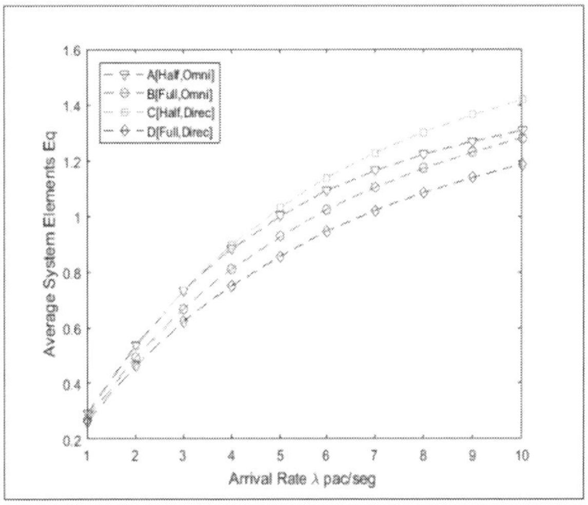

Figure 7. Average Number of packets in the System.

VI. CONCLUSION

In this paper, we presented a first approximate Markovian analytical model to evaluate the performance of four operation modes in a line wireless multihop network, considering half and full duplex operations and omnidirectional and directional antennas, including a new IBFD mode proposed in [9], where this mode was analyzed based only on simulation.

We considered a scenario with no buffer (no queue in the servers). In this scenario, we conclude that the use of full duplex operation with directional antennas mode has the best performance in terms of blocking probability and the average number of packets in the system and the mode using half duplex operation with directional antennas has the best performance in terms of capacity and throughput.

For future works, we intend to analyze the performance of a system considering buffer (queues) in the servers.

Acknowledgment

This work was partially supported by Finep, with resources from Funttel, Grant No. 01.14.0231.00, under the Radiocommunication Reference Center (Centro de Referência em Radiocomunicações - CRR) project of the National Institute of Telecommunications (Instituto Nacional de Telecomunicações - Inatel), Brazil.

References

[1] M. Heino et al., "Recent advances in antenna design and interference cancellation algorithms for in-band full duplex relays," IEEE Communications Magazine, vol. 53, no. 5, 2015, pp. 91–101.

[2] K. M. Thilina, H. Tabassum, E. Hossain, and D. I. Kim, "Medium access control design for full duplex wireless systems: challenges and approaches," IEEE Communications Magazine, vol. 53, no. 5, 2015, pp. 112–120.

[3] M. S. Amjad and O. Gurbuz, "Linear Digital Cancellation with Reduced Computational Complexity for Full-Duplex Radios," in Wireless Communications and Networking Conference (WCNC). IEEE, 2017, pp. 1–6.

[4] E. Ahmed and A. M. Eltawil, "All-digital self-interference cancellation technique for full-duplex systems," IEEE Transactions on Wireless Communications, vol. 14, no. 7, 2015, pp. 3519–3532.

[5] X. Huang and Y. J. Guo, "Radio Frequency Self-Interference Cancellation With Analog Least Mean-Square Loop," IEEE Transactions on Microwave Theory and Techniques, vol. 65, no. 9, 2017, pp. 3336–3350.

[6] M. S. Sim et al., "Nonlinear self-interference cancellation for full-duplex radios: From link-level and system-level performance perspectives," IEEE Communications Magazine, vol. 55, no. 9, 2017, pp. 158–167.

[7] Y. Liu et al., "A Full-Duplex Transceiver With Two-Stage Analog Cancellations for Multipath Self-Interference," IEEE Transactions on Microwave Theory and Techniques, vol. 65, no. 12, 2017, pp. 5263–5273.

[8] M. Jain et al., "Practical, real-time, full duplex wireless," in Proceedings of the 17th annual international conference on Mobile computing and networking. ACM, 2011, pp. 301–312.

[9] K. Miura and M. Bandai, "Node architecture and MAC protocol for full duplex wireless and directional antennas," in Personal Indoor and Mobile Radio Communications (PIMRC), 23rd International Symposium on. IEEE, 2012, pp. 369–374.

Fundamental Analysis for Cooperative Reception Scheme using Mobile Aerial Base Stations in Wireless Sensor Networks

Shintaro Mori
Department of Electronics Engineering and Computer Science
Fukuoka University
8-19-1, Nanakuma, Jonan-ku, Fukuoka 814-0180, Japan
e-mail: smori@fukuoka-u.ac.jp

Abstract—**The Internet of Things (IoT) and emerging wireless sensor networks (WSNs) have been widely adopted in various fields and are attracting attention. In addition, low power wide area (LPWA) technologies have shown great advances and are applicable to IoT and WSN solutions. LPWA-based WSNs are effective when wireless data transmissions are sent at long periodic time intervals. However, vast amounts of forwarding data cannot be handled due to collision and congestion. To overcome this technical issue, in this paper, we propose a novel cooperative (hybrid) reception scheme using mobile aerial base stations (MBSs) mounted on unmanned aerial vehicles (UAVs). Moreover, we fundamentally demonstrate that the proposed mechanism can improve frame-reception probability based on exhaustive computer simulation. As a result, the proposed scheme achieves up to 8.32-times better performance than a comparable scheme without using MBSs.**

Keywords-wireless sensor network; unmanned aerial vehicle; low power wide area network; mobile aerial base station

I. Introduction

As one of the fastest growing technologies, the Internet of Things (IoT) promises to revolutionize the way we live and work, and advanced wireless sensor network (WSN) systems have become technically easy to build in the past several years. With this background, there is great potential to meet the huge demands for IoT systems. However, major challenges remain, such as the tradeoff between low energy consumption and extensive wireless area coverage. Notably, typical sensor node (SN) devices have become tiny and cheap, including resource-constrained processing modules and small batteries with a limited energy budget [1].

To construct a long-lived WSN system, most studies adopt such measures as cooperative communication techniques, network coding schemes, clustering mechanisms, and so on. On the other hand, other solutions require the emergence of a new-type of architecture. Low power wide area (LPWA) network [2][3] techniques represent a novel wireless network paradigm that complements traditional cellular and short-range wireless communications in addressing the diverse requirements of IoT applications. These techniques include, for example, long-range wide area network (LoRa WAN) [4], Sigfox [5], and narrowband IoT (NB-IoT) [6].

A variety of LPWA technologies can provide the means to sense and collect environmental data anywhere and anytime: several kilometers-order coverage areas, narrowband channel occupancy, periodical transmission, and the unsophisticated physical (PHY) and media access control (MAC) protocols. In fact, at the PHY layer, a low-bit-rate and noise-robust modulation scheme, such as the binary phase shift keying (BPSK) method and the (Gaussian) frequency shift keying ((G)FSK) method, is typically used. In addition, LPWA systems commonly use the radio frequency of sub-GHz bands, such as 915 MHz for the USA, 868 MHz for the EU, and 920 MHz for Japan. Furthermore, at the MAC layer, a pure-ALOHA procedure is commonly adopted, where data are sent if a node has data to send, collisions occur when any new data are released while any node is transmitting, and both of these data are lost. To investigate the effectiveness of LPWA systems, Adelantado et al. [7] surveyed the capabilities and limitations of LoRa WAN systems. Bor et al. [8] experimentally demonstrated that the current LPWA scheme could not provide sufficient performance for typical smart city deployment, that is, 120 nodes per 0.038 km^2. At the same time, conventional LPWA-based WSN systems can operate effectively even if the PHY and MAC protocols are constructed by a simple procedure that only requires data transmitted at a sufficiently long-interval for uploading requests. However, in the near-future, we cannot expect vast amounts of forwarding data to be handled based on a traditional scheme due to collision and congestion.

In this paper, as a way to overcome this technical issue, we propose a novel cooperative (hybrid) reception scheme by using mobile aerial base stations (MBSs) mounted on unmanned aerial vehicles (UAVs), such as drones and small planes [9][10]. The goal of this paper is to present a fundamental analysis technique for improving the probability of frame reception. Its performance for UAV-mounted MBSs in LPWA-based WSNs is still unknown. Nevertheless, our study shows significant results from our preliminary analysis.

Regarding related studies, Li and Cai [11] proposed an MBS-based offloading mechanism for solving the problem of increased traffic volume in heterogeneous cellular networks. Sharma et al. [12] investigated the same concept, but they proposed a user-driven MBS deployment scheme. For the MBS placement's and UAV trajectory's decision formula, Lyu et al. [13] proposed a placement algorithm to minimize the number of MBSs needed to provide wireless coverage. Furthermore, Mozaffari et al. [14] and Alzenad [15] expanded the technique of Lyu et al. [13] for the 3D location scenario. On the other hand, another study of Mozaffari et al. [16] investigated a topic similar to that taken up in this paper. In that work, they did not take into account the MAC protocol design, and their simulation was conducted under a traditional

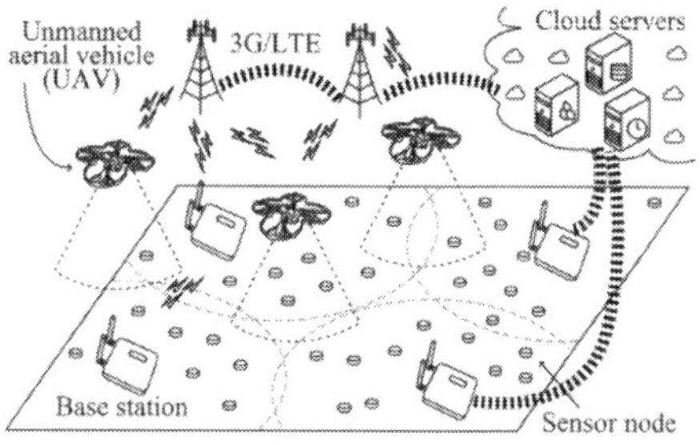

Figure 1. Network model of proposed scheme

WSN usage, with the radio frequency set to the 2-GHz industry science medical (ISM) band and 500 SNs distributed over a 1 km^2 area. — In the proposed scheme, the radio frequency is set to 920 MHz (i.e., a sub-GHz band) and up to 500,000 SNs are distributed.

The remainder of this paper is organized as follows. Section II describes the proposed scheme. Section III provides computer simulation result. Finally, in Section IV, we summarize our findings and conclude the paper.

II. Proposed Scheme

In the proposed scheme (Figure 1), the SNs periodically transmit the sensing data, which their neighbor base stations (BSs) receive and forward to the cloud servers. In addition, the UAV flies at the edge of the cell coverage area, which offers a poor radio-propagation environment, as well as the gap area outside the BSs' coverage range and the hotspot area where the sensing data are generated at a greater rate than in the surrounding area. We assume that BSs, MBSs, and cloud servers are ideally connected with each other through mobile cellular networks, and we focus on the wireless links between SNs and BSs and between SNs and MBSs. Moreover, the BSs and MBSs are provided with sufficient power supply, while the SNs have a strictly limited battery capacity, since the battery exchange cost is non-remunerative and relatively expensive due to use of cheap hardware devices. Therefore, ensuring sophisticated and intelligent transmission control in the SN device is not realistic. In other words, the proposed concept using UAV-mounted MBSs that cooperatively operate with legacy BSs at the receiver side might be a reasonable idea.

In the rest of this section, we explain how to improve the frame-reception probability by using the proposed mechanism. As shown in Figure 2 (a), we assume that three SN devices ($\mathbb{A}$, $\mathbb{B}$, and $\mathbb{C}$) are deployed within the BS's coverage cell, where $\mathbb{A}$ and $\mathbb{B}$ are located at the same distance from the BS while $\mathbb{C}$ is located in the cell-edge area at a farther distance, and that the UAV aviates in the border region between adjacent cells. In this case, as shown in Figure 2 (b), we assume three MAC procedure scenarios: typical transmission, collision occurring in the hotspot, and long-distance data transmission in the cell-edge region. We found that the proposed scheme can work effectively in the latter two scenarios.

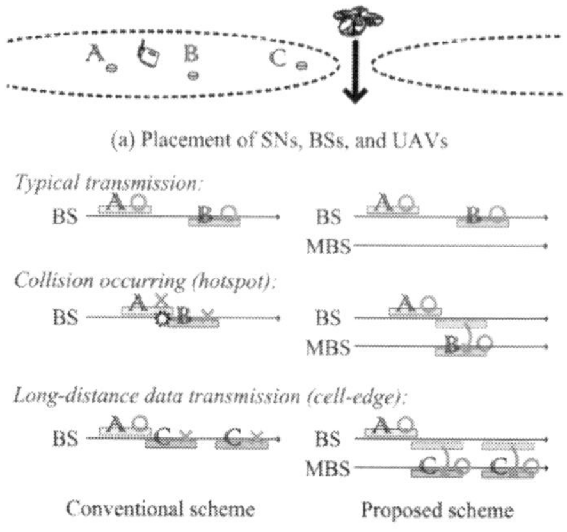

Figure 2. Typical scenarios in which proposed scheme operates

For the typical transmission and collision occurring in the hotspot scenario, the conventional LPWA-based WSN system works without causing collisions due to its sparse channel allocation requests. According to the increased SN, in Figure 2 (b), $\mathbb{B}$ tries to send its frame while $\mathbb{A}$ transmits its own frame; consequently, both $\mathbb{A}$'s frame and $\mathbb{B}$'s frame are lost due to the pure-ALOHA feature. In this situation, their frames should be retransmitted after random back-off time, which might contribute to additional frame collisions. In the proposed scheme, if the MBS's channel were by chance not busy and $\mathbb{B}$'s frame could be moved from the BS to the MBS, both frames might be successfully transferred. Here, among $\mathbb{A}$, $\mathbb{B}$, BSs, and MBSs, the wireless links are selected in the shared radio frequency band. On the other hand, $\mathbb{B}$ sends its frame via an exclusive radio channel different from that for $\mathbb{A}$'s frame. Hence, we can assume that $\mathbb{A}$ and $\mathbb{B}$ can be communicated with BSs and MBSs without interference.

For long-distance data transmission in the cell-edge scenario, $\mathbb{C}$'s frame request does not fatally affect $\mathbb{A}$'s frame transmission. In other words, $\mathbb{C}$'s frame is inevitably lost regardless of the scenario. In the proposed scheme, since MBSs can collect the cell-edge node's frame, such as $\mathbb{C}$'s frame, the overall frame-reception probability can be improved.

The proposed scheme does not check the availability of the MBS channel in order to avoid system complexity for the SN device; instead, we consider compatibility with the traditional LPWA's MAC protocol like the pure-ALOHA procedure. On the other hand, to further improve throughput, we should introduce an intelligent frequency-sharing mechanism for use among SNs, BSs, and MBSs: This remains our important future work.

III. Computer Simulation

In this section, we demonstrate the fundamental performance of our proposed mechanism, i.e., the ability to improve frame-reception probability, using an exhaustively prepared computer simulator implemented in C++ language.

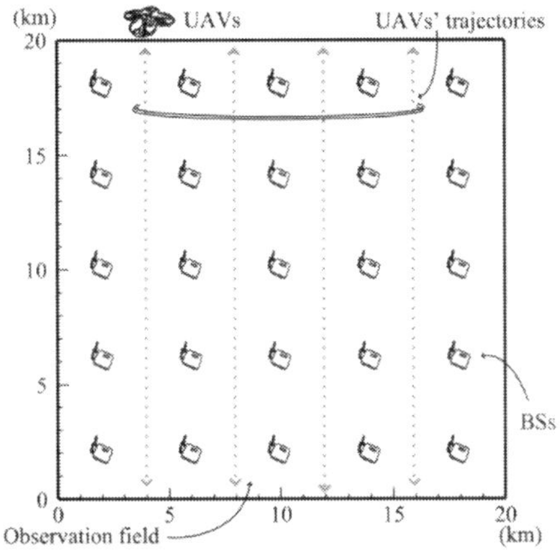

Figure 3. Deployment and trajectory of SNs, BSs, and MBSs (UAVs)

A. Simulation model

In the computer simulation model (Figure 3), BSs are deployed in the lattice (grid) pattern, MBSs (on UAVs) aviate between BSs, and SNs are randomly scattered over the surface of the observation area. We assume that the UAVs can aviate at all times by changing to alternate aircraft along the given fixed trajectory (red line in Figure 3). The detailed simulation parameters are summarized in Table I. Individual SNs generate the sensing data with equal frequency, and the parameter settings of the MAC layer are set based on the Japanese LoRa WAN specifications [17]. For frame reachability, we calculate the received signal-to-noise ratio (SNR) based on the manner described in Section III.B, and we compare the obtained SNR with the required SNR based on the manner given in Section III.C.

B. Radio propagation model

In our computer simulation, we calculated the receiver side's signal strength based on the distance between the transmitter side and the receiver side. According to the typical link budget formula [18], the received signal strength in decibel can be calculated as

$$P_{\mathrm{RX}} = P_{\mathrm{TX}} - L_{\mathrm{TX}} + G_{\mathrm{TX}} - L_{\mathrm{P}}(d) + G_{\mathrm{RX}} - L_{\mathrm{RX}} \,, \qquad (1)$$

where, at the transmitter and receiver sides, respectively, P_{TX} and P_{RX} denote electrical radio powers, L_{TX} and L_{RX} denote electrical power loss in the physical circuit and impedance mismatching, and G_{TX} and G_{RX} denote antenna gains.

In (1), $L_{\mathrm{P}}(d)$ denotes radio propagation loss, and it can generally be represented as

$$L_P(d) = \alpha + 10 \cdot \beta \cdot \log_{10}(d) + \mathcal{S} \,, \qquad (2)$$

where d denotes the distance between terminals, $\mathcal{S}$ denotes shadowing variation, and both α and β are given by individual radio propagation models. In this paper, we select the model of Erceg et al. [19] for the link between SNs and BSs and the model of Amorim et al. [20] for the link between SNs and MBSs. These models were formulated based on experimental measurements, and we separately used them by considering the difference between line-of-sight (LOS) propagation (for SNs-MBSs) and non-LOS (NLOS) propagation (for SNs-BSs).

TABLE I. SIMULATION PARAMETERS

Terms		Values
Observation area		Square, 20 km × 20 km
Sensor node	Number of SNs	1,000–500,000
	Trans. interval	1,200 s (= 20 min.)
Base station	Number of BSs	25
	Antenna height	$h_{\mathrm{BS}} = 50.0$ m
UAV	Number of aircrafts	20
	Altitude	120 m
	Velocity	5.56 m/s (= 20 km/hr.)
MAC layer	Protocol	pure ALOHA
	Number of channels	3
	Transmission time	4 s
	Max retrans. num.	3
	Max back-off time	30 s
	Frame length	$\ell = 50$ byte (= 400 bit)
	Req. frame error prob.	$P_{\mathrm{e}} = 0.5$ %, 1 %, 2 %, 5 %
PHY layer	Modulation method	BPSK, Binary FSK
	Error control coding	NA
	Radio frequency	920 MHz ($\lambda = 0.326$ m)
	Channel model	Rayleigh fading
	Radio-propagation model	Erceg's model (SN–BS) Amorim's model (SN–UAV)
Parameters of Erceg's model (Flat surface ground, light tree density)		$a = 3.6$, $b = 0.005$, $c = 20.0$, $\varepsilon = 0.59$, $d_0 = 100$ m, $\mu_{\mathcal{S}} = 8.2$, $\sigma_{\mathcal{S}} = 1.6$
Parameters of Amorim's model		$\sigma_{\mathcal{S}} = 3.4$
Link-budget constant parameters	Transmission power	$P_{\mathrm{TX}} = 13.0$ dBm (20 mW)
	Antenna gain	$G_{\mathrm{TX}} = 0$ dBi, $G_{\mathrm{RX}} = 3.53$ dBi
	Circuit loss	$L_{\mathrm{TX}} = L_{\mathrm{RX}} = 0$ dB

Consequently, the parameters of α, β, and $\mathcal{S}$ in (2) can be characterized as follows:

Erceg et al.'s model: $\mathcal{S}$ is a random variable with normal distribution of $\mathcal{N}(\mu_{\mathcal{S}}, \sigma_{\mathcal{S}}^2)$, and both α and β can be calculated as

$$\begin{cases} \alpha = 20\log_{10}(4\pi d_0/\lambda) \,, \\ \beta = (a - bh_{\mathrm{BS}} + c/h_{\mathrm{BS}}) + \varepsilon \cdot z \,, \end{cases} \qquad (3)$$

where h_{BS} denotes the antenna height of BS, λ denotes the carrier radio wavelength, and a, b, c, d, and ε denote the constant values depending on the surrounding environment [19]. In addition, z is a random variable with a normal distribution of $\mathcal{N}(0, 1)$.

Amorim's model: $\mathcal{S}$ is a random variable with normal distribution of $\mathcal{N}(0, \sigma_{\mathcal{S}}^2)$, and both α and β are given by $\alpha = 35.3$ and $\beta = 2.0$, depending on the UAV altitude [20].

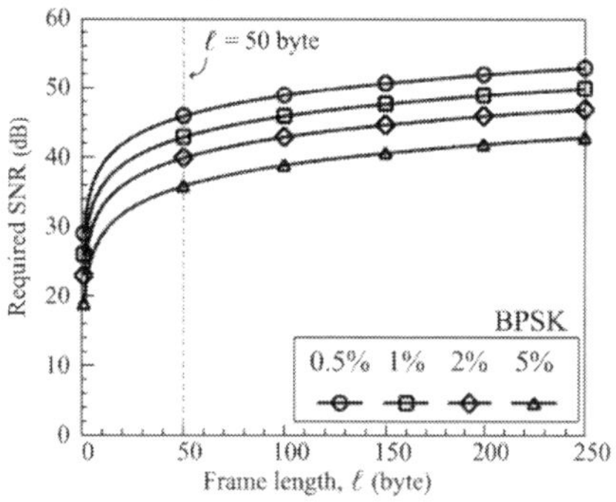

Figure 4. Frame length, ℓ, versus required SNR for BPSK method

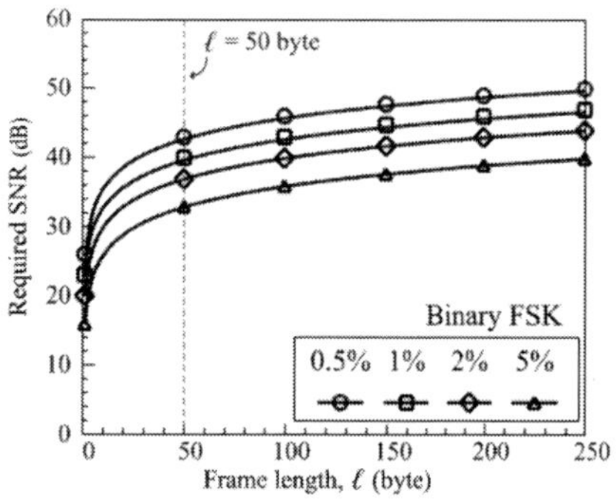

Figure 5. Frame length, ℓ, versus required SNR for Binary FSK method

C. Required SNR calculation

In this paper, we consider the BPSK method and Binary FSK method as the modulation scheme. In general, the bit error probability, p_b, under the Rayleigh fading environment can be theoretically calculated [18] as follows:

$$\begin{cases} p_b = \left[1 - \sqrt{\gamma/(1+\gamma)}\,\right]/2 & \text{(BPSK)}, \\ p_b = \left[1 - \sqrt{\gamma/(2+\gamma)}\,\right]/2 & \text{(Binary FSK)}, \end{cases} \quad (4)$$

where γ denotes SNR, and the relationship between γ and P_{RX} is given by

$$\gamma = P_{RX}/\kappa\tau_o\,, \quad (5)$$

where κ (= 4.0 × 10^{-21} W/Hz) denotes Boltzmann's constant value and τ_o (K) denotes the system device's absolute temperature. Therefore, by letting ℓ (bit) denote frame length, we can calculate the frame error probability, p_e, using (4) as

$$p_e = 1 - (1 - p_b)^{\ell}\,. \quad (6)$$

Figures 4 and 5 show the calculation results for the frame length, ℓ, versus the required SNR when the p_e values are

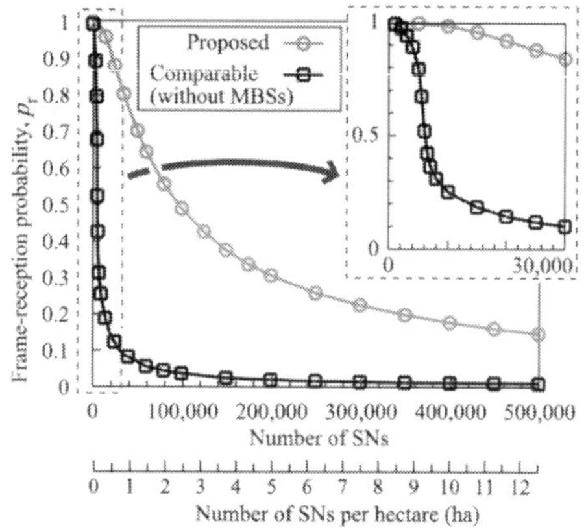

Figure 6. Number of SNs versus frame-reception probability

0.5%, 1%, 2%, and 5% for the BPSK and Binary FSK methods, respectively, based on the above procedure.

D. Numerical result

When the frame error probability is 0.5% and ℓ = 50 bytes (i.e., the maximum LoRa frame length transmitted in the airtime allowed by Japanese regulations [17]), based on Figures 4 and 5, we can obtain the required received power as -126 dBm and -129 dBm for the BPSK and Binary FSK methods, respectively. In (5), the required P_{RX} can be obtained as 43 dBm and 46 dBm based on Figures 4 and 5, and in the general condition, $\kappa\tau_o$ is given as -172 dBm.

Figure 6 shows the number of SNs (and number of SNs per hectare) versus frame-reception probability, p_r, which is calculated as

$$p_r = N_r \,/\, N_{all}\,, \quad (7)$$

where N_r and N_{all} denote the number of successfully received frames and the number of all generated frames, respectively. Consequently, in the comparable scheme without using MBSs, the frame-reception probability was dramatically degraded. This is because frame collisions and retransmissions significantly increased as they exceeded the multiple access capability of the pure-ALOHA method. We believe this phenomenon led to the same conclusion reached in Adelantado et al. [7] and C. Bor et al. [8].

On the other hand, the proposed scheme could reduce the worse degradation in the frame-reception probability curve, even if the SNs increased. When the required frame-reception probabilities were 0.9, 0.8, and 0.5, the proposed scheme with MBSs could increase the number of SNs (and per hecare) by 5.77, 7.00, and 15.8 times, respectively, compared to the scheme without MBSs, while still keeping the same farme reception rate in the end. Finally, the proposed scheme achieved up to 8.32 times better performance in frame-reception probability than the comparable scheme.

IV. Conclusion

In this paper, we proposed a novel cooperative (hybrid) reception scheme using UAV-mounted mobile aerial base stations for LPWA-based WSNs. Computer simulation demonstrated that the proposed scheme achieved up to 8.32 times better performance than a comparable scheme without using MBSs in terms of the frame-reception probability. In future work, we should consider such issues as an extended receiver-side cooperation mechanism, MBS placement and algorithms for detetmining the UAV's flight path and aircraft selection.

References

[1] G. Anastasi, M. Conti, M. Di Francesco, and A. Passarella, "Energy Conservation in Wireless Sensor Networks: A Survey," *Ad Hoc Networks*, vol. 7, no. 3, pp. 537–568, May 2009.

[2] U. Raza, P. Kulkarni, and M. Sooriyabandara, "Low Power Wide Area Networks: An Overview," *IEEE Commun. Surveys & Tutorials*, vol. 19, no. 2, pp. 855–873, Second-quarter 2017.

[3] H. Wang and A. O. Fapojuwo, "Survey of Enabling Technologies of Low Power and Long Range Machine-to-Machine Communications," *IEEE Commun. Surveys & Tutorials*, vol. 19, no. 4, pp. 2621–2639, Fourth-quarter 2017.

[4] LoRa, https://www.lora-alliance.org/ [retrived: Mar. 2018].

[5] Sigfox, https://www.sigfox.com/ [retrived: Mar. 2018].

[6] Y. P. E. Wan et al., "A Primer on 3GPP Narrowband Internet of Things," *IEEE Commun. Mag.*, vol. 55, no. 3, pp. 117–123, Mar. 2017.

[7] F. Adelantado et al., "Understanding the Limits of LoRaWAN," *IEEE Commun. Mag.*, vol. 55, no. 9, pp. 34–40, Sept. 2017.

[8] M. C. Bor, U. Roedig, T. Voigt, and J. M. Alonso, "Do LoRa Low-Power Wide-Area Networks Scale," *Proc. the 19th Int. Conf. Modeling, Analysis, and Simulation of Wireless and Mobile Syst. (MSWiM'16)*, Nov. 2016, pp. 59–67, doi: 10.1145/2988287.2989163.

[9] A. T. Erman, L. V. Hoesel, P. Havinga, and J. Wu, "Enabling Mobility in Heterogeneous Wireless Sensor Networks Cooperating with UAVs for Mission-critical Management," *IEEE Wireless Commun.*, vol. 15, no. 6, pp. 38–46, Dec. 2008.

[10] Y. Zeng, R. Zhang, and T. J. Lim, "Wireless Communications with Unmanned Aerial Vehicles: Opportunities and Challenges," *IEEE Commun. Mag.*, vol. 54, no. 5, pp. 36–42, May 2016.

[11] Y. Li and L. Cai, "UAV-assisted Dynamic Coverage in Heterogeneous Cellular System," *IEEE Network*, vol. 31, no. 4, pp. 56–61, July–Aug. 2017.

[12] V. Sharma, M. Bennis, and R. Kumar, "UAV-assisted Heterogeneous Networks for Capacity Enhancement," *IEEE Commun. Lett.*, vol. 20, no. 6, pp. 1207–1210, June 2016.

[13] J. Lyu, Y. Zeng, R. Zhang, and T. J. Lim, "Placement Optimization of UAV-mounted Mobile Base Stations," *IEEE Commun. Lett.*, vol. 21, no. 3, pp. 604–607, Mar. 2017.

[14] M. Mozaffari, W. Saad, M. Bennis, and M. Debbah, "Efficient Deployment of Multiple Unmanned Aerial Vehicles for Optimal Wireless Coverage," *IEEE Commun. Lett.*, vol. 20, no. 8, pp. 1647–1650, Aug. 2016.

[15] M. Alzenad, A. El-Keyi, F. Lagum, and H. Yanikomeroglu, "3-D Placement of an Unmanned Aerial Vehicle Base Station (UAV-BS) for Energy-Efficient Maximal Coverage," *IEEE Wireless Commun. Lett.*, vol. 6, no. 4, pp. 434–437, Aug. 2017.

[16] M. Mozaffari, W. Saad, M. Bennis, and M. Debbah, "Mobile Unmanned Aerial Vehicles (UAVs) for Energy-Efficient Internet of Things Communications," *IEEE Trans. Wireless Commun.*, vol. 16, no. 11, pp. 7574–7589, Nov. 2017.

[17] ARIB STD-T108, https://www.arib.or.jp/english/ [retrived: Mar. 2018].

[18] J. G. Proakis, *Digital Communications*, McGraw-Hill, Jan. 2008.

[19] V. Erceg et al, "An Empirically Based Path Loss Model for Wireless Channels in Suburban Environment," *IEEE J. Sel. Areas in Commun.*, vol. 17, no. 7, pp. 1205–1211, July 1999.

[20] R. Amorim et al., "Radio Channel Modeling for UAV Communication Over Cellular Networks," *IEEE Wireless Commun. Lett.*, vol. 6, no. 4, pp. 514–517, Aug. 2017.

Performance Evaluation of TCP Variants with Packet Reordering

Yutaka Fukuda
Information Science Center,
Kyushu Institute of Technology
1-1 Sensui-cho, Tobata,
Kitakyushu 804-8550, Japan
Email: fukuda@isc.kyutech.ac.jp

Daiki Nobayashi
Faculty of Engineering,
Kyushu Institute of Technology
1-1 Sensui-cho, Tobata-ku,
Kitakyushu 804-8550, Japan
Email: nova@ecs.kyutech.ac.jp

Takeshi Ikenaga
Faculty of Engineering,
Kyushu Institute of Technology
1-1 Sensui-cho, Tobata-ku,
Kitakyushu 804-8550, Japan
Email: ike@ecs.kyutech.ac.jp

***Abstract*—Packet reordering in a short fixed period is considered in this paper. We believe that data will be transmitted dynamically and in parallel in the near future, which will require more frequent periodic packet reordering. This in turn will lead to unnecessary retransmissions and throughput degradation to the TCP (Transmission Control Protocol). There has been much research to improve the TCP performance with packet reordering, but the considered reorder intervals have been based on measurements on the existing Internet, and the short, fixed reorder intervals caused by the flexible transmission schemes have not been studied sufficiently. Therefore, in this paper, we vary the fixed reorder interval from within the Round-Trip Time (RTT) to over the RTT, and evaluate the communication performance of TCP NewReno and Cubic. From the simulation results, we show that the performance of TCP Cubic is highly affected by the packet reordering.**

Keywords–TCP; Cubic; NewReno; packet reordering.

I. Introduction

Packet reordering is out-of-order packet arrival at the receiver. Namely, the destination receives a packet in a different order from its sending one. Although there are several causes, one of the main reasons for packet reordering is that some packets take different paths because of route oscillations over the network layer. TCP (Transmission Control Protocol) addresses this issue by performing sequence control and sends back duplicate ACKs (Acknowledgments) to report the packet gap. However, the TCP sender assumes packet loss after receiving three duplicate ACKs from the receiver, and decreases the transmission rate, which causes a substantial throughput degradation. To avoid this performance deterioration, various methods have been proposed in previous studies [4]–[10].

In contrast, recent development trends in network technologies, in addition to the usual communication performance metrics, such as fault tolerance and delay, have included multipath routing for a variety factors such as power savings. Furthermore, research and development are also being conducted extensively on maintaining communication while simultaneously using different types of media on mobile devices, such as LTE and IEEE 802.11 wireless LAN. Networks in the future are therefore expected to move further toward dynamic multipath routing, which will generate more packet reordering along the path and change the reordering pattern. Especially, packet reordering may occur continuously at regular intervals because of, for example, simultaneous multipath use in order to achieve high-speed and efficient communication. However, to the best of the authors' knowledge, the impact of packet reordering occurring at short, regular intervals on the performance of TCP communication has not been previously studied.

Therefore, the objective of this paper is to study the impact of packet reordering occurring at regular intervals on the performance of TCP communication. Specifically, this paper examines the communication performance when frequent packet reordering occurs continuously within and over the Round-Trip Time (RTT) using NewReno and Cubic as TCP congestion control algorithms, and shows the requirement to adapt the packet reordering from simulation results.

The remainder of the paper is organized as follows. Section 2 discusses the related studies. Section 3 describes the simulation model and the packet reordering schemes used in this paper. Section 4 presents the communication performances of TCP NewReno and Cubic when packet reordering occurs, and Section 5 summarizes our conclusions.

II. Related Work

Many studies [1]–[3] show actual measurements of packet reordering occurrence on the Internet. When a packet arrives out of order, the TCP receiver sends out a duplicate ACK on the missing packet. If at least three duplicate ACKs arrive, then the TCP sender interprets them as packet loss, and retransmits the packet indicated by the duplicate ACK. Then, fast recovery is triggered with fast retransmit, and congestion window *cwnd* is set to half its value, which causes significant performance degradation. To date, there have been many studies [5]–[10] aimed at solving this problem.

Proposed solutions for packet reordering are classified as follows: (1) dynamically control the number of duplicate

ACKs to enter fast recovery [4], [6], [7]; (2) detect the occurrence of packet reordering by the TCP timestamp option and restore the reduced *cwnd* and *ssthresh* to their original values [5]; and (3) detect packet loss not by duplicate ACKs but by using timers [8]. The advantages and disadvantages of these proposed solutions, as well as their evaluation through a simulation study, are provided in detail in Leung et al. [9]. In addition, Feng et al. [10] evaluated the performance of the proposed solutions for packet reordering in a high-speed communication environment.

To evaluate the performance of the proposed solutions, these previous studies use actual measurements on the Internet. In simulations, they vary the packet delay between relay routers to invoke packet reordering. However, we believe that data packets will be transmitted more dynamically and in parallel to achieve effective performance on the near-future Internet, which will cause more frequent periodic packet reordering. To the best of the authors' knowledge, TCP communication performance with frequent and continuous packet reordering within and over the RTT has not been studied sufficiently.

III. Simulation Model

In this study, we use the network simulator ns-3 [11] after adding a packet reordering function. The simulation topology for the simulation is given in Figure 1. The sending terminal S sends TCP segments with a size of 1,500 bytes to the receiving terminal D. It is assumed that each TCP flow is used for greedy file transfer. Assuming concurrent use of multiple paths, packet reordering was modeled to occur at the bottleneck link between routers R_1 and R_2 with a link bandwidth of 10 Mb/s and a delay of 5 ms. In contrast, the link bandwidth of the access links between each terminal and routers R_1 and R_2 is 100 Mb/s with a delay of 15 ms, resulting in an RTT of 70 ms between the terminals. The TCP congestion control algorithms used for the study are NewReno [12] [13] and the Linux-standard Cubic [14], [15]. Simulation time is 10.2 s, and TCP starts transmission at 0.2 s after starting the simulation.

In previous studies, the setting of the packet reordering interval is based on arrival distributions obtained by actual measurements. In contrast, in this paper, we assume that reordered packets arrive predetermined interval or more. Specifically, if the buffer size of R_1 is larger than the predetermined variable RI (Reorder Interval), then the head of line packet in R_1 is moved behind by the RI packet size. Note that other packets are not reordered until transmission of the moved packet is completed.

Reordering behavior in our study is illustrated in Figure 2. First, assume that there are 11 packets in R_1, packets 10 to 20, as shown in Figure 2(a) and RI = 4. Since the buffer size is 11, which is larger than RI, and head of line packet 10 has not been reordered before, packet reordering occurs and packet 10 is moved behind by RI = 4 packets as shown in Figure 2(b). Packets are thereafter sequentially transmitted until packet 10 as shown in Figure 2(c). After packet 10 is transmitted, six packets, packets 15 to 20, still remain in R_1. Since the packet reordering condition is satisfied, the head of line packet 15 is moved behind

TABLE I. SIMULATION CONDITIONS

Segment Size	1,500 bytes
RTT	70 ms
Reorder Interval	4–100 packets (Minimum 4.8–120 ms intervals)
TCP variants	NewReno, Cubic
Simulation time	10.2 s
Simulator	ns-3

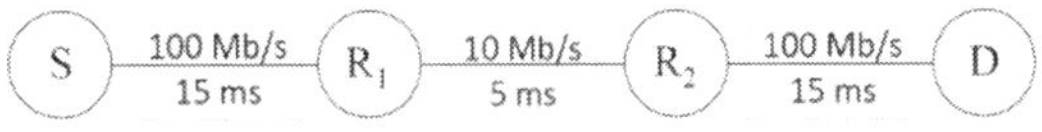

Figure 1. Simulation model.

by 4 packets as shown in Figure 2(d). Based on this scheme, packet reordering occurs and packets at every RI are moved backward if the buffer size of R_1 is larger than RI.

In the simulation, RI was set from 4 to 100 packets. Note that since the TCP segment size is 1,500 bytes and the link bandwidth between R_1 and R_2 is 10 Mb/s, the forwarding time of one packet is 1,500 bytes × 8 bits/10 Mb/s = 1.2 ms. Thus, if RI = 4, then packets are reordered at intervals of 1.2 ms × 4 = 4.8 ms. Moreover for RI = 4, since the RTT between terminals is 70 ms, reordering can occur $70/4.8 \simeq 14$ times at most within one RTT. The simulation conditions given above are shown in Table I.

IV. Simulation Results and Discussion

The simulation results are presented in this section. We set the buffer size of relay router R_1 sufficiently in order not to lose packets, and the impact of packet reordering alone on the performance of TCP communication is studied. Next, we show how packet reordering impacts communication performance both when RI is within and over RTT.

A. Fundamental Characteristics

As a preliminary step, throughput was measured when packet reordering does not occur under the same simulation conditions. A throughput of 9.54455 Mb/s was confirmed for both Cubic and NewReno. Figure 3 shows the normalized throughput (= throughput with packet reordering / throughput without packet reordering) when RI is varied from 4 to 100. Figure 4 shows the number of fast recovery events.

From Figure 3, normalized throughput of both NewReno and Cubic are not strictly increasing, since the packet reordering pattern in each RI is different. However, the occurrence of packet reordering caused throughput to decrease by a maximum of approximately 50 % for NewReno and a maximum of approximately 65 % for Cubic. The throughput performance of Cubic is lower than that of NewReno except for RI = 30. In addition, Figure 4 also shows that packet reordering causes fast recovery for RI below 100. Moreover, a shorter RI corresponds to a larger number of fast recovery events. Note that for RI = 100, Figure 4 shows that there is no fast recovery, and since packet reordering does not occur at R_1, the normalized

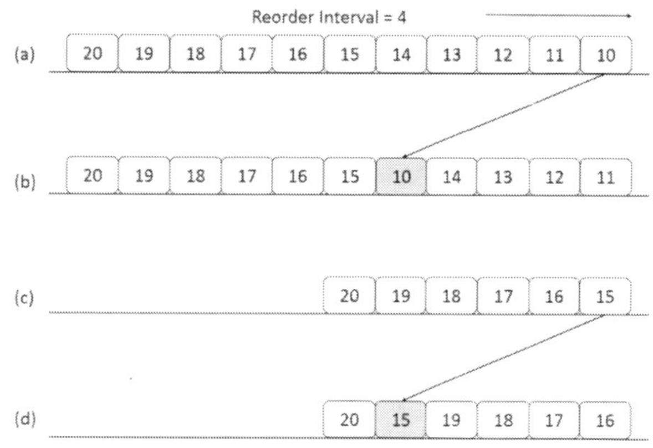

Figure 2. Packet reordering.

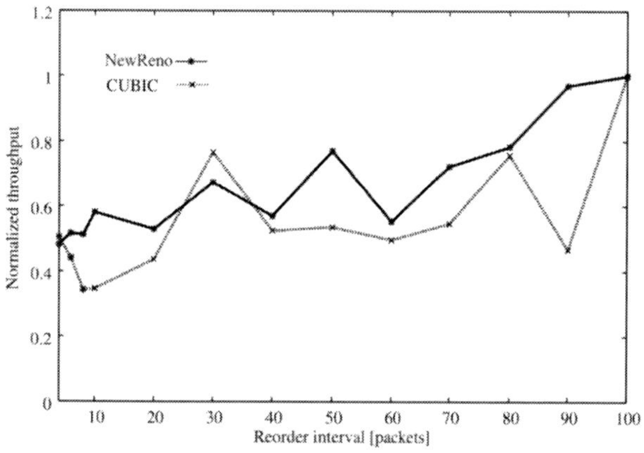

Figure 3. Normalized throughput [Mb/s].

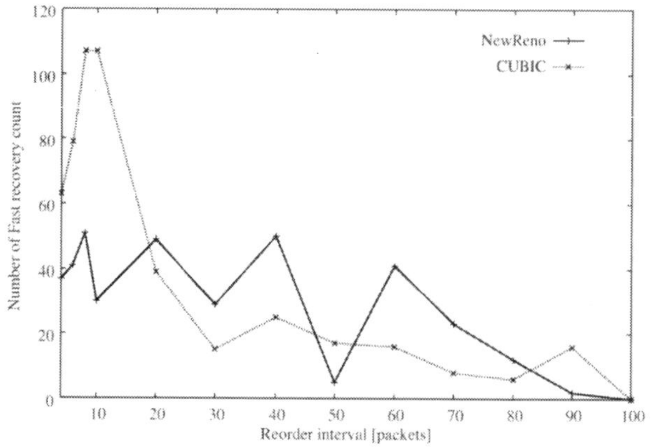

Figure 4. Fast recovery count.

throughputs of both TCP variants are equal to 1. Furthermore, a comparison of Figures 3 and 4 reveals that, for Cubic, throughput performance deteriorates regardless of the number of fast recovery events. We can therefore consider that both frequent occurrence of packet reordering (small RI) and occurrence of packet reordering with a large *cwnd* (large RI) affect throughput performance for Cubic. Thus, in the next section, we examine the behavior of NewReno and Cubic for different RIs.

B. For RI shorter than RTT

We first consider the case that RI is 8 (1.2 ms $\times$ 8 = 9.6 ms), where the interval for packet reordering is shorter than RTT. The *cwnd* of NewReno and Cubic are shown in Figures 5 and 6, respectively. *cwnd* increases even after fast recovery due to packet reordering in TCP NewReno, whereas *cwnd* fluctuates at a low range in TCP Cubic, as illustrated by Figures 5 and 6. To show their behaviors in more detail, the time range between 2 and 2.3 s is shown in Figures 7 and 8. Figure 7 shows that, after fast recovery is invoked because of packet reordering, NewReno sets *cwnd* to half its value before fast recovery and continues communication in congestion avoidance mode. In contrast, Cubic repeatedly decreases *cwnd* to its initial value of 2 after fast recovery, as demonstrated in Figure 8.

To understand Cubic's behavior, *cwnd* from 0 to 2 s is considered in Figure 9. As shown in the figure, in Cubic, the size of *cwnd* after fast recovery is gradually reduced until it falls to the minimum value of 2. This is because Cubic updates *cwnd* and *ssthresh* according to the following equation [15].

$$cwnd = ssthresh = max(\frac{cwnd \times \beta}{BICTCP\_BETA\_SCALE}, 2) \quad (1)$$

We use $\beta = 819$ and $BICTCP\_BETA\_SCALE = 1024$ for the simulation, thus multiplicative decrease factor is 0.8. Based on (1), *cwnd* with successive fast recovery gradually becomes smaller and eventually converges to the minimum value of 2, which significantly reduces throughput. These results show that, for frequent packet reordering, the throughput performance of TCP Cubic is highly affected by the packet reordering because Cubic updates *cwnd* based on (1).

C. For RI longer than RTT

In this section, we consider the case that RI is 80 (1.2 ms $\times$ 80 = 96 ms), where the interval for packet reordering is longer than RTT. The *cwnd* for each congestion control algorithm is shown in Figures 10 and 11. Figure 10 shows that NewReno can send packets in congestion avoidance mode even after the occurrence of packet reordering. In contrast, as shown in Figure 11, increase of *cwnd* in Cubic occurs intermittently in the range between 2 and 8 s. In Cubic, *cwnd* can be increased after receiving the number of ACKs given by *cnt*. The count variable *cnt* is calculated according to the following equation [15].

$$\begin{aligned} &if \quad (cwnd < W(t + RTT) \\ &\qquad cnt = \frac{cwnd}{W(t+RTT) - cwnd} \quad (2) \\ &else \\ &\qquad cnt = 100 \times cwnd \quad (3) \end{aligned}$$

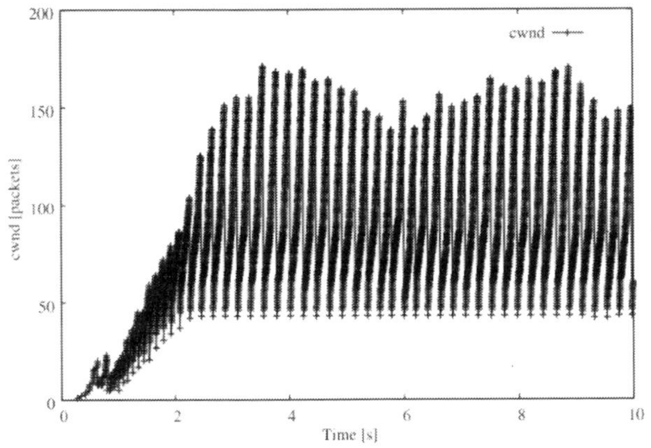

Figure 5. TCP NewReno (RI = 8).

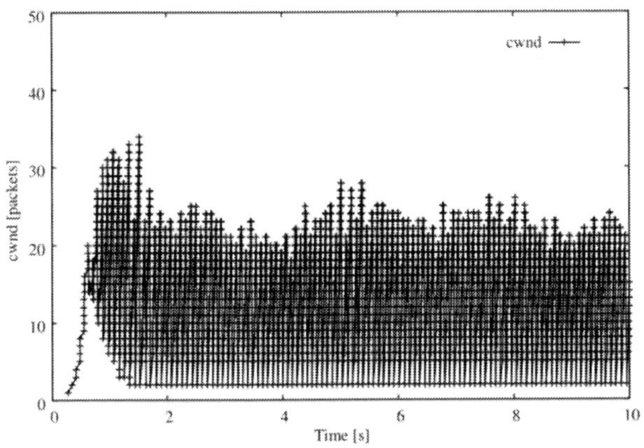

Figure 6. TCP Cubic (RI = 8).

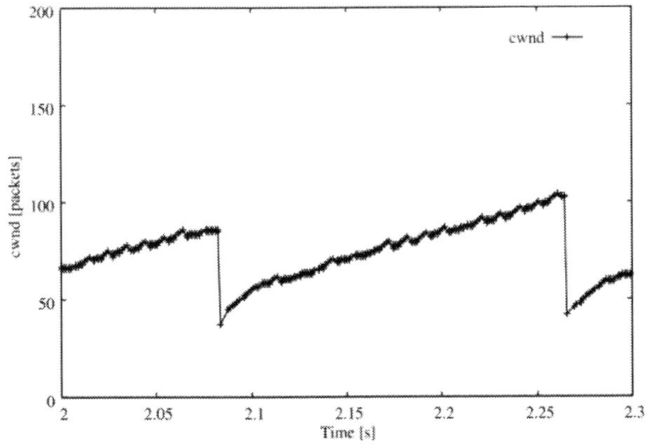

Figure 7. TCP NewReno (RI = 8; 2.0–2.3 s).

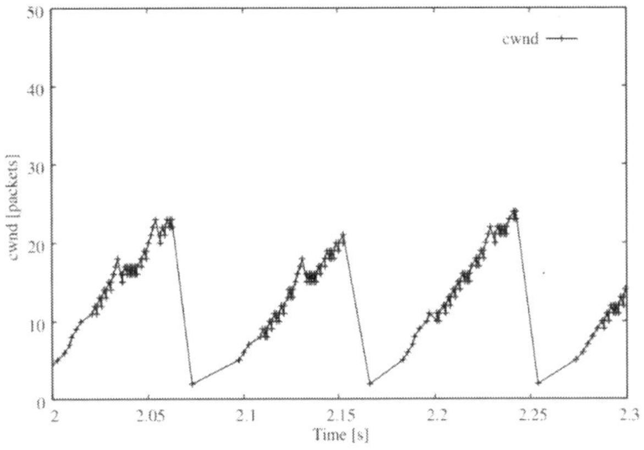

Figure 8. TCP Cubic (RI = 8; 2.0–2.3 s).

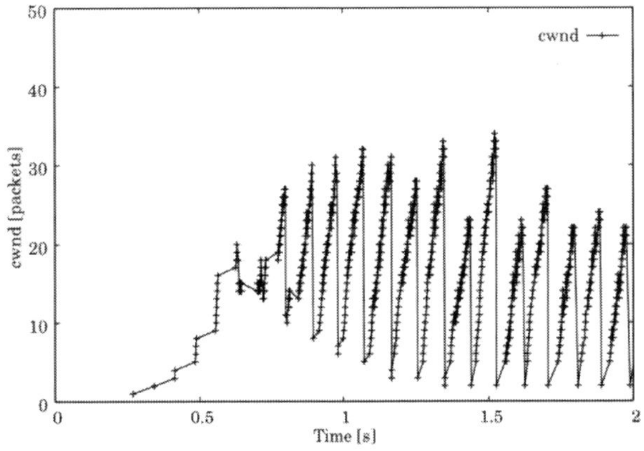

Figure 9. TCP Cubic (RI = 8; 0–2.0 s).

Based on (2) and (3), cnt becomes large if $cwnd$ becomes somewhat large and the difference between $W(t+\mathrm{RTT})$ and $cwnd$ is small. In other words, a large number of received ACKs is required to increase $cwnd$. For the case of RI = 80 considered in this section, the value of cnt is relatively large because packet reordering occurs when $cwnd$ has increased to some extent. Thus, the $cwnd$ increase is intermittent for a long period of time, whereas NewReno can increase $cwnd$ with normal congestion avoidance mode. In order to improve the performance of TCP Cubic when packet reordering occurs with large $cwnd$, different packet loss detection aproach is required.

From these simulation results, we have shown that the throughput performance of Cubic may deteriorate considerably when packet reordering occurs at intervals longer than RTT and $cwnd$ is large, even if the number of packet reordering events per unit time is small. Furthermore, results of Sections 4.2 and 4.3 show that there is a need for packet loss detection that does not rely on duplicate ACKs and a transmission method with higher tolerance to packet reordering, whereas the cause for the lower throughput in Cubic varies depending on how packet reordering occurs.

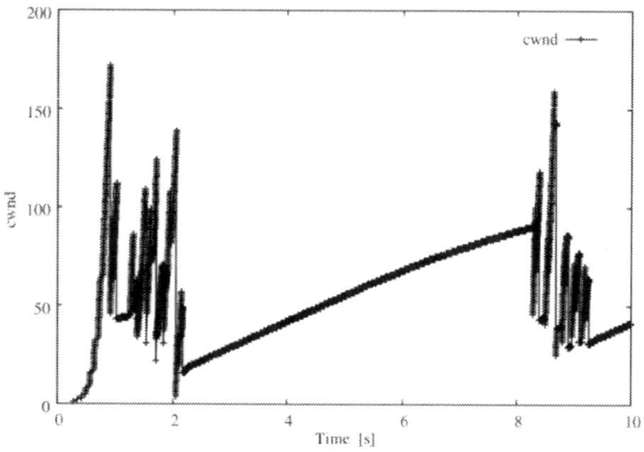

Figure 10. TCP NewReno (RI = 80).

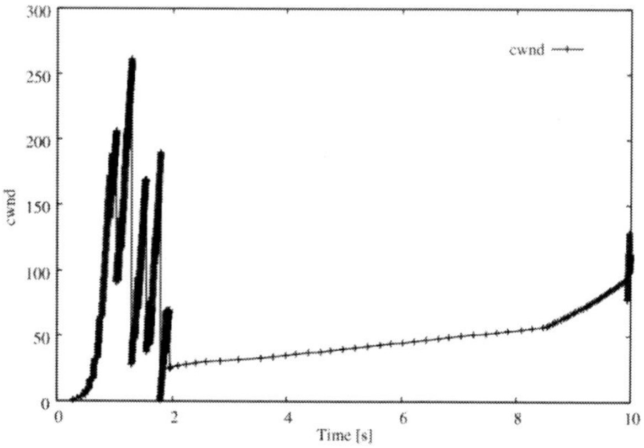

Figure 11. TCP Cubic (RI = 80).

V. Conclusion

In this paper, we examined the impact of packet reordering occurring at very short regular intervals on the communication performances of TCP NewReno and Cubic. Implemented on ns-3, packet reordering was designed to occur at each predetermined RI interval and head of line packet move to RI packets. RI was then varied so that it was within or over RTT to study the throughput and number of fast recovery events due to packet reordering. For an RI smaller than RTT, the throughput for Cubic decreases considerably since Cubic continually reduces *cwnd* and *ssthresh* when duplicate ACKs are detected due to frequent packet reordering. For an RI larger than RTT, the throughput performance of Cubic also deteriorates substantially when packet reordering occurs with a large *cwnd* even if the number of packet reordering events per unit time is small. Specifically, in congestion avoidance mode, NewReno can increase the *cnwd* by 1 segment for each RTT, whereas Cubic cannot increase *cwnd* until the predetermined number of ACKs are received. These simulation results indicate that both a packet loss detection scheme which does not rely on duplicate ACKs and a method to maintain packet transmission in spite of packet reordering are vital. Future work includes evaluations of other TCP variants, such as Compound TCP and TCP-PR [8], which detects packet loss using timers rather than duplicate ACKs, in the same packet reordering environment as in this paper. In addition, congestion control algorithms with high tolerance to packet reordering should be considered.

Acknowledgments

This work was supported in part by a JSPS KAKENHI Grant-in-Aid for Scientific Research (C) (Research Project No. 16K00129).

References

[1] X. Zhou and P. V. Mieghem, "Reordering of IP Packets in Internet," Passive and Active Network Measurement: 5th International Workshop, PAM 2004, pp. 237-246, Antibes Juan-les-Pins, France, Apr., 2004.

[2] L. Gharai, C. Perkins, and T. Lehman, "Packet reordering, high speed networks and transport protocol performance," In Proceedings of the 13th International Conference on Computer Communications and Networks (IEEE Cat. No. 04EX969), pp. 73-78, Chicago, IL, USA, Oct. 11-14, 2004.

[3] N. M. Piratla and A. P. Jayasumana, "Metrics for packet reordering: a comparative analysis," International Journal of Communication Systems, Vol. 21, No. 1, pp. 99-113, 2008.

[4] E. Blanton and M. Allman, "On making TCP more robust to packet reordering," ACM SIGCOMM Computer Communication Review, Vol. 32, No. 1, pp. 20-30, 2002.

[5] R. Ludwig and R. H. Katz, "The Eifel algorithm: making TCP robust against spurious retransmissions," ACM SIGCOMM Computer Communication Review, Vol. 30, No. 1, pp. 30-36, Jan. 2000.

[6] M. Zhang, B. Karp, S. Floyd, and L. Peterson, "RR-TCP: a reordering-robust TCP with DSACK," In Proceedings of the 11th IEEE International Conference on Network Protocols, pp. 95-106, Nov., 4-7, 2003.

[7] K. C. Leung and C. Ma, "Enhancing TCP performance to persistent packet reordering," Journal of Communications and Networks, Vol. 7, No. 3, pp. 385-393, Sept. 2005.

[8] S. Bohacek, J. P. Hespanha, J. Lee, C. Lim, and K. Obraczka, "A new TCP for persistent packet reordering," IEEE/ACM Transaction on Networking, Vol. 14, No. 2, pp. 369-382, Apr. 2006.

[9] K. C. Leung, V. O. K. Li, and D. Yang, "An overview of packet reordering in Transmission Control Protocol (TCP): problems, solutions, and challenges," IEEE Transactions on Parallel and Distributed Systems, Vol. 18, No. 4, pp. 522-535, Apr. 2007.

[10] J. Feng, Z. Ouyang, L. Xu, and B. Ramamurthy, "Packet reordering in high-speed networks and its impact on high-speed TCP variant," Computer Communications, Vol. 32, No. 1, pp. 62-68, Jan. 2009.

[11] "Network Simulator ns-3," http://www.nsnam.org/ retrieved: Mar. 2018.

[12] S. Floyd and T. Henderson,"RFC2582: the NewReno modification to TCP's fast recovery algorithm," RFC, 1999.

[13] S. Floyd, T. Henderson, and A. Gurtov, "RFC3782: the NewReno modification to TCP's fast recovery algorithm," RFC, 2004

[14] I. Rhee and L. Xu, "CUBIC: a new TCP friendly high-speed TCP variant," SIGOPS Operating System Review, Vol. 42, No. 5, pp. 64-74, Jul. 2008.

[15] B. Levasseur, M. Claypool, and R. Kinicki, "A TCP CUBIC implementation in ns-3," In Proceedings of the 2014 Workshop on ns-3 (WNS3'14), Atlanta, Georgia, USA, May 7, 2014.

A Multirate Loss Model of Quasi-Random Input for the X2 Link of LTE Networks

Panagiotis I. Panagoulias[1], Ioannis D. Moscholios[1], Michael N. Koukias[2] and Michael D. Logothetis[2]
1. Dept. of Informatics and Telecommunications, University of Peloponnese, Tripolis, Greece
Emails: panagoulias@uop.gr, idm@uop.gr
2. WCL, Dept. of Electrical and Computer Engineering, University of Patras, Patras, Greece
Emails: mkoukias@upatras.gr, mlogo@upatras.gr

Abstract—**In this paper, first we review a multirate loss model, whereby we can assess the call-level Quality of Service (QoS) of the Long Term Evolution (LTE) X2 link supporting calls of different service-classes with fixed bandwidth requirements. The X2 interface connects directly two neighboring evolved NodeBs and is mainly responsible for the transfer of user-plane and control-plane data during a handover. In the model, the X2 interface is modelled as a link of fixed capacity. Handover calls are accepted in the X2 link whenever available bandwidth exists. Secondly, we propose a multirate loss model where calls arrive in the X2 link according to a quasi-random process and compete for the available bandwidth under the Complete Sharing (CS) policy. The CS policy allows calls to enter the system when available bandwidth exists. We propose recursive formulas for the calculation of time and call congestion probabilities as well as link utilization for the CS policy.**

Keywords-LTE; X2; Quasi-random process; congestion; recursive formula.

I. Introduction

Long Term Evolution (LTE) networks provide increased throughputs via better spectrum exploitation and the use of multiple antennas, minimized latencies and a relatively simplified (the so-called "flat") architecture for the Evolved Universal Mobile Telecommunication System (UMTS) Terrestrial Radio Access Network (E-UTRAN) [1].

The main components of an LTE network are the Evolved Packet Core (EPC) and the E-UTRAN. The EPC is responsible for the management of the core network components and the communication with the external network. The E-UTRAN provides air interface, via evolved NodeBs (eNBs), to a User Equipment (UE) and acts as an intermediate node handling the radio communication between the UE and the EPC. Each eNB covers a specific cell and exchanges traffic with the core network through the S1 interface. An active UE is quite likely to cross the boundary of the source cell, causing a handover. A handover is the process of a seamless transition of the UE's radio link from the source eNB to one of its neighbors. During this transition, the direct logical interface (link) between two neighboring eNBs – the X2 link – is used, for the user data arriving to the source eNB via the S1 link, to be transferred to the target eNB (Figure 1).

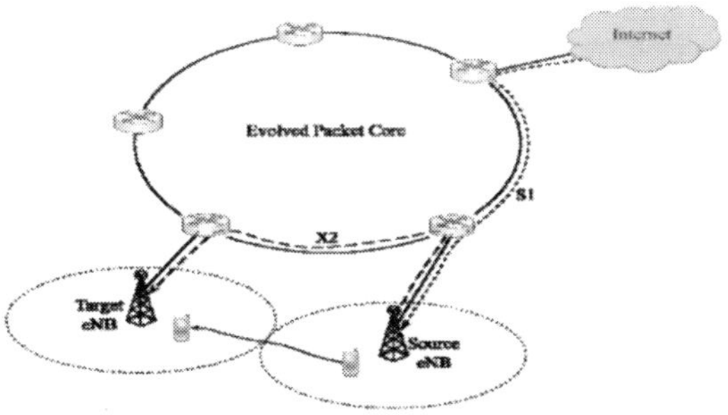

Figure 1. The S1 interface and the X2 interface between source and target eNBs.

The X2 interface is mainly used for the handover operation but it also supports load management and inter-cell interference coordination functions. However, considering that load management requires a constant but negligible bandwidth and assuming homogeneous LTE networks, in which interference coordination is not used [2] [3], we consider only the bandwidth required for the handover support. Based on the above, the X2 link carries both control and user plane traffic. However, according to [4][5], control plane traffic is negligible compared to user plane traffic. Therefore, we study herein user plane traffic only.

The determination of congestion probabilities in the X2 link can be based on multirate teletraffic loss models [2] [4][5]. In [2], a simple model is proposed by Blogowski, Klopfenstein and Renard (BKR model) that studies the impact of UE mobility in congestion probabilities. A circular source cell is considered, that accommodates a finite number of users, who generate quasi-random handover traffic [6] and have different bandwidth requirements. All UEs are considered having a constant velocity and moving in a straight line. The X2 link is modeled as a link of fixed capacity that accepts handover calls if their total bandwidth requirement is available upon their arrival. The calculation of congestion probabilities is based on analytical formulas that take into account UEs mobility, but can be complex in the case of large systems with large capacities and many service-classes. This is because enumeration and processing of the state space are required. In [4], a richer stochastic model is proposed by Widjaja and La Roche (WLR model), which is based on a fluid mobility model [7][8] and the classical Erlang Multirate Loss Model (EMLM) [9][10]. Calls arrive in the X2 link according to a Poisson process, have fixed bandwidth requirements and compete for the available bandwidth under the Complete Sharing (CS policy). In the CS policy, a call is accepted in the system if its bandwidth requirement is available. Otherwise, the call is blocked and lost without further affecting the system. Although the BKR and WLR models provide similar congestion probability results, we adopt the WLR model since: a) basic performance measures including congestion probabilities, link utilization and average number of calls in the system can be recursively determined, without the need of state space processing (which is essential in [2]), b) various other bandwidth sharing policies (e.g., the bandwidth reservation policy, also known as guard channel policy, [11]-[16], the multiple fractional channel reservation policy [17]-[19] or the threshold policy [20]-[26]) can be applied in the X2 link, based on [4] and c) various handover arrival processes can be studied, e.g., the quasi-random arrival process, the batched Poisson process or an ON-OFF process [27]-[32]. Finally, in [5], a multirate loss model is proposed, based on the EMLM, assuming that traffic in the X2 link is elastic. Elastic traffic refers to calls whose allocated bandwidth is not fixed during their lifetime in the system. To model the bandwidth sharing policy in the case of elastic traffic the processor sharing discipline is considered [33]-[40].

In this paper, we study the X2 link at call-level and analyze it as a multirate loss system. To this end, we extend the WLR model to include the quasi-random arrival process (WLR-q model). In the quasi-random process, calls are generated by a finite number of users, a realistic assumption in the case of handover calls. Thus, the quasi-random process is smoother than the random (Poisson) process where calls are generated by an infinite number of users [12], [41]-[45].

This paper is organized as follows: In Section II, we review the WLR model of [4]. In Section III, we propose the WLR-q model. In Section IV, we present analytical TC probabilities results for the proposed model and the model of [4]. We conclude in Section V.

II. Review of The WLR Model

Consider a circular source cell of radius R, which accommodates Poisson arriving calls of K different service-classes. Calls of service-class k (k=1,…,K) follow a Poisson process with arrival rate λ_k and have a generally distributed service time, μ_k^{-1}. Contrary to the BKR model, in the WLR model a fluid mobility model is considered for the determination of the offered traffic-load in the X2 link.

The fluid mobility model of [4] considers traffic flow as the flow of a fluid. Such a model can be used to model the behavior of macroscopic movement (i.e., the movement of an individual UE is considered of little significance) [8]. This fluid mobility model formulates the amount of traffic flowing out of a circular region of a source cell to be proportional to the population density within that region, the average velocity, and the length of the region boundary. For a circular region with a population density of ρ_k (UEs of service-class k per km^2), an average velocity of v_k, and a diameter of $L=2\pi R$, the UE crossing rate per unit time, CR_k, from a source to any neighbor cell is:

$$CR_k = \rho_k v_k L/\pi = 2\rho_k v_k R \qquad (1)$$

Based on the above and assuming Poisson handover traffic, the offered traffic-load of service-class k calls, a_k, in the X2 link equals [4]:

$$a_k = p_A(k)\frac{\rho_k v_k L}{\pi}\delta = 2p_A(k)\rho_k v_k R\delta \qquad (2)$$

where: $p_A(k) = \lambda_k/(\lambda_k + \mu_k)$ is the probability that a service-class k UE is active (i.e., when there exists a Radio Resource Control (RRC) connection between a UE and eNB) and δ is the interruption time of the radio link between the source eNB and the UE.

Let b_k be the data rate of an active service-class k UE and n_k be the in-service service-class k UEs in the X2 link. By defining the corresponding vectors $\boldsymbol{n} = (n_1,...,n_k,...,n_K)$ and $\boldsymbol{b} = (b_1,...,b_k,...,b_K)$ then the occupied bandwidth j in the X2 link can be expressed as:

$$j = \boldsymbol{nb} = \sum_{k=1}^{K} n_k b_k,\ \ j = 0,1,...,C_{X2} \qquad (3)$$

To determine the X2 link occupancy distribution, $q(j)$, it is assumed that UEs compete for the available bandwidth under the CS policy. Following the analysis of the EMLM, the un-normalized values of $q(j)$'s can be determined by the classical Kaufman-Roberts recursive formula [9][10]:

$$q(j) = \begin{cases} 1 \ for\ j=0 \\ \frac{1}{j}\sum_{k=1}^{K} a_k b_k q(j-b_k) \ for\ j=1,...,C_{X2} \\ 0 \ otherwise \end{cases} \qquad (4)$$

Based on $q(j)$'s we calculate the Time Congestion (TC) probabilities of service-class k, B_k, by the formula [4]:

$$B_k = \sum_{j=C_{X2}-b_k+1}^{C_{X2}} G^{-1} q(j) \qquad (5)$$

where: $G = \sum_{j=0}^{C_{X2}} q(j)$ is the normalization constant.

TC probabilities are determined by the proportion of time the system is congested and measured by an outside observer. Call Congestion (CC) probabilities refer to the probability that a UE is blocked and lost. Due to the assumption of Poisson arrivals, TC and CC probabilities coincide (PASTA property, [6]).

III. The Proposed WLR-q Model

In the WLR model, calls compete for the available bandwidth of the X2 link under the CS policy. In this section, we extend the WLR model by considering the case of quasi-random traffic.

Consider the X2 link of fixed capacity C_{X2} that accommodates K different service-classes. Calls of service class k (k =1,...,K) require b_k channels and come from a finite source population N_k while the mean arrival rate of service-class k idle sources is $\lambda_{k,fin} = (N_k - n_k)s_k$ where n_k is the number of in-service calls and s_k is the arrival rate per idle source. Assuming a population density of $\rho_k = N_k / \pi R^2$ for a circular region and that the UEs are always active, then the total offered traffic load of service-class k is $2\frac{N_k v_k \delta}{\pi R}$ while the offered traffic-load per idle source of service-class k is given by $a_{k,fin} = 2v_k\delta / \pi R$ (in erl). This arrival process is known as a quasi-random process [6]. If $N_k \rightarrow \infty$ for k = 1,...,K, and the total offered traffic-load remains constant, then the arrival process becomes Poisson.

The global balance equation for state $\boldsymbol{n}=(n_1,\ldots,n_k,\ldots,n_K)$, expressed as *rate into state* $\boldsymbol{n}$ = *rate out of state* $\boldsymbol{n}$, is given by:

$$\sum_{k=1}^{K}(N_k - n_k + 1)s_k P(\boldsymbol{n}_k^-) + \sum_{k=1}^{K}(n_k + 1)\delta^{-1}P(\boldsymbol{n}_k^+) = \sum_{k=1}^{K}(N_k - n_k)s_k P(\boldsymbol{n}) + \sum_{k=1}^{K} n_k \delta^{-1} P(\boldsymbol{n}) \quad (6)$$

where:
$\boldsymbol{n}_k^+ = (n_1,\ldots,n_{k-1},n_k+1,n_{k+1},\ldots,n_K)$ $\boldsymbol{n}_k^- = (n_1,\ldots,n_{k-1},n_k-1,n_{k+1},\ldots,n_K)$ and $P(\boldsymbol{n}), P(\boldsymbol{n}_k^-), P(\boldsymbol{n}_k^+)$ are the probability distributions of the corresponding states $\boldsymbol{n}, \boldsymbol{n}_k^-, \boldsymbol{n}_k^+$, respectively.

The proposed model has a Product Form Solution (PFS) for the determination of the steady state probabilities $P(\boldsymbol{n})$ due to the fact that local balance exists between adjacent states $\boldsymbol{n}_k^-, \boldsymbol{n}$ or $\boldsymbol{n}, \boldsymbol{n}_k^+$. The local balance equations, for k=1,...,K, are of the form:

$$(N_k - n_k + 1)a_{k,fin} P(\boldsymbol{n}_k^-) = n_k P(\boldsymbol{n}) \quad (7)$$

where: $a_{k,fin} = s_k \delta$.

The PFS that satisfies both (6) and (7) is the following:

$$P(\boldsymbol{n}) = G^{-1}\left(\prod_{k=1}^{K}\binom{N_k}{n_k}a_{k,fin}^{n_k}\right) \quad (8)$$

where $G \equiv G(\boldsymbol{\Omega}) = \sum_{\boldsymbol{n}\in\boldsymbol{\Omega}}\left(\prod_{k=1}^{K}\binom{N_k}{n_k}a_{k,fin}^{n_k}\right)$.

To avoid the complex calculations based on the PFS, we prove a recursive formula for the calculation of the X2 link occupancy distribution, $q_{fin}(j)$, of the proposed WLR-q model. By definition:

$$q_{fin}(j) = \sum_{\boldsymbol{n}\in\boldsymbol{\Omega}_j} P(\boldsymbol{n}) \quad (9)$$

where $\boldsymbol{\Omega}_j$ is the set of states whereby the occupied bandwidth is exactly j, i.e. $\boldsymbol{\Omega}_j = \{\boldsymbol{n}\in\boldsymbol{\Omega} : \boldsymbol{nb} = j\}$ and $\boldsymbol{\Omega}$ is the system's state space, $\boldsymbol{\Omega} = \{\boldsymbol{n} : 0 \le \boldsymbol{nb} \le C_{X2},\ k = 1,\ldots,K\}$.

Since $j=\boldsymbol{nb} = \sum_{k=1}^{K} n_k b_k$ we write (9) as follows:

$$j q_{fin}(j) = \sum_{k=1}^{K} b_k \sum_{\boldsymbol{n}\in\boldsymbol{\Omega}_j} n_k P(\boldsymbol{n}) \quad (10)$$

To determine the $\sum_{\boldsymbol{n}\in\boldsymbol{\Omega}_j} n_k P(\boldsymbol{n})$ in (10), we sum both sides of (7) over $\boldsymbol{\Omega}_j$:

$$\sum_{\boldsymbol{n}\in\boldsymbol{\Omega}_j}(N_k - n_k + 1)a_{k,fin}P(\boldsymbol{n}_k^-) = \sum_{\boldsymbol{n}\in\boldsymbol{\Omega}_j} n_k P(\boldsymbol{n}) \quad (11)$$

The left hand side of (11) can be written as:

$$\sum_{\boldsymbol{n}\in\boldsymbol{\Omega}_j}(N_k - n_k + 1)a_{k,fin}P(\boldsymbol{n}_k^-) = N_k \sum_{\boldsymbol{n}\in\boldsymbol{\Omega}_j} a_{k,fin}P(\boldsymbol{n}_k^-) - \sum_{\boldsymbol{n}\in\boldsymbol{\Omega}_j}(n_k - 1)a_{k,fin}P(\boldsymbol{n}_k^-) \quad (12)$$

Since $\sum_{\boldsymbol{n}\in\boldsymbol{\Omega}_j} a_{k,fin}P(\boldsymbol{n}_k^-) = a_{k,fin}q_{fin}(j-b_k)$ the first term of the right hand side of (12) becomes:

$$N_k \sum_{\boldsymbol{n}\in\boldsymbol{\Omega}_j} a_{k,fin}P(\boldsymbol{n}_k^-) = N_k a_{k,fin} q_{fin}(j-b_k) \quad (13)$$

The second term of the right hand side of (12) is written as:

$$\sum_{\boldsymbol{n}\in\boldsymbol{\Omega}_j}(n_k - 1)a_{k,fin}P(\boldsymbol{n}_k^-) = a_{k,fin}y_{k,fin}(j-b_k)q_{fin}(j-b_k) \quad (14)$$

where $y_{k,fin}(j-b_k)$ is the average number of service-class k calls in state $j-b_k$.

Based on (13) and (14), (12) becomes:

$$\sum_{\boldsymbol{n}\in\boldsymbol{\Omega}_j}(N_k - n_k + 1)a_{k,fin}P(\boldsymbol{n}_k^-) = a_{k,fin}\left(N_k - y_{k,fin}(j-b_k)\right)q_{fin}(j-b_k) \quad (15)$$

Equation (11) due to (15) takes the form:

$$\left(N_k - y_{k,fin}(j-b_k)\right)a_{k,fin}q_{fin}(j-b_k) = \sum_{\boldsymbol{n}\in\boldsymbol{\Omega}_j} n_k P(\boldsymbol{n}) \quad (16)$$

Equation (10) due to (16) is written as:

$$jq_{fin}(j) = \sum_{k=1}^{K} \left(N_k - y_{k,fin}(j-b_k) \right) a_{k,fin} b_k q_{fin}(j-b_k) \quad (17)$$

In the recursive formula of (17), the values of $y_{k,fin}(j-b_k)$ are not known. To determine them, we use a lemma of [46]. According to that lemma, two stochastic systems are equivalent and result in the same congestion probabilities, if they have: a) the same traffic description parameters $(K, N_k, a_{k,fin})$ where k=1,…,K and b) exactly the same set of states.

Our purpose is, therefore, to find a new stochastic system, whereby we can determine $y_{k,fin}(j-b_k)$. The bandwidth (channel) requirements of calls and the capacity in the new stochastic system are chosen according to the following two criteria: 1) conditions (a) and (b) are valid and 2) each state has a unique occupancy j.

Based on the above, state j is reached via the previous state $j-b_k$. Thus, $y_{k,fin}(j-b_k) = n_k - 1$ and (17) is given by:

$$q_{fin}(j) = \begin{cases} 1, & for\ j=0 \\ \frac{1}{j}\sum_{k=1}^{K}(N_k - n_k + 1) a_{k,fin} b_k q_{fin}(j-b_k), & for\ j=1,...,C_{X2} \\ 0, & otherwise \end{cases} \quad (18)$$

In (18), the values of n_k are unknown. The determination of n_k's requires the state space determination of the equivalent system, a complex procedure especially for large capacity systems that accommodate many service-classes. Because of this we approximate n_k in state j, $n_k(j)$, as $y_k(j)$, when Poisson arrivals are considered, i.e., $n_k(j) \approx y_k(j)$. Thus, we determine $q_{fin}(j)$'s via the formula:

$$q_{fin}(j) = \begin{cases} 1, & for\ j=0 \\ \frac{1}{j}\sum_{k=1}^{K}(N_k - y_k(j-b_k)) a_{k,fin} b_k q_{fin}(j-b_k), & for\ j=1,...,C_{X2} \\ 0, & otherwise \end{cases} \quad (19)$$

where the values of $y_k(j)$'s are given by:

$$y_k(j) = \begin{cases} \frac{a_k q(j-b_k)}{q(j)} & for\ \ j \geq b_k \\ 0 & otherwise \end{cases} \quad (20)$$

As far as the values of $q(j)$'s in (20) are concerned, they can be determined by (4).

Having determined $q_{fin}(j)$'s we calculate the TC probabilities of service-class k calls, B_k, as follows:

$$B_k = \sum_{j=C_{X2}-b_k+1}^{C_{X2}} G^{-1} q_{fin}(j) \quad (21)$$

where: $G = \sum_{j=0}^{C_{X2}} q_{fin}(j)$ is the normalization constant.

CC probabilities of service-class k, $B_{CC,k}$, can be determined via (21) where $q_{fin}(j)$'s are calculated (via (19)) for a system with N_k - 1 traffic sources. As far as the X2 link utilization, U_{X2}, is concerned, it is given by:

$$U_{X2} = \sum_{j=1}^{C_{X2}} jG^{-1} q_{fin}(j) \quad (22)$$

The following algorithm summarizes the order of TC probability and X2 link utilization calculations in the proposed WLR-q model:

1) Determine $q(j)$'s via (4).
2) Determine $y_k(j)$'s via (20).
3) Determine $q_{fin}(j)$'s via (19).
4) Determine B_k's via (21) and U_{X2} via (22).

IV. Numerical Results

In this section, we compare the analytical results of TC probabilities, obtained by the proposed WLR-q model for various values of velocity and cell radius. For comparison, we also present the corresponding analytical results obtained in the case of the WLR model.

Consider an X2 link of capacity C_{X2} = 50 channels that accommodates calls (handovers in progress) of K=3 service-classes with channel requirements: b_1 = 1, b_2 = 5 and b_3 = 12, respectively. Calls of each service-class arrive in the link according to a quasi-random process and are generated by a finite number of sources, N_k = 50, for k=1, 2, 3 (it is supposed that, at any moment, the total number of active users inside a cell -who are candidate to perform a handover- along with those performing a handover, is constant). Furthermore, let δ = 0.05 sec, and velocities v_1 = v_2 = v_3 = 30 km/h. In the x-axis of Figures 2-4, the velocity of all users increases in steps of 2 km/h. So, point 1 refers to: (v_1, v_2, v_3) = (30, 30, 30) while point 11 to: (v_1, v_2, v_3) = (50, 50, 50).

Figures 2-4 present the analytical TC probabilities of each service-class for three different values of the cell radius R = 150, 200 and 250 m. Based on these results, we conclude that: 1) TC probabilities are lower in the case of quasi-random traffic (WLR-q model) compared to the corresponding TC probabilities obtained in the case of the Poisson process (WLR model). 2) The increase of velocity increases TC probabilities, since it is more probable for a call to make a handover. 3) The increase of R reduces TC probabilities since it becomes less likely that a call will make a handover.

V. Conclusion

We review a multirate loss model for the call-level analysis of the X2 link in LTE networks. The X2 link is modelled as a multirate loss system that accommodates handover calls from different service-classes with fixed bandwidth requirements. Handover calls are accepted in the X2 link whenever available bandwidth exists. Otherwise, call blocking occurs. Furthermore, we propose a multirate loss model for the call-level analysis of the X2 link when the arrival process becomes quasi-random. We provide recursive formulas for the calculation of various performance measures including TC and CC probabilities. As a future work, we intend to study the applicability of the bandwidth reservation and the multiple fractional channel reservation policies in the proposed model.

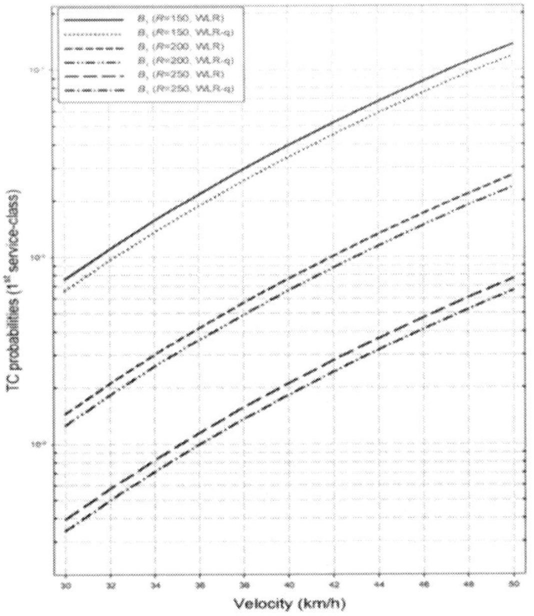

Figure 2. TC probabilities of the 1st service-class.

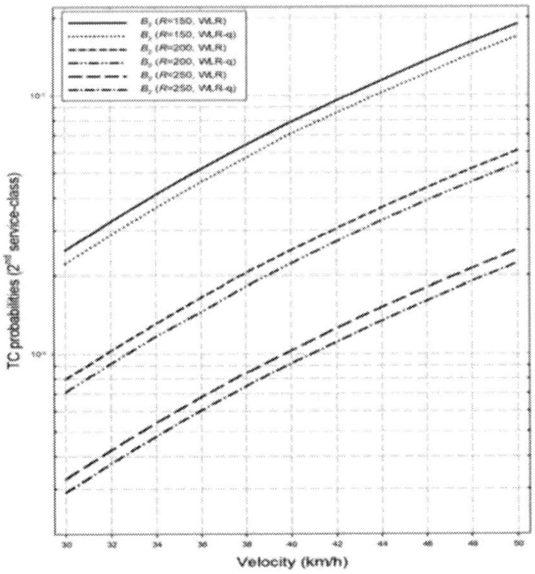

Figure 3. TC probabilities of the 2nd service-class.

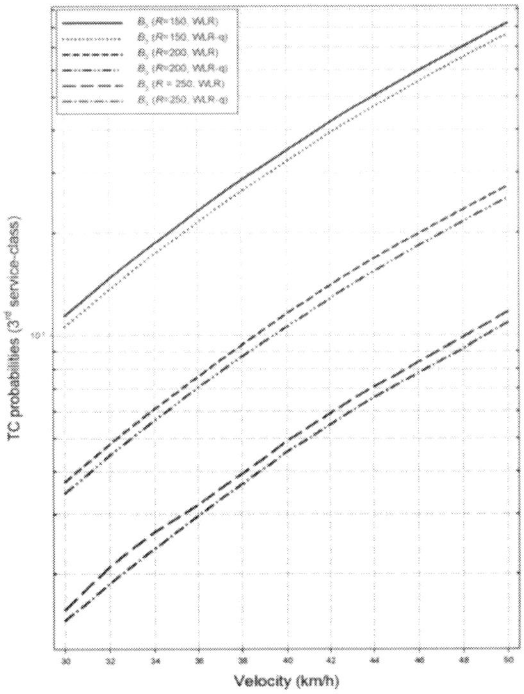

Figure 4. TC probabilities of the 3rd service-class.

REFERENCES

[1] H. Holma and A. Toskala, LTE for UMTS: Evolution to LTE – Advanced, Wiley, New York, 2011.

[2] A. Blogowski, O. Klopfenstein, and B. Renard, "Dimensioning X2 backhaul link in LTE networks", Proc. IEEE ICC, Ottawa, Canada, pp. 2768-2773, June 2012.

[3] M. Peng, D. Liang, Y. Wei, J. Li, and H. Chen, "Self-configuration and self-optimization in LTE-advanced heterogeneous networks", IEEE Commun. Magazine, 51 (5), pp. 36-45, May 2013.

[4] I. Widjaja and H. Roche, "Sizing X2 bandwidth for Inter-connected eNBs", Proc. IEEE VTC Fall, Anchorage, Alaska, USA, pp. 1-5, Sept. 2009.

[5] B. Renard, S. Elayoubi, and A. Simonian, "A dimensioning method for the LTE X2 interface", Proc. IEEE Wireless Commun. and Networking Conf., Shanghai, China, pp. 2718-2723, April 2012.

[6] H. Akimaru and K. Kawashima, Teletraffic - Theory and Applications, 2nd edn. Springer, Berlin, 1999.

[7] V. Frost and B. Melamed, "Traffic modeling for telecommunications networks", IEEE Commun. Magazine, 32 (3), pp. 70-81, March 1994.

[8] D. Lam, D. Cox, and J. Widom, "Teletraffic modeling for personal communications services", IEEE Commun. Magazine, 35 (2), pp. 79-87, Feb. 1997.

[9] J. Kaufman, "Blocking in a shared resource environment", IEEE Trans. Commun., 29 (10), pp. 1474-1481, Oct. 1981.

[10] J. Roberts, "A service system with heterogeneous user requirements," in: G. Pujolle (Ed.), Performance of Data Communications Systems and Their Applications, North Holland, Amsterdam, pp. 423-431, 1981.

[11] J. Roberts, "Teletraffic models for the Telecom 1 Integrad Services Network", Proc. 10th ITC, paper 1.1-2, Montreal, Canada, 1983.

[12] M. Stasiak, M. Glabowski, A. Wisniewski and P. Zwierzykowski, Modeling and Dimensioning of Mobile Networks, Wiley, New York, 2011.

[13] I. Moscholios, J. Vardakas, M. Logothetis, and A. Boucouvalas, "A Batched Poisson Multirate Loss Model Supporting Elastic Traffic under the Bandwidth Reservation Policy", Proc. IEEE ICC, Kyoto, Japan, pp. 1-6, June 2011.

[14] I. Moscholios, J. Vardakas, M. Logothetis, and A. Boucouvalas, "QoS Guarantee in a Batched Poisson Multirate Loss Model Supporting Elastic and Adaptive Traffic", Proc. IEEE ICC 2012, Ottawa, Canada, pp. 1281-1286, June 2012.

[15] I. Moscholios, J. Vardakas, M. Logothetis, and M. Koukias, "A Quasi-random Multirate Loss Model supporting Elastic and Adaptive Traffic under the Bandwidth Reservation Policy", Int. Journal on Advances in Networks and Services, 6 (3&4), pp. 163-174, 2013.

[16] V. Abdulova and I. Aybay, "Performance evaluation of non-prioritized and prioritized call admission control schemes in wireless cellular networks", Wireless Personal Commun., 78 (1), pp. 69-84, Sept. 2014.

[17] F. Cruz-Pérez, J. Vázquez-Ávila, and L. Ortigoza-Guerrero, "Recurrent formulas for the multiple fractional channel reservation strategy in multi-service mobile cellular networks", IEEE Commun. Letters, 8 (10), pp. 629-631, Oct. 2004.

[18] J. Vázquez-Ávila, F. Cruz-Pérez, and L. Ortigoza-Guerrero, "Performance analysis of fractional guard channel policies in mobile cellular networks", IEEE Trans. Wireless Commun., 5 (2), pp. 301-305, March 2006.

[19] I. Moscholios, "Congestion Probabilities in Erlang-Engset Multirate Loss Models under the Multiple Fractional Channel Reservation Policy", Image Processing & Communications, 21 (1), pp. 35-46, 2016.

[20] D. Tsang and K. Ross, "Algorithms to determine exact blocking probabilities for multirate tree networks", IEEE Trans. Commun., 38 (8), pp. 1266-1271, Aug. 1990.

[21] J. Ni, D. Tsang, S. Tatikonda, and B. Bensaou, "Optimal and structured call admission control policies for resource-sharing systems", IEEE Trans. Commun., 55 (1), pp. 158-170, Jan. 2007.

[22] I. Moscholios, M. Logothetis, J. Vardakas, and A. Boucouvalas, "Performance metrics of a multirate resource sharing teletraffic model with finite sources under the threshold and bandwidth reservation policies", IET Networks, 4 (3), pp. 195-208, May 2015.

[23] V. Abdulova and I. Aybay, "Prioritized new call threshold policy for wireless cellular networks" Wireless Personal Commun., 85 (4), pp. 2549-2563, Dec. 2015.

[24] I. Moscholios, V. Vassilakis, M. Logothetis, and A. Boucouvalas, "A probabilistic threshold-based bandwidth sharing policy for wireless multirate loss networks" IEEE Wireless Commun. Letters, 5 (3), pp. 304-307, June 2016.

[25] I. Moscholios, V. Vassilakis, M. Logothetis, and A. Boucouvalas, "State-dependent Bandwidth Sharing Policies for Wireless Multirate Loss Networks", IEEE Transactions on Wireless Communications, 16 (8), pp. 5481-5497, August 2017.

[26] I. Moscholios, M. Logothetis, and S. Shioda, "Performance Evaluation of Multirate Loss Systems Supporting Cooperative Users with a Probabilistic Behavior", IEICE Transactions on Communications, E100-B (10), pp. 1778-1788, October 2017.

[27] J. Kaufman and K. Rege, "Blocking in a shared resource environment with batched Poisson arrival processes", Performance Evaluation, 24 (4), pp. 249-263, Feb. 1996.

[28] I. Moscholios, G. Kallos, V. Vassilakis, and M. Logothetis, "Congestion Probabilities in CDMA-based networks supporting batched Poisson input traffic", Wireless Personal Commun., 79 (2), pp. 1163-1186, Nov. 2014.

[29] I. Moscholios, V. Vassilakis, and P. Sarigiannidis, "Performance Modelling of a Multirate Loss System with Batched Poisson Arrivals under a Probabilistic Threshold Policy", IET Networks, DOI: 10.1049/iet-net.2017.0216 , Online ISSN 2047-4962 Available online: 07 February 2018.

[30] M. Mehmet-Ali, "Call-burst blocking and call admission control in a broadband network with bursty sources", Performance Evaluation, 38 (1), pp. 1-19, Sept. 1999.

[31] I. Moscholios, P. Nikolaropoulos, and M. Logothetis, "Call level blocking of ON-OFF traffic sources with retrials under the complete sharing policy", Proc. 18th ITC, Berlin, Germany, Sept. 2003, pp. 811-820.

[32] I. Moscholios, M. Logothetis, and G. Kokkinakis, "Call-burst blocking of ON-OFF traffic sources with retrials under the complete sharing policy", Performance Evaluation, 59 (4), pp. 279-312, March 2005.

[33] S. Yashkov and A. Yashkova, "Processor sharing: a survey of the mathematical theory", Automation and Remote Control, 68 (9), pp. 1662-1731, Sept. 2007.

[34] L. Lei, C. Lin, J. Cai, and X. Shen, "Flow-level performance of opportunistic OFDM-TDMA and OFDMA networks", IEEE Trans. Wireless Commun., 7 (12), pp. 5461-5472, Dec. 2008.

[35] S. Yong, W. Song, and Z. Zhong, "Resource allocation for aggregate multimedia and healthcare services over heterogeneous multi-hop wireless networks", Wireless Personal Commun., 69 (1), pp. 229-251, March 2013.

[36] I. Moscholios, J. Vardakas, M. Logothetis, and A. Boucouvalas, "Congestion probabilities in a batched Poisson multirate loss model supporting elastic and adaptive traffic", Annals of Telecommun., 68 (5), pp. 327-344, June 2013.

[37] I. Moscholios, M. Logothetis, J. Vardakas, and A. Boucouvalas, "Congestion Probabilities of Elastic and Adaptive Calls in Erlang-Engset Multirate Loss Models under the Threshold and Bandwidth Reservation Policies", Computer Networks, 92 (1), pp. 1-23, December 2015.

[38] I. Moscholios, M. Logothetis, and A. Boucouvalas, "Blocking Probabilities of Elastic and Adaptive Calls in the Erlang Multirate Loss Model under the Threshold Policy", Telecommunication Systems, 62 (1), pp. 245-262, May 2016.

[39] S. Elayoubi, Y. Khadraoui, B. Baynat, and T. En-Najjary, "Flow level performance evaluation in mobile networks: Analytical modeling and empirical validation", Computer Communications, 108, pp. 27-35, Aug. 2017.

[40] I. Dimitriou, "Dynamic balancing in finite processor sharing queues with guard bandwidth policy, multiclass retrial users and signals", Performance Evaluation, 114, Sept. 2017.

[41] I. Moscholios, M. Logothetis, and P. Nikolaropoulos, "Engset Multi-Rate State-Dependent Loss Models", Performance Evaluation, 59 (2-3), pp. 247-277, February 2005.

[42] M. Glabowski, "Modelling of state-dependent multirate systems carrying BPP traffic", Annals Telecommun., 63 (7), pp. 393-407, August 2008.

[43] I. Moscholios, G. Kallos, M. Katsiva, V. Vassilakis, and M. D. Logothetis, "QoS Equalization in a W-CDMA Cell Supporting Calls of Infinite or Finite Sources with Interference Cancelation", Journal of Telecommunications and Information Technology (JTIT), 3, pp. 63-70, 2014.

[44] I. Moscholios, V. Vassilakis, M. Logothetis, and J. Vardakas, "Erlang-Engset Multirate Retry Loss Models for Elastic and Adaptive Traffic under the Bandwidth Reservation Policy", Int. Journal on Advances in Networks and Services, 7 (1&2), pp. 12-24, July 2014.

[45] V. Vassilakis, I. Moscholios, and M. Logothetis, "Uplink Blocking Probabilities in Priority-Based Cellular CDMA Networks with Finite Source Population", IEICE Transactions on Communications, vol. E99-B (6), pp. 1302-1309, June 2016.

[46] G. Stamatelos and J. Hayes, "Admission control techniques with application to broadband networks", Computer Commun., 17 (9), pp. 663-673, Sept. 1994.

A Novel Ranging Method using Bimodal Gaussian Distributed RSSI Measurements

Jing Jing Wang
Kyungpook National University
Graduate school of Electronics Engineering,
Daegu, South Korea
Email: wjj0219@naver.com

Jun Gyu Hwang
Kyungpook National University
Graduate school of Electronics Engineering,
Daegu, South Korea
E-mail: cjstk891015@naver.com

KwangEog Lee
Agency for Defense Development (ADD)
Datian, South Korea
E-mail: kelee@add.re.kr

Joon Goo Park
Kyungpook National University
Graduate school of Electronics Engineering,
Daegu, South Korea
E-mail: jgpark@knu.ac.kr

Abstract—**The ranging method based on Received Signal Strength Indicator (RSSI) widely uses indoor positioning technology of Wireless Sensing Network (WSN) because of low cost and low complexity. The primary challenge is how to overcome some of the phenomena that affect signal propagation in a real environment, such as multipath, diffraction, and absorption. Also, it makes the positioning method more accurate. We are interested in the fact that influences on RSSI measurements from indoor propagation environments can be another ranging error source. In other words, to improve the ranging accuracy, the factors influencing RSSI measurements should be minimized or compensated. In this paper, we propose a method using bimodal Gaussian distribution to get more accurate estimated RSSI. The proposed method uses RSSI measurements with bimodal Gaussian distributed characteristics in a reference position. The experimental results in the proposed method show that more precise results are achieved compared with the existing method.**

Keywords— RSSI; bimodal gaussian; attenuation log model.

I. INTRODUCTION

In recent years, wireless network technologies, such as Wi-Fi, ZigBee, Bluetooth, iBeacon have been rapidly developed and widely used [1][2][3]. According to the signal transmission intensity attenuation, phase difference, time delay based on wireless network positioning technology can estimate the location of the mobile node in the wireless network coverage area to provide positioning services. The indoor positioning technology using RSSI measurements is focused in this research area because of its high positioning accuracy. It is also compliant with GPS (Global Positioning System) in precise positioning area [4]. Due to the complexity of indoor environments, the positioning error is relatively large compared to that of outdoor GPS. Other indoor positioning methods such as Ultrasonic [5], Ultra-wideband [6] and so on, which are restricted by the cost and application condition, are hard to meet the general demands of indoor positioning.

Ranging algorithms are divided into two categories according to the method of distance measurement in wireless sensor networks. One is a ranging-based algorithm, and the other is a range-free algorithm. The former method measures RSS (Received Signal Strength), (Time of Arrival), TDOA (Time Difference of Arrival), etc. and calculates or estimates the distance between node and reference [7]. The latter one utilizes the relationship of geometric location information between receiving nodes and the transmitting nodes to estimate the distance.

The positioning algorithm based on more precisely calculated or estimated distance information can provide higher positioning accuracy. The RSSI attenuation log model, which is easily influenced by various factors in propagation environments, is generally used for distance estimation.

A suitable method that not only efficiently improves the positioning error but also expands the measurement range of indoor positioning is needed.

The rest of the paper is structured as follows. In Section II, the RSSI-based ranging method is introduced. In Section III, the statistics of RSSI measurements are analyzed. In Section IV, a new attenuation log model using RSSI measurements with bimodal Gaussian distributed characteristics in a reference position is proposed and its experimental results are given in Section V. Conclusions are given in Section VI.

II. RSSI-BASED RANGING METHOD

In positioning theory, one of the techniques related to ranging is to estimate the distance between two points by the signal strength between the transmitting point and the receiving point. Most devices can currently obtain RSSI. WSN does not require additional hardware support, and it does not affect the energy consumption, the size of the nodes and the cost of the nodes. Therefore, WSN technology and RSSI technology are very suitable for rough ranging.

In free space, RSSI is inversely proportional to the square of the distance d between the receiving point and the transmitting point. The relationship can be expressed using the famous Friis formula [8]:

$$P_r(\mathrm{d}) = \frac{P_t G_t G_r \lambda^2}{(4\pi)^2 d^2 L} \qquad (1)$$

In Equation (1), $P_r(\mathrm{d})$ is the received power, and the unit is watts. P_t is the transmit power, and the unit is watts. G_t is the transmit antenna gain. G_r is the gain of the receiving antenna. λ is the wavelength of the transmitted signal and the unit is meter. L is a loss parameter that has nothing to do with the propagation environment. In fact, the system loss parameters represent the total loss of the actual system hardware. It includes transmission lines, filters, and antennas.

In general, L is greater than one. However, if we assume that the system hardware has no loss, we can let L = 1. From (1), we can observe that the attenuation of the received power is exponential with the distance. So, the free-space path loss can be directly derived from Equation (1) without any system loss.

$$PL_F(\mathrm{d})[\mathrm{dB}] = 10\log\left(\frac{P_t}{P_r}\right) = -10\log\left(\frac{G_t G_r \lambda^2}{(4\pi)^2 d^2}\right) \quad (2)$$

If we ignore the antenna gain and let $G_t = G_r = 1$, Equation (2) can be written as:

$$PL_F(\mathrm{d})[\mathrm{dB}] = 10\log\left(\frac{P_t}{P_r}\right) = 20\log\left(\frac{4\pi d}{\lambda}\right) \quad (3)$$

In a free-space model, the average received signal is in a logarithmic relationship with the distance d between the transmitter and the receiver in all environments. In fact, a more general path loss model can be constructed using the environment-dependent signal attenuation factor to change the free-space path loss model. The mathematical expression of signal attenuation log model is as follows:

$$PL_{LN}(d) = \mathrm{PL}(d_0) + 10nlg\left(\frac{d}{d_0}\right) + X_0 \quad (4)$$

where d represents the distance from the transmitting node to the receiving node, and the unit is m. d_0 is the unit distance and usually takes 1m. $PL_{LN}(d)$ is the path loss after a distance of d, and the unit is dBm. $\mathrm{PL}(d_0)$ is the path loss after the unit distance, and the unit is dBm. X_0 is Gauss random number for a mean of 0, and its standard deviation range is 4~10. When the n value is smaller, the signal attenuation in the transmission process is smaller, and the signal can spread farther away. The range is generally between 2 and 4. Figure 1 shows the signal attenuation model for indoor positioning.

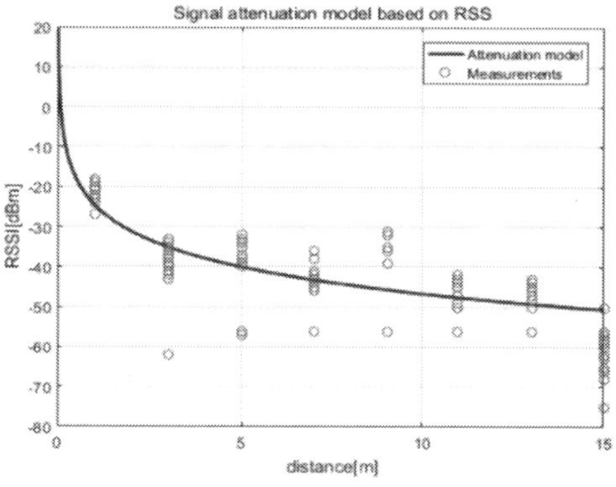

Figure 1. Signal attenuation model for indoor positioning

III. STATISTICS OF RSSI MEASUREMENTS

The relevant research shows that the relationship between the RSSI and the transmission distance of the wireless signal is closely related and stochastic characteristics of RSSI measurements follow a particular rule pattern.

From the point of view of the probability density function property, the measured RSSI data were analyzed. We collected RSSI measurements every two meters and analyzed them by comparing with the stochastic distribution model. After thorough analysis, we can find that most of the RSSI measurements at a fixed location conform to Gaussian distributions or bimodal Gaussian distributions. At the same time, there is a small part of abnormal RSSI values. Figures 2-5 give the probability density distributions of RSSI measurements at 1m, 5m, 9m, and 13m.

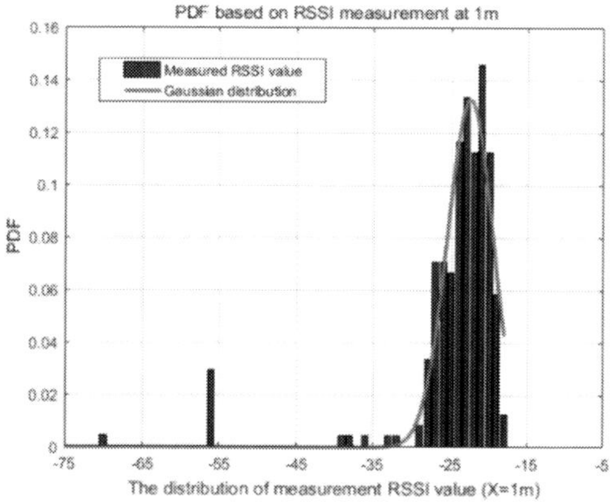

Figure. 2. Probability density function of RSSI measurements at 1m

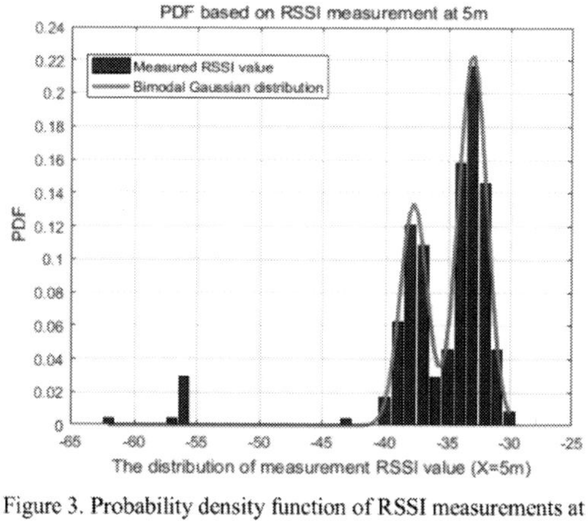

Figure 3. Probability density function of RSSI measurements at 5m

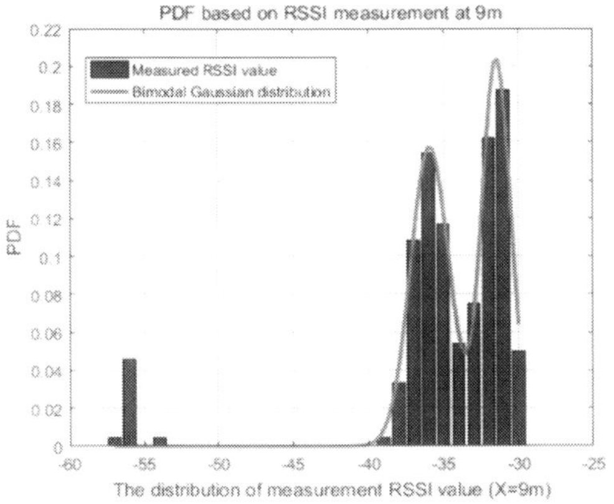

Figure. 4. Probability density function of RSSI measurements at 9m

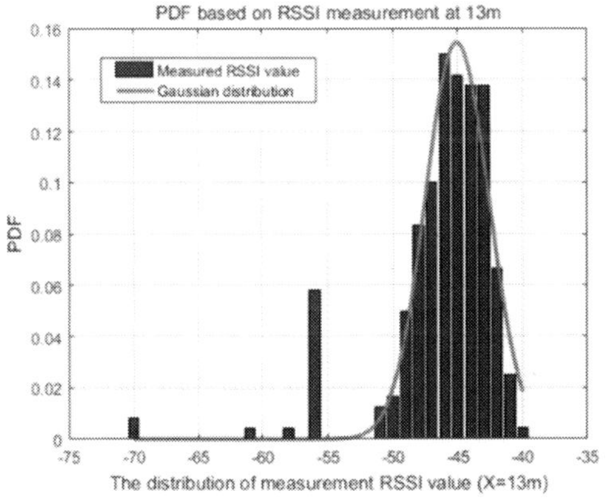

Figure. 5. Probability density function of RSSI measurements at 13m

IV. A New Attenuation RSSI Log Model

The existing RSSI attenuation log model utilizes the mean value of the RSSI measurements at a reference point for its derivation. Relevant research shows that the RSSI mean value is close to the representative RSSI value at that point. Although this value is close to the representative RSSI value, we find that there is some difference caused by some error sources in indoor environments. For its analysis, we collect 240 RSSI measurements at every reference point.

By analyzing Figures 2-5, after removing a small part of outliers, we can find that the RSSI values measured at 1m and 13m show Gaussian distributed characteristics and those at 5m and 9m conform to the bimodal Gaussian distribution.

Therefore, we propose a new RSSI attenuation log model, which can provide more precise ranging information. The derivation procedures are presented below.

Firstly, we conducted an analysis based on the nature of the collected RSSI values, then filtered out the abnormal value, which produces a big difference with the average.

Secondly, according to Equation (5), we can get a Gaussian distribution model and Bimodal Gaussian distribution model of the RSSI measurements at a reference point.

Thirdly, according to Equation (7), we weigh filtered RSSI measurements which comply with bimodal Gaussian distribution to get the RSSI estimate at the reference point.

Finally, we propose a new RSSI attenuation log model, which is valid for up to 15m range.

We take out this part of the RSSI value. Then, we calculate the estimated RSSI value according to the selected RSSI measurement values at a fixed point. We obtain estimates based on bimodal Gaussian distribution or Gaussian distribution respectively by processing 240 RSSI data from 1 meter to 15 meters. The equation of mixed Gaussian distribution is expressed as:

$$\mathrm{F(x)} = a_1 \frac{1}{\sqrt{2\pi}\sigma_1} e^{-\frac{(x-\mu_1)^2}{2\sigma_1{}^2}} + a_2 \frac{1}{\sqrt{2\pi}\sigma_2} e^{-\frac{(x-\mu_2)^2}{2\sigma_2{}^2}}, \quad (5)$$

$$where, (\sigma > 0)$$

The maximum value of the first peak is Max_1, and the maximum value of the second peak is Max_2. If

$$Min \leq \frac{Max_1 + Max_2}{2} \quad (6)$$

Min is the minimum value between two peaks in Equation (6). At this time, the 240 RSSI measurements we have obtained are Gaussian distributions. Otherwise, they are bimodal Gaussian distributions.

$$RSSI_{Bimodal\ Gauss} = \frac{a_1}{a_1 + a_2}\mu_1 + \frac{a_2}{a_1 + a_2}\mu_2 \quad (7)$$

$$RSSI_{Gauss} = \frac{\sum_{i=1}^{m} RSSI_{max_i} P_i}{\sum_{i=1}^{m} P_i} \quad (8)$$

where $P_i \geq 0.04$ and $RSSI_{max_i} \geq RSSI_{max_{i+1}}$

We use the above method to get the estimated value of RSSI at the reference point.

A new attenuation log model can be composed using the estimated RSSI values obtained from 240 RSSI measurement values at a reference point in linear regression model.

V. Experimental Results

In experiments, we use ipTIME N3004 as a node and place those nodes at the height of 0.2m on the ground. To reduce the impact of ground reflection on the received RSSI value and the ranging error, the reference node is also placed at 0.2m height. Broadcom 802.11 wireless network card built-in notebook computer is used as a mobile node and is located 1m away from a fixed node for measurement start. The considered reference points are 2m apart sequentially to each other. At each reference point, 240 times measurement processes are executed. The experiments were carried out in the third-floor corridor of Kyungpook National University IT1 Building, as shown in Figure 6.

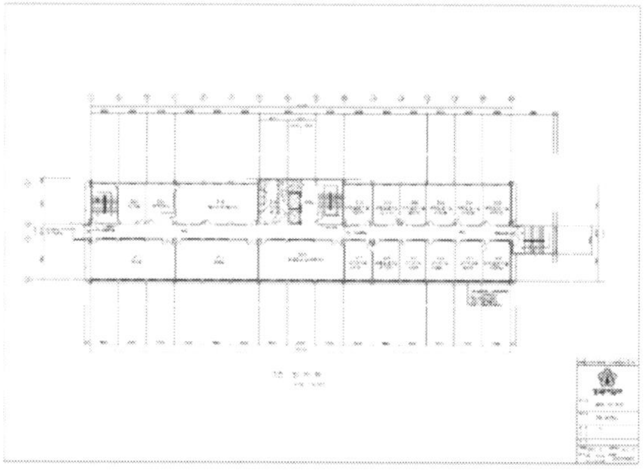

Figure 6. Kyungpook National University IT-1 building

We compare the performance of the proposed RSSI attenuation log model with that of an existing attenuation log model.

We calculate RSSI values at reference points using mean filtering and bimodal Gaussian filtering for 240 measurement samples at each reference point. Then, we can obtain an existing RSSI attenuation log model and the proposed RSSI attenuation log model like below

Parameters of existing RSSI model: A = -23.84, n = 2.206

Parameters of proposed RSSI model: A = -21.81, n = 2.326

The attenuation log model curve is fitted according to filtered RSSI values at reference points. After that, we can obtain a proposed RSSI attenuation log model, which is valid in range of 1m to 15m, as shown in Figure 7. The red line is the proposed RSSI attenuation log model.

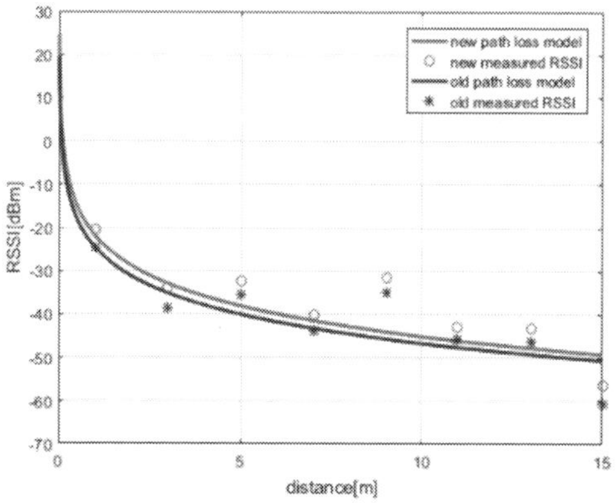

Figure 7. Fitted RSSI-distance curve using the proposed method and mean filtering

According to Figure 7, we can calculate distances of unknown nodes by obtaining RSSI values of those corresponding nodes. For performance, we compare distances of unknown nodes calculated by the proposed method and the existing one. The comparison results are shown in Table 1.

TABLE 1. COMPARISON OF THE DISTANCE MEASUREMENT ERRORS OF THE PROPOSED METHOD AND MEAN FILTERING METHOD

Distance (m)	Measure Distance Mean Filtering Method(m)	Measure Distance The Proposed Method(m)	Improved The Range Error(m)	Reduction rate (%)
1m	0.234	0.105	0.129	12.9%
3m	1.724	1.4621	0.2617	8.73%
5m	1.564	1.2521	0.311	6.23%
7m	1.5	0.9076	0.5924	8.46%
9m	5.746	4.3488	1.3976	15.53%
11m	1.613	0.909	0.704	43.7%
13m	2.667	1.802	0.864	32.4%

From Table 1, we can find that the proposed RSSI attenuation log model provides more accurate distance information compared with an existing RSSI attenuation model. Experimental results show that the range error decreases more evidently beyond the range of 10m, which indicates that the proposed method can extend the applicable range. At the same time, the proposed method reduces the distance error at 11 meter reference point by 0.704m.

From the comparison results, we can conclude that the proposed method improves the ranging accuracy to a certain extent and reduces the influence of more substantial ranging errors due to other factors, such as obstacles.

V. CONCLUSION

In this paper, we propose a novel RSSI attenuation model based on bimodal Gaussian filtering. The proposed method produces more accurate distance information and is applicable for more extended ranging case compared with an existing RSSI attenuation log model method, which is based on simple mean filtering.

ACKNOWLEDGMENT

This work has been supported by the National GNSS Research Center program of Defense Acquisition Program Administration and Agency for Defense Development.

REFERENCES

[1] A. Note, "ZigBee," *Electronics*, vol. 14, pp. 67–77, 2008.
[2] B. A. Miller, "Bluetooth Technology," in *Handbook of Computer Networks*, vol. 2, 2011, pp. 790–801.
[3] M. Kouhne and J. Sieck, "Location-Based Services with iBeacon Technology," in *Proceedings - 2nd International Conference on Artificial Intelligence, Modelling, and Simulation, AIMS 2014*, 2014, pp. 315–321.
[4] A. El-rabbany, *Introduction to GPS: The Global Position System*. 2006.
[5] F. Ijaz and H. Yang, "Indoor positioning: A review of indoor ultrasonic positioning systems," *Adv. Commun. Technol.*, pp. 1146–1150, 2013.

[6] L. Zhang and G. Yang, "Ultra-wide-band based indoor positioning technologies," *Shuju Caiji Yu Chuli/Journal Data Acquis. Process.*, vol. 28, no. 6, pp. 706–713, 2013.
[7] R. Yamasaki, A. Ogino, T. Tamaki, T. Uta, N. Matsuzawa, and T. Kalo, "TDOA location system for IEEE 802.11b WLAN," in *IEEE Wireless Communications and Networking Conference, WCNC*, 2005, vol. 4, pp. 2338–2343.
[8] V. Mathuranathan, "Log Distance Path Loss or Log Normal Shadowing Model," *Channel Modelling*, 2013. [Online]. Available: http://www.gaussianwaves.com/2013/09/log-distance-path-loss-or-log-normal-shadowing-model/. [retrieved April 2018]

Context Aware Group Key Management Model for Internet of Things

Hussein Harb, Ashraf William, Omayma A. El-Mohsen
Switching Department
National Telecommunication Institute
Cairo, Egypt
E-mail: Hussein.Harb@nti.sci.eg, awilliam@nti.sci.eg, Omayma.mohsen@nti.sci.eg

Abstract—**Internet of Things (IoT) devices are resource constrained. Therefore, many IoT applications rely on multicast in their transmission to preserve IoT node resources. However, security is a main concern in critical applications such as actuators control. Consequently, the multicast traffic has to be secured. Multicast security requires an efficient and scalable Group Key Management (GKM) protocol. In case of IoT, the situation is more difficult because of the dynamic nature of IoT scenarios. This paper introduces a new model for GKM based on using a context aware security server accompanied by a group of key distribution servers. The model efficiently distributes group encryption keys to IoT devices to secure the multicast sessions. The proposed solution is mathematically evaluated relative to the Logical Key Hierarchy (LKH) protocol. The comparison shows that the proposed model efficiently enhanced the performance for both the members and the key servers regarding load and key storage cost.**

Keywords—Internet of Things; Group Key Management; Context Awareness.

I. INTRODUCTION

The Internet of Things (IoT) refers to billions of interconnected smart objects equipped with sensors or actuators. Existing and evolving communication protocols are used to enable services to such smart objects and allow them to communicate among each other and with backend users of the Internet during different activities of sensing and controlling. IoT networks, without intelligence, are just wireless sensor networks. Intelligence in IoT is achieved using context awareness. Context awareness, as defined in [1], is the ability of a system to provide information or services to users using information of a certain entity where the entity can be a person, place, piece of software, or an object.

On the other hand, the IoT is naturally a resource-constrained network regarding Central Processing Unit power, memory, and energy. Therefore, many of the IoT application scenarios rely on multicast operation to preserve bandwidth and enhance the sensing and control operation among the sensors and the actuators. For example group communication is used in; smart meter applications, in building safety, in home automation and intelligent transportation systems.Multicast transmits data efficiently between one sender or multiple senders to multiple receivers. However, the constrained nature and the massive size of the IoT network make it vulnerable to many security attacks.

In order to multicast information among a certain group securely, the traffic should be encrypted. So, a common group key should be shared among all members of the group. Whenever membership changes, the group key should be updated. Hence, during the registration process, it is necessary to have strong authentication mechanisms to acquire the identity of the participants prior to distributing the key material. Thus, the main concern is around key management, key distribution, and access control for the key material [2].

Group Key Management (GKM) protocols are divided into three categories: centralized, decentralized, and distributed key management protocols [2]-[4]. Nevertheless, all the conventional GKM protocols under the above mentioned categories do not suit the dynamic nature of the IoT scenarios and applications. Consequently, many research directions are carried out to adapt these protocols to IoT networks [5]-[7]. Yet, most of the research related to GKM focuses on adapting these protocols by working on just one or two of the IoT aspects such as mobility, scalability, constrained nature of devices, application nature, network access technology, or addressing. They ignore that the majority of IoT scenarios need to work on most of these aspects combined together and they lack the ability to address the resulting issues of such combination.

In this paper, a new GKM security model is proposed, i.e., CASMA (Context-Aware Secured Multicast Architecture), to work with different IoT applications and to suite the dynamic nature of the IoT scenarios. CASMA relies on adding intelligence to the security operation by using a Context Aware Security Server (CASS) that is responsible for managing the secure multicast session and group key distribution operation. The key distribution operation itself is carried out through a set of Key Distribution Servers (KDS). The CASS collects context information from both members (sensors or actuators) and KDSs, and analyses it to assign those members to the appropriate KDS that will be able to serve them best, while controlling load balancing which improves both performance and scalability.

The solution advantages can be summarized in the following:

- CASMA is an open model that is not tied to a specific protocol or algorithm and can deploy any of the current or future protocols or algorithms.
- The allocation process is based on context-awareness, which improves both performance and scalability.
- It can be deployed for both private and public application scenarios.
- It provides load balancing control among key servers.
- It overcomes key servers' failover.

The rest of the paper is organized as follows: Section II describes background information related to the secured multicast operation and the protocols used to achieve it along with an overview of the current related research directions concerning GKM in IoT scenarios. Section III covers the proposed GKM model architecture and operation. Section VI presents a mathematical evaluation and analysis of the proposed GKM model performance. Finally, Section V concludes the paper and proposes future research directions.

II. BACKGROUND AND RELATED WORK

A. *Secured Multicast Operation*

In order to secure multicast traffic, a security policy is set up by Group Owner (GO) and passed to a trusted entity; the Group Controller and Key server (GCKS), which will manage the group security operation. Next, the group members register with the GCKS. Their registration is accepted only if they meet the security parameters defined in the security policy set up by the GO. At this time, group members are eligible for keys download.

The aim of such process is that all authorized users download the same key that is used to encrypt and decrypt multicast data messages. This shared key is called Traffic Encryption Key (TEK). In order to preserve the secrecy of the multicast data and to achieve forward and backward secrecy, the TEK needs to be updated periodically or each time a member joins/leaves the multicast group according to the rekeying mechanism defined in the group security policy [2]-[4]. Each authorized member that shares the TEK may need to download additional Keys, called Key Encryption Key (KEK) and Group Encryption Key (GEK), which facilitates the update of the TEK.

B. *Group Key Management Protocols*

Protecting group information is achieved by defining the security policy by the GO and enforcing it among group members. This is accomplished by using protocols such as Group Security Association Key Management Protocol (GSAKMP) [8] or Group Domain of Interoperation (GDOI) [9]. The GO creates the security policy rules for the group and expresses them in a policy token that is passed to the GCKS. The GCKS enforces such a policy by granting access only to members that fulfill the security policy. In this case, members will have the right to download the group keys. Whenever membership changes, the keys need to be updated according to the mechanism defined in the security policy. In general, protocols used in group key management update can be classified into centralized, decentralized, and distributed group management protocols.

In centralized group key management protocols, there is only one GCKS responsible for group key distribution and update. The GCKS shares a pairwise key with each member of the group and distributes group keys to group members on a point-to-point basis. Examples of protocols working in centralized fashion are Group Key Management Protocol (GKMP), Logical Key Hierarchy (LKH), LKH+, One-way Function Tree (OFT), Centralized Flat Table (CFT), and Efficient Large-Group Key (ELK) [2]-[4].

In decentralized group key management protocols, the large group is divided into small subgroups. A group key is shared among all group members and every subgroup has its own subgroup key. The GCKS serves all members of the group. On the other hand, every subgroup has its subgroup key sever, which manages the subgroup key. Examples of protocols working in decentralized fashion are Scalable Multicast Key Distribution (SMKD), Iolus, Dual-Encryption Protocol (DEP), MARKS, Kronos, and Intra-Domain Group Key Management protocol (IGKMP) [2]-[4].

In distributed group management protocols, many members in the group are responsible for new group key generation and distribution. It has no group controller. The group key can be generated in a contributory fashion, where all members aid in generating the group key. However, this process becomes difficult as group members increase or if the key is generated by one of the members, which is not secure. The distributed group key management protocols are the most complex and difficult ones. Examples of distributed protocols are Group Diffie–Hellman Key Exchange (G-DH), Conference Key Agreement (CKA), Distributed Logical Key Hierarchy (DLKH), Distributed One-way Function Tree (DOFT), and Diffie–Hellman Logical Key Hierarchy (DH-LKH) [2]-[4].

C. *Related Work*

Most of the research work carried out in this domain is either very specific to an application or a rekeying protocol. For example, in [5] Li et al. focus on Privacy Preservation in Smart Buildings of the Smart Grid. It is based on Tree Group Deffie-Helman (TGDH) evaluating fault tolerance and performance. The paper assumed that the key server and the trust center are always available; it doesn't state how security is maintained in case of their failure.

Similarly, Agrawal [6] works on Secure Key Distribution Protocols in Smart Meter application focusing on preventing man-in-the-middle attack. The paper introduces just a security analysis with no performance evaluation.

In [7], a centralized approach to distribute and manage group keys in ad hoc networks and Internet of Things is used. The proposal is applied to Vehicle-to-Vehicle communications in Vehicular Ad hoc Networks measuring the communication cost. The paper proposes performing batch leave operation based on a pre-determined leave time stated by members while joining the group. The paper assumes that each member knows the exact time to leave the group, which is not always the case. Also, the paper ignores leave events due to communication loss.

It is obvious that most of the research work carried out is tied to a certain type of application such as smart grids, Internet of vehicles, etc., none of which is generic. In addition, those researches work on just one or two aspects of IoT assuming that the conditions of the application scenario is static which is not the case for IoT application scenarios which have dynamic and varying nature regarding the network access technology, type of application, state of members and key servers and the load on them.

This raises the motivation to introduce our GKM model that adapts to the dynamic nature of IoT scenarios regarding application nature and scenario conditions.

III. THE PROPOSED GKM MODEL

This section presents the new proposed solution. In subsection A, the new key management architecture, CASMA, is introduced. Next, subsection B explains its operation.

A. *CASMA Architecture*

The CASMA model is based on the IGKMP protocol architecture [2]-[4][10]. IGKMP is a decentralized key management protocol in which subgroups are called areas. Each area has one subgroup controller called Area Key Distributer (AKD). A common controller, i.e., Domain Key Distributer (DKD), is responsible for generating the group key and facilitating the co-ordination between AKDs. Each member belongs to one area only and registers with one AKD according to the location.

The CASMA architecture is shown in Figure 1. CASMA follows the International Telecommunication Union IoT architecture reference model defined in [11]. According to the model, the architecture is composed of a Device layer, Network layer, Service Support and Application Support layer, and finally an Application layer.

CASMA is based on using a CASS server and a set of KDSs. Here, The KDSs are the DKD and the Zone Key Distribution servers (ZKDs). The DKD; as in IGKMP; is responsible for TEK generation and update, while the ZKDs replace the AKDs found in IGKMP. The ZKDs are the subgroup controller of their zones, where the zone represents the ZKD with its registered members. They are not tied to a certain area or location as is the case for AKDs. All these servers lie in the Service Support and Application Support Layer of the IoT Reference Model, as shown in Figure 1.

The CASS server acts as the trusted entity that is responsible for managing the security sessions, while the KDSs are responsible for key distribution and update.

The CASS collects context information from both members (sensors or actuators) and KDSs and stores it in its database. The information collected from sensors includes location, access network, multicast group to join, application accessed and load on KDSs and their availability. On the other hand, the information from KDSs is that related to the supported multicast groups and the number of members associated with each group.

The CASS server analyses the collected information and uses it to assign those members to the appropriate ZKD that will be able to serve them best, while controlling load balancing. This information is periodically updated. Therefore, the allocation process is based on intelligent context-awareness, which improves both performance and scalability.

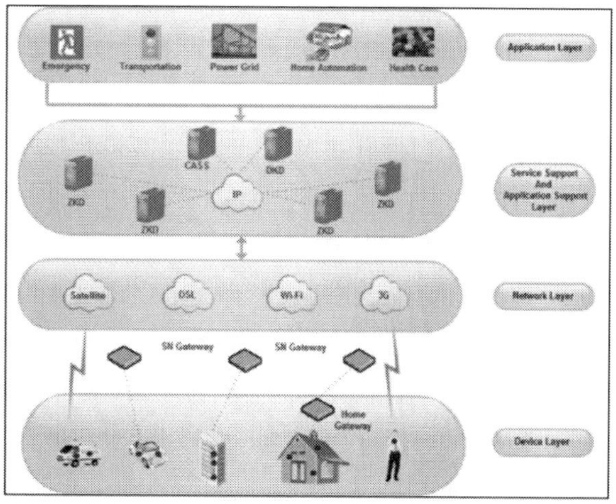

Figure 1. CASMA Architecture

CASS roles can be defined as follows:

- Acts as a Trusted Entity for security operation.
- Manages the operation of key distribution.
- Contains profile for context information of registered member (status, location, access network, multicast application running).
- Contains profile for context information of ZKDs (status, location, multicast groups supported, number of registered members in each group).
- Collects context information from members and KDSs and stores it. This information includes:
  - Access Network (Wi-Fi, Zigbee, 3G and 4G)
  - Geographical location
  - Multicast group to join
  - Load on ZKD servers
- Analyses collected information and uses it to assign the members to the appropriate KDS that will be able to serve them best, while controlling load balancing.
- Receives members' query-to-join requests.
- Assigns members (actuator nodes) to the appropriate ZKD to register with according to analyzed context information.
- Keeps track of active ZKDs.
- Assigns alternative ZKD to members in case of the main ZKD failure.
- Adjusts periodic rekey time according to application and network conditions.

ZKD roles are as follows:

- Communicates with CASS Server, DKD, and members.
- Receives request to join messages from members.
- Each ZKD Creates a zone that contains itself and the members that register with it.
- Shares a unique key; Member-Private-Key (MbrPKey) with each accompanied member. This key is used to provide a secure unicast channel between the ZKD and the member.
- Shares a common Zone group Key (ZKey) between itself and all accompanied members. This key is used to assist TEK distribution from the ZKD to the associated members.
- The MbrPKey and the ZKey as shown in Figure 2 are both generated and downloaded from the ZKD to the members during the registration process.
- Shares a unique key ZKDkey with the DKD. This key is used to provide secure unicast channel between the ZKD and the DKD.
- Shares a common Domain group Key (DGkey) between the DKD and all ZKDs. This is used to assist in the distribution of TEK from the DKD to all ZKDs.
- The ZKDKey and the DGKey as shown in Figure 2 are both generated and downloaded from the DKD to the ZKDs during the registration process between ZKD and DKD.
- Updates members with TEK during rekeying.

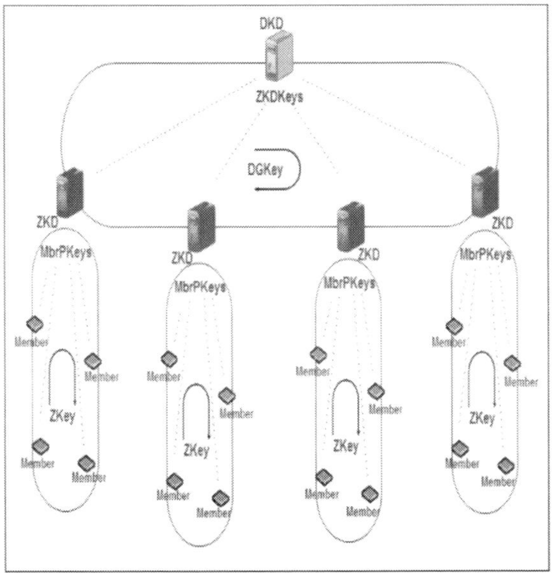

Figure 2. Architecture Keys

DKD roles are defined as follows:

- Communicates with the CASS Server and the ZKDs.
- Shares the unique ZKDkey with each ZKD.
- Shares the common multicast DGkey with all ZKDs.
- Generates the TEK and transmit it to the ZKDs over a secured channel.
- Notified by the CASS in case of membership change or periodic rekeying.
- Updates TEK according to membership change or periodic rekeying.
- Keeps track of key synchronization among ZKDs.

It is worth mentioning that within each zone, rekeying can take place using the above mentioned MbrPKey and Zkey. It can also take place using any of the centralized rekeying protocols mentioned in Section II-B (LKH, LKH+, OFT, CFT, and ELK). This solution can be implemented in either private application scenarios, such as buildings automation, smart home, and buildings safety or public application scenarios, such as in smart cities and Internet of vehicle applications.

B. CASMA operation

The following explains the rekeying operation in CASMA solution. This process takes place whether periodically or due to member change.

Member Join:

With every new member joining the group, the group key needs to be changed in order to assure backward secrecy (new members have no access to previous secured data). The messages flow is shown in Figure 3.

First, the new member (Actuator) sends a "Query-to-Join" request to the CASS server. The CASS server analyses its database and selects the appropriate ZKD according to the scenario logic. The address of the assigned ZKD is sent to the joining member in the "Query-Response" message.

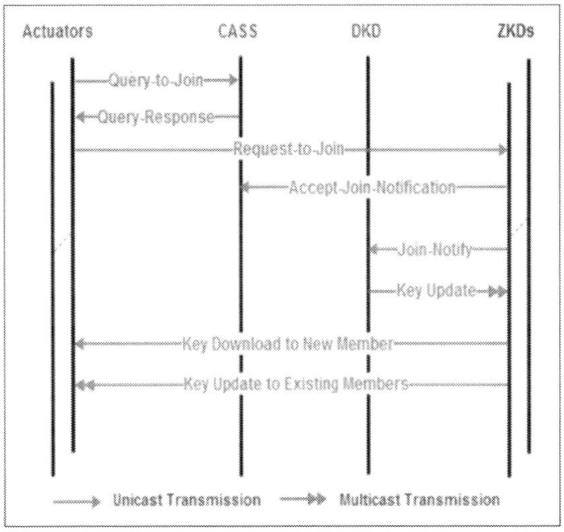

Figure 3. Join Multicast Group Message Flow

Second, the member sends a "Request-to-Join" message to the assigned ZKD. The ZKD authenticates the joining member and ensures that it meets the security policy specification. If it succeeds, the ZKD sends an "Accept-Join-Notification" message to the CASS server to update its database with the context information related to the ZKD (number of accompanied members relative to the multicast group) and to the member (successfully registered with the assigned ZKD).

Third, the ZKD sends a "Join-Notify" message to the DKD to update the TEK. Consequently, the DKD performs key update and multicasts the new key to all ZKDs encrypted with the DGkey. Finally, the ZKDs extract the TEK and multicast it to their zone members encrypted using their Zone key. Simultaneously, the ZKD with the new joining member updates its ZKey and sends the new keys (TEK and ZKey) to the new member encrypted with its private key (MbrPKey).

Member Leave:

When a member leaves a group, the multicast key and its zone key need to be updated to assure forward secrecy (the leaving member has no access to forthcoming data transmitted). The messages flow is shown in Figure 4.

First, the leaving member (Actuator) sends a "Leave" request to its ZKD. Second, The ZKD forwards the "Leave" request to the DKD to perform TEK update. Third, the ZKD sends a "Leave_Notification" message to the CASS server to update its context information database indicating that the load on this ZKD is decremented by the effect of the leaving member. Fourth, the ZKD creates a new ZKey and sends this key to each one of the remaining zone members encrypted by each member private key (MbrPKey). This is represented by the zone key download operation taking place on the zone existing members throughout all ZKDs. Fifth, the TEK update takes place when the DKD creates the new TEK and multicasts it to all ZKDs encrypted by the DGkey. Finally, each ZKD decrypts this message carrying the TEK, re-encrypts it using its ZKey, and multicasts it to its zone existing members.

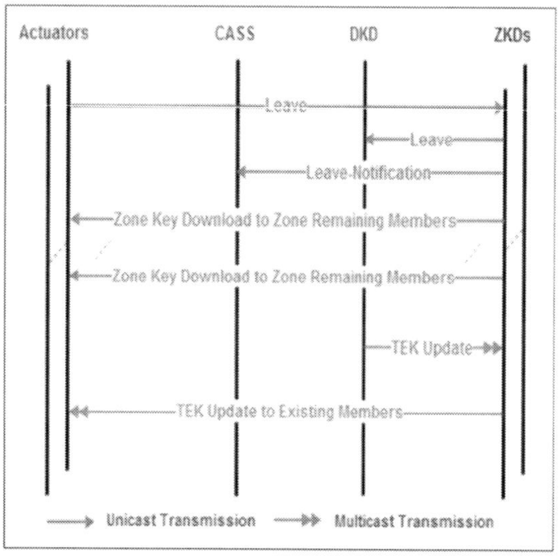

Figure 4. Leave Multicast Group Message Flow

Periodic Rekeying:

The CASS server periodically informs the DKD server to update the Keys to avoid security breaches. By keeping track of the server status, the CASS informs the DKD about the appropriate time for rekeying to avoid network and server loading as shown in Figure 5. As a result the DKD creates the new TEK and multicasts it to all ZKDs encrypted by the DGkey. Each ZKD decrypts this message carrying the TEK, re-encrypts it using its ZKey, and multicasts it to its zone members. Furthermore, the CASS can adjust the time interval needed for periodic rekeying according to application type and strength of the encryption key.

IV. Performance Analysis

As previously mentioned in Section III-A, rekeying within each zone can take place using one of the centralized key management protocols. Consequently and in order to evaluate the performance of CASMA, a comparison is held between two cases. In the first one, LKH is used in the traditional centralized way. In the second case, LKH protocol is used for rekeying within each zone in CASMA.

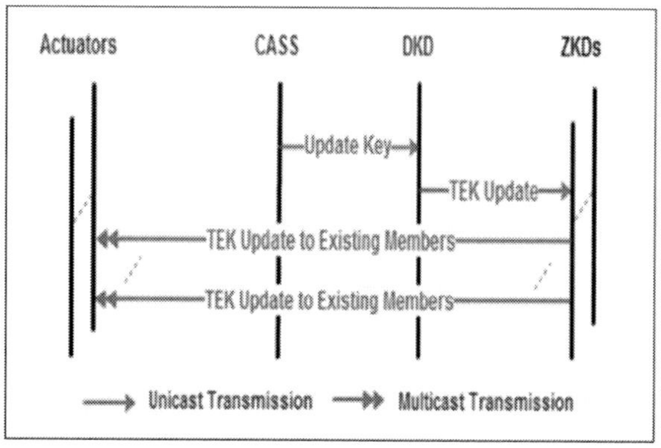

Figure 5. Periodic Rekeying Message Flow

The LKH protocol is chosen for comparison as it is considered one of the most efficient rekeying protocols. The operation of LKH as shown in Figure 6 begins by building a hierarchal key tree with members acting as leaves and the GKCS acting as the root of the tree. Each node in the tree represents a key in the key hierarchy. The root key is the TEK used to secure the group data. The leaf key is the unique key shared between the node and the key server. The intermediate nodes represent keys that are a set of KEKs used to help in the distribution and update of TEK. According to the tree structure, each member stores all the keys in the path from itself to the root. With members change, all the keys in its path need to be changed to maintain forward and backward secrecy [12].

In our evaluation, the LKH key tree is built as a balanced binary tree where each node has just two children. The context information that is used here by the CASS server for members' distribution among ZKDs is the load on these servers. The members register with the first ZKD until a threshold level is reached. Next, the members will begin to register with the next ZKD. The threshold level used in this evaluation is sixteen. In a balanced binary tree, this threshold gives rise to five keys to be stored in each member per multicast group. This is considered appropriate for such constrained devices.

The evaluation studies two critical parameters for multicast security in IoT: storage cost in members and key servers and communication cost during the join and leave operations.

A. *Storage Cost*

Storage cost is defined as the number of keys stored in each member and in the key servers.

Member Keys:

According to the LKH protocol, each member stores $\log_2(n)+1$ keys, where n represents the number of members [12]. In our proposal, each zone implements LKH. Accordingly, the number of keys stored in each member is $\log_2(n_{mz})+2$, where n_{mz} represents the number of members in each zone. This number originates from the fact that, each zone member stores $\log_2(n_{mz})+1$ keys according to LKH (which covers the individual MbrPKey and Zkey). Additionally, each member stores the global TEK.

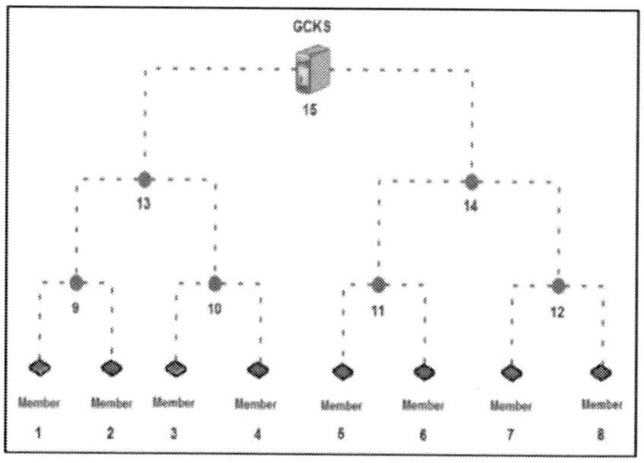

Figure 6 LKH Architecture

Figure 7 shows the members storage cost for both traditional LKH and CASMA. In traditional LKH, as the number of members increases, the number of stored keys also increases. In our proposal, the members are distributed among many ZKDs with a maximum number of sixteen members per zone. This leads to a maximum of six keys to be stored per zone member. As a result, much less keys are stored in members using CASMA compared to the traditional LKH protocol.

Server Keys:

In traditional LKH, there is only one key server that stores 2n-1 keys [12]. In CASMA, there are two types of servers: the DKD and the ZKDs. For the ZKD, the number of keys stored is $2n_{mz}+2$. This number originates from implementing LKH within the zone, which gives rise to $2n_{mz}-1$ stored keys in each ZKD. Additionally, each ZKD stores three extra keys; the Zkey, the ZKDkey, and the TEK. Adding these three keys to the existing 2n-1 keys results in $2n_{mz}+2$ keys stored in each ZKD. For the DKD, the number of keys stored is n_z+2, where n_z is the number of ZKDs. This number represents the individual ZKDkey of each ZKD in addition to the DGkey and TEK.

Figure 8 shows the key servers storage cost. For the single key server in traditional LKH, the storage load increases linearly with the addition of new members. For CASMA, the load is nearly constant. This is due to the distribution of members among several servers. CASMA is clearly much more efficient as it balances the load among the servers and avoids overloading a single server. Hence, it outperforms in terms of scalability. Furthermore, members are re-assigned to other servers in case their primarily assigned server fails providing resilience and redundancy.

Table I summarizes the comparison of the key storage for CASMA versus traditional LKH.

TABLE I. COMPARISON OF STORAGE COST

	Member	Key Server	
		DKD	ZKD
CASMA	$\log_2(n_{mz})+2$	n_z+2	$2n_{mz}+2$
LKH	$\log_2(n)+1$	2n-1	

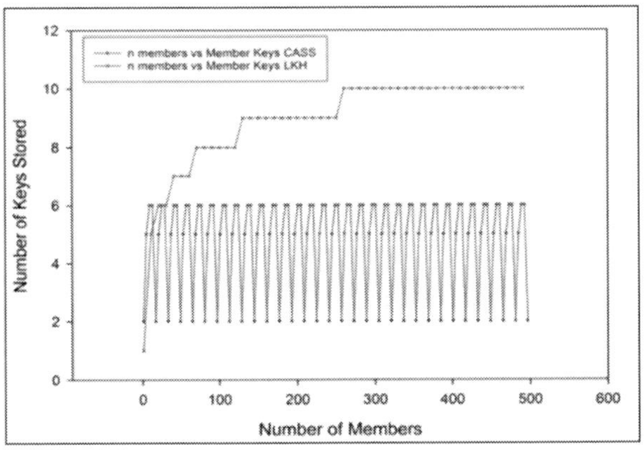

Figure 7. Multicast Group Members Storage Cost

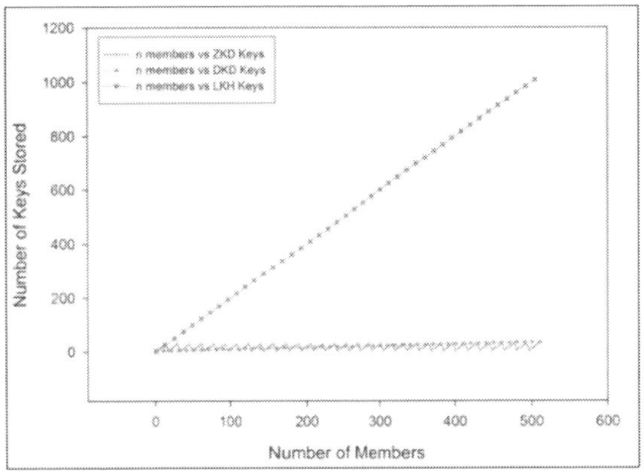

Figure 8. Multicast Group Key Servers Storage Cost

Both Figures 7 and 8 show the great memory savings achieved by the CASMA model.

B. Communication Cost

Communication cost is defined as the number of required rekeying messages sent by the key servers during the join and leave operations.

Communication Cost during Join operation:

In LKH, the number of join messages is $2*\log_2(n)$ with single key distribution per message [12]. On the other hand, when a new member joins the group in CASMA, the DKD multicasts the new TEK to all ZKDs in one message. In the unaffected zones, the ZKD multicasts this TEK to its zone members in only one message as well. For the zone with the new joining member, the ZKD updates the other members with the new ZKey according to LKH with $2*\log_2(n_{mz})$ messages. Additionally, it multicasts the new TEK to all zone members using the new ZKey. Therefore, the total number of messages transmitted by this ZKD is $2*\log_2(n_{mz})+1$.

The number of Join messages versus the number of members is shown in Figure 9 for both CASMA and traditional LKH protocols. The number of messages sent by ZKD in CASMA does not exceed 9, which is less than half the number sent by LKH server in LHK. CASMA surpasses traditional LKH in accommodating large groups of members and is hence more scalable.

Communication Cost during Leave operation:

For a binary tree and a single key distribution per message, the number of leave messages in LKH is $(2*\log_2(n))-1$ messages [12]. In CASMA, when a member in a certain zone leaves the group, the ZKD in this zone updates the ZKey of its tree using $(2*\log_2(n_{mz}))-1$ messages. Next, the DKD multicasts the new TEK to all ZKDs using one message. Finally, all ZKDs multicast the new TEK to their zone members in one message too. This includes the ZKD with the leaving member. As a result, the total number of messages transmitted by the ZKD with the leaving member equals $(2*\log_2(n_{mz}))$.

Figure 10 shows the communication cost versus the number of members for both CASMA and traditional LKH protocols. Once again, the number of messages sent by ZKD servers in CASMA is less than half the number of messages sent by LKH server in LHK. The new proposal surpasses traditional LKH in scalability.

Table II summarizes the comparison of the communication cost for the new proposal versus traditional LKH.

TABLE II. COMPARISON OF COMMUNICATION COST IN KEY SERVERS

	Join Messages			Leave Messages		
CASMA	DKD	ZKD	ZKD*	DKD	ZKD	ZKD*
	1	1	$2*\log_2(n_{mz})+1$	1	1	$2*\log_2(n_{mz})$
LKH	$2*\log_2(n)$			$2*\log_2(n)-1$		

ZKD*: ZKD with joining or leaving member

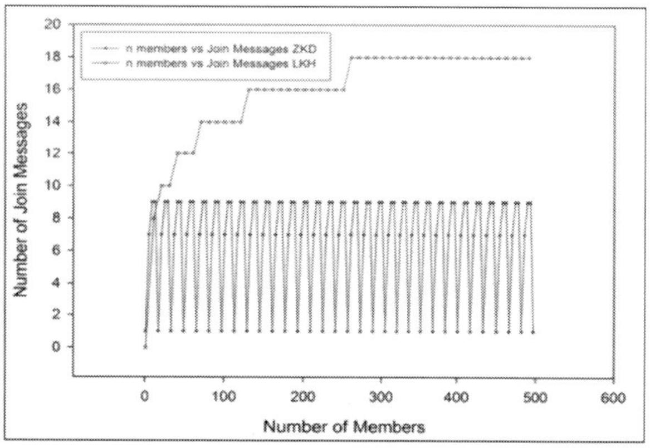

Figure 9. Join Messages Communication Cost

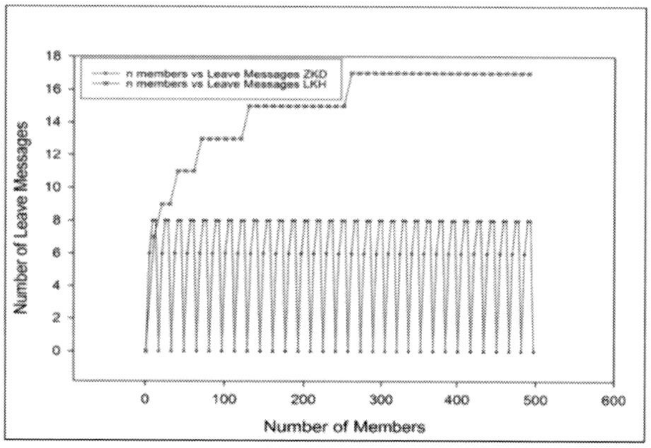

Figure 10. Leave Messages Communication Cost

Both Figures 9 and 10 show the great reduction in the number of messages during the join and leave operation in the CASMA model.

V. CONCLUSION AND FUTURE WORK

This paper introduces a new GKM security model; CASMA. The model deals with the dynamic nature of IoT application scenarios using a context aware security server. This server assigns members to the appropriate key server to register with and obtain the keying materials based on collected context information. The proposal is evaluated by measuring and comparing both communication and storage costs of CASMA to the traditional LKH protocol. The evaluation shows a significant improvement in performance, scalability, resilience, and redundancy when CASMA is used instead of traditional LKH.

REFERENCES

[1] G. D. Abowd et al., "Towards a better understanding of context and context-awareness", Proceedings of the 1st international symposium on Handheld and Ubiquitous Computing, London, UK, 1999, pp. 304–307.

[2] R. Barskar and M. Chawla, "A Survey on Efficient Group Key Management Schemes in Wireless Networks", Indian Journal of Science and Technology, Vol 9(14), April 2016.

[3] B. Jiang and X. Hu, "A Survey of Group Key Management", International Conference on Computer Science and Software Engineering, 2008.

[4] S. Rafaeli and D. Hutchison, "A Survey of Key Management for Secure Group Communication", Journal ACM Computing Surveys (CSUR), Volume 35 Issue 3, Pages 309-329, September 2003.

[5] D. Li, Z. Aung, S. Sampalli, J. Williams and A. Sanchez, "Privacy Preservation Scheme for Multicast Communications in Smart Buildings of the Smart Grid", Journal, Smart Grid and Renewable Energy (SGRE),Vol 4 No. 4, July 2013.

[6] N. Agrawal, "Secure Key Distribution Protocol with Smart Meter", International Journal of Current Engineering and Technology, Vol.5, No.5, Oct 2015.

[7] L. Veltri, S. Cirani, S. Busanelli and G. Ferrari, "A novel batch-based group key management protocol applied to the Internet of Things", Elsevier Journal, Ad Hoc Networks, Volume 11, Issue 8, November 2013, Pages 2724–2737.

[8] Harney, Meth and Colegrove, "GSAKMP: Group Secure Association Key Management Protocol", RFC 4535, June 2006.

[9] Weis, Rowles and Hardjono, "The Group Domain of Interpretation", RFC 6407, October 2011.

[10] T. Hardjono, B. Cain, and L. Monga, "Intra-domain Group key Management for Multicast Security", IETF internet Draft, September 2000.

[11] International Telecommunication Union - ITU-T Y.2060 - (06/2012) - Next Generation Networks - Frameworks and functional architecture models - Overview of the Internet of things.

[12] D. Wallner, E. Harder and R. Agee, "Key Management for Multicast: Issues and Architecture", RFC 2627, June 1999.

A Study on How Coarse-grained Clock System Influences NDN Rate-based Congestion Control

Toshihiko Kato, Kazuki Osada, Ryo Yamamoto, and Satoshi Ohzahata
University of Electro-Communications
Tokyo, Japan
e-mail: kato@is.uec.ac.jp, osada@net.is.uec.ac.jp, ryo_yamamoto@is.uec.ac.jp, ohzahata@is.uec.ac.jp

Abstract—**Named Data Networking (NDN) is a widely adopted future Internet architecture that focuses on large scale content retrieval. The congestion control is one of the hot research topics in NDN, and the rate-based congestion control method is considered to be well suited. From the viewpoint of implementation, however, the rate-based method has an issue that it requires the fine-grained clock management. This is hard to implement in off-the-shelf computers. This paper evaluates the performance in the case that consumers use a coarse-grained clock system. We use the Stateful Forwarding as a target, which is a rate-based method proposed by the group proposing NDN. The simulation results show that a coarse-grained clock system increases congestion. This paper also proposes a smooth Interest sending scheme under a coarse-grained clock system, which relieves congestion.**

Keywords- NDN; Congestion Control; Rate Control; Clock Management.

I. INTRODUCTION

Named Data Networking (NDN) [1] is widely adopted as a platform for the future Internet architecture well suited for large scale content retrieval. The fundamental adopted in NDN is the name of required content, not the address of hosts containing the content. NDN uses two types of packets in all communications: Interest and Data. A consumer requesting a content sends an Interest packet containing the content name. A producer providing the corresponding content data returns a Data packet to the consumer. NDN routers transferring the Data packet cache the packet for future redistribution [2].

The congestion control is one of the hot research topics in NDN [3]. It is also a hot topic in TCP, but the mechanisms in TCP congestion control are limited to the congestion window management at end nodes [4], and the explicit congestion notification, which is recently introduced [5]. In contrast, the NDN congestion control introduces a variety of techniques. The receiver-driven window-based congestion control method is similar to that in TCP. Here, congestion is detected by timeout [6][7] or the congestion notification [8], and the window for Interest packets are managed heuristically, e.g., through an Additional Increase and Multiplicative Decrease (AIMD) mechanism. In NDN, the rate-based congestion control method is also studied actively. Here, a consumer and routers maintain a rate, by which Interest packets are transmitted contiguously. The rate is determined heuristically by use of congestion notification [9]-[11] or by the explicit rate reporting [12]-[14].

In NDN, the Round-Trip Time (RTT) between an Interest packet and the corresponding Data packet changes largely because of the Data packet caching at routers. The window-based congestion control method needs to determine a window size corresponding to the delay and bandwidth product, but the delay changes in NDN. Therefore, it is pointed that the rate-based method is more appropriate for NDN congestion control.

From the viewpoint of implementation, however, the rate-based congestion control method has some problems. Since the transmission speed in recent data links becomes high, such as 1 Gbps and 4 Gbps, the fine-grained clock management is required in the rate-based congestion control. For example, if the Data packet size is 10,000 bits and the link speed is 1 Gbps, the duration of one Data packet transmission is 10 micro seconds. It is supposed that higher precision clock will be required to control the Interest packet sending timing. On the other hand, the fine-grained clock management is hard to implement in off-the-shelf computers. TCP implementation uses 200 msec and 500 msec clocks for the delayed acknowledgement and retransmission, respectively [15]. So, it is considered that implementing rate-based mechanism with micro second order clock is extremely hard.

In this paper, we discuss how a coarse-grained clock system influences the NDN rate-based congestion control. We adopt the Stateful Forwarding [9] as a target system of evaluation, because it is implemented in ndnSIM, which is a widely used network simulator of NDN. Moreover, we propose a method to send Interest packets more smoothly even in the coarse-grained clock environment.

The rest of this paper is organized as follows. Section II explains the related work on NDN congestion control and discusses clock management. Section III describes the simulator base performance evaluation of the Stateful Forwarding over the coarse-grained clock system. Section IV gives our proposal of smooth Interest packet sending even if the coarse-grained clock management is used. In the end, Section V concludes this paper.

II. RELATED WORK

A. *Related work on NDN congestion control*

As described above, the congestion control methods in NDN are categorized as the window-based and the rate-based methods. The Interest Control Protocol (ICP) [6] and the Content Centric TCP (CCTCP) [7] are examples of the traditional TCP like window-based method, where a consumer sends Interest packets with the limitation of window size, and window size is changed according to the AIMD mechanism triggered by Data packet reception and congestion detected by timeout. The Chunk-switched Hop Pull Control

Protocol (CHoPCoP) [8] is another window-based method. It introduces explicit congestion notification with random early marking instead of timeout-based congestion detection, and the Interest sending control is done at a consumer with the window size changed by the AIMD mechanism. Although the window-based methods are simple, the window size itself may not be optimum when many Data packets are cached in different routers.

On the other hand, the rate-based methods are classified into the non-deterministic scheme, which uses the AIMD mechanism to determine the Interest sending rate, and the explicit rate notification scheme, in which intermediate routers report the optimum rate to a consumer. The Stateful Forwarding (SF) [9] is an example of the former scheme. SF introduces a negative acknowledgment (NACK) packet as a response to an Interest packet, which is generated when a router detects congestion. A consumer and a router manage the Interest sending rate locally by AIMD, and it decreases the rate when an NACK packet is received. The Stateful Forwarding with NACK suppressing [10] is a modification of SF. It resolves a problem that SF suffers from excessive rate reduction invoked by continuous NACK packets generated within one congestion event. The Practical Congestion Control (PCON) scheme [11] uses the CoDel active queue management scheme [16], which watches out the delay of packets in sending queues, to detecting congestion. When congestion is detected, a router signals this to consumers and downstream routers by explicitly marking Data packets. In respond to it, the alternative path forwarding or rate reducing is done by downstream routers or consumers, respectively.

In contrast with those non-deterministic methods, new methods have emerged that enable routers to report a maximum allowed Interest sending rate. In the Explicit Congestion Notification (ECN) based Interest sending rate control method proposed in [12], a consumer uses a minimum rate among the reported rates from all intermediate routers. In the Hop-By-Hop Interest Shaping (HoBHIS) [13], routers decide the maximum allowed Interest sending rate independently and accordingly shape Interest packet. The maximum allowed rate is also reported to a consumer and this allow a consumer to send Interest packets without invoking congestion. The Multipath-aware ICN Rate-based Congestion Control (MIRCC) [14] introduces a similar per-link Interest shaper at every router and rate reporting to consumer. It takes account of the case that a flow uses multipath transfer. In those methods, the maximum allowed rate is calculated from the parameters including link capacity and utilization, queue size, inflated Interest rate and average RTT. They are able to control Interest transmission so as to suppress congestion and to provide higher throughput compared with other rate-based methods.

B. Discussions on clock management

Although the rate-based congestion control methods are capable to provide better performance than the window-based method, they have implementation issues. In order to control the timing to send Interest packets, timers need to be implemented that expire when Interest packets are sent out. If the link speed is high and there are a lot of content retrieval flows, the timeout values of those timers become small and the timeout timing will be random. In order to implement those timers over off-the-shelf computers, the fine-grained clock mechanism and multiple timers realized by timer interrupt handler are required. However, they will introduce large processing overhead and reduce processing throughput drastically.

In order to avoid this problem, TCP protocol processing uses very rough clock mechanism, as described above. The Asynchronous Transfer Mode (ATM) [17], a legacy scheme standardized in the framework of broadband integrated services digital network, uses rate-based control for sending ATM cells. However, they do not use clock mechanism but adopt a way that null cells are inserted between cells with user data in order to pace user data cell flows.

Yamamoto [18] tackled a similar issue for high speed TCP data transfer. He pointed out that the TCP over Gigabit link requires the rate control as well as the window control but the clock-based rate control provides large processing overhead for terminals. So, he introduced pause packets over Gigabit Ethernet, corresponding to null cells in ATM, that are used only between end nodes and switching hubs. This approach can be adopted only over the dedicated link and cannot be applied to the shared media type link like high speed wireless LAN.

Kato and Bandai mentioned the similar issue on the processing overhead of fine-grained clock management for the rate-based congestion control, but they took an approach that exploits a hop-by-hop window control [19].

III. PERFORMANCE EVALUATION WITH COARSE-GRAINED CLOCK

Based on the discussions in Section II.B, we evaluate how the rate-based NDN congestion control works when the clock granularity is large. We adopt SF [9] as a target rate-base scheme because it is implemented by its proposer over ndnSIM version 1.0 [20], which uses C++ as a programming language. This section discusses the performance when the clock management becomes coarse-grained.

A. Experimental configuration

(1) Software implementation

Currently, ndnSIM has several versions; 1.0, and 2.0 through 2.4. Although SF is proposed by the research group who is maintaining ndnSIM, we believe that SF is implemented only in ndnSIM 1.0. Moreover, there are some bugs and problems in ndnSIM 1.0. For evaluating the influence by coarse-grained clock system, we added the followings to the current ndnSIM software.

- Support of AIMD like rate control

  SF mentions the rate control using AIMD as one possible candidate, but ndnSIM does not implement it. So, we have implemented it in the module managing Interest and Data packets (the `ForwardingStrategy` class) in the following way. The start value of Interest sending rate is given manually. When a router receives a Data packet, it increases the rate by one, under the limitation that it does not exceed the link speed at the outgoing interface. When receiving a NACK packet, it halves the current rate, under

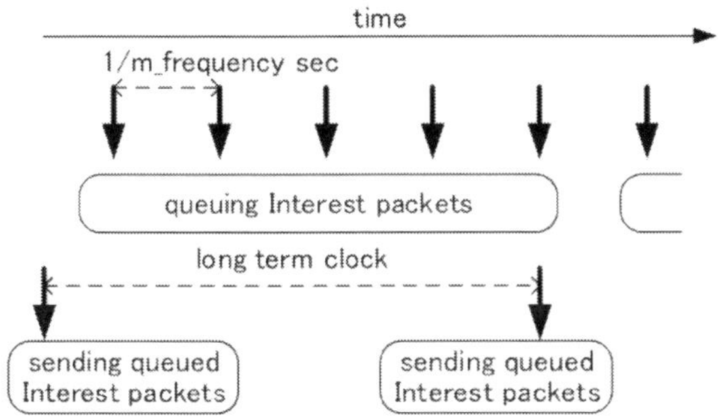

Figure 1. Implementation scheme of coarse-grained clock system.

the limitation that the minimum value of Interest sending rate is 1 packet/s.

It should be noted that the intermediate routers do not provide a shaping function that transmits Interest packets in a fixed rate. Instead, it provides a policing function that checks whether the Interest sending rate exceeds the limit or not. In order to handle a variable sending rate, the policing is performed by use of a leaky bucket.

- Use of constant bit rate (CBR) type consumer

ndnSIM 1.0 provides three types of consumers: rate based (the `ConsumerCbr` class), window based (the `ConsumerWindow` class) and batch type (the `ConsumerBatches` class). We decided to use the `ConsumerCbr` class and have added the AIMD like rate control on it. This class uses a protected static variable `m_frequency` as the Interest sending rate. We changed the variable in the same way described above in the `OnData()` and `OnNack()` methods, which are the methods called when a Data packet and an NACK packet is received, respectively.

- Emulation of coarse-grained clock system

In NDN, the rate control is implemented in the classes `Consumer` and `ConsumerCbr`; the `Consumer` class is the superclass of `ConsumerCbr`. The sending of Interest packets with a specific rate is implemented in the `ScheduleNextPacket()` method of the `ConsumerCbr` class. In this method, the `SendPacket()` method of the `Consumer` class is invoked periodically, every `1.0/m_frequency` seconds. The `SendPacket()` method sends one Interest packet actually.

We emulated a course-grained clock system in the `Consumer` class in the following way (see Figure 1).

- A clock system with longer tick, such as 100 ms, is implemented in the `Consumer` class. It calls itself periodically with the `Schedule()` method of the `Simulator` class.
- We also introduced a queue storing Interest packets temporarily. This queue is implemented using the `list` class.
- In the `SendPacket()` method, Interest packets are stored in the queue, instead of being sent actually.

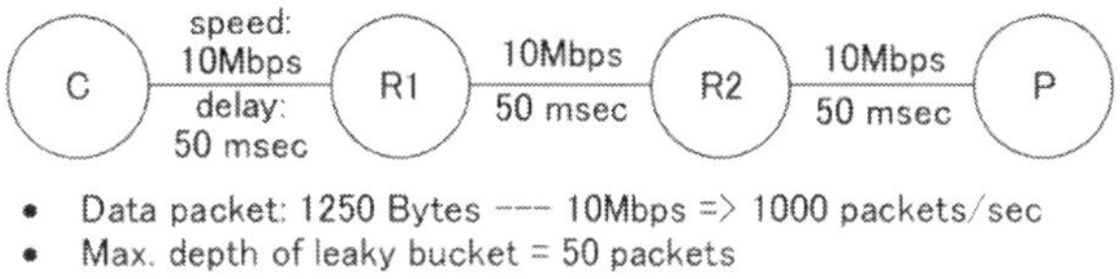

Figure 2. Network configuration and conditions.

- When the longer clock tick is invoked, all the queued Interest packets are transmitted actually.

(2) Experimental setting

We conducted the performance evaluation in the network configuration shown in Figure 2, which is a linear configuration where one consumer (C), two routers (R1 and R2), and one producer (P) are connected via 10 Mbps link with 50 msec propagation delay. The length of a Data packet is 1250 bytes, and the link speed corresponds 1,000 packets/sec. As described above, a consumer and routers maintain leaky bucket for policing the Interest packet flow. The arriving Interest packet is thrown into the leaky bucket conceptually, and, if the depth of the bucket becomes larger than the maximum value, a NACK packet is replied for the Interest packet. In our experiment, the maximum depth is set to 50 packets.

Under these conditions, we evaluated the cases that the coarse-grained clock is 50 msec, 100 msec, and 200 msec. In all the evaluation runs, the consumer starts from 200 packets/sec as the Interest sending rate. Each evaluation run takes 10 sec.

B. Perforamce evaluation results

Figure 3 shows the time variation of the sequence number contained in the name of requested content. It corresponds to the number of content request in a content retrieval flow. Each value is plotted when the corresponding Interest packet is sent. Figure 4 shows the time variation of the Interest sending rate at the consumer. In this figure, each value is plotted when the consumer receives a Data or NACK packet and it changes the value of Interest sending rate.

Figures 3 (a) and 4 (a) show the results of the original SF implementation. The sequence number is increasing steadily. The Interest sending rate starts from 200 packets/sec and goes to 1,000 packets/sec, the maximum value corresponding to the link speed. These results show that the rate-based congestion control works well.

Figures 3 (b) and 4 (b) show the results when the coarse-grained clock system is used and the clock tick is 50 msec. The sequence number is also increasing steadily, but there are several drops in the Interest sending rate. The rate starts from 200 packets/sec and goes to 1,000 packets/sec, but it drops to 500 packets/sec at 3.2 sec. This is triggered by a NACK packet generated locally inside the consumer. That is, the consumer also maintains the leaky bucket for policing the Interest packet flow. When the Interest sending rate is 1,000 packets/sec and the clock tick is 50 msec, fifty Interest packets are generated in one moment by the application, and rush into the leaky bucket. Since the maximum depth of the bucket is 50 packets, all of them are stored in the bucket and leaked in

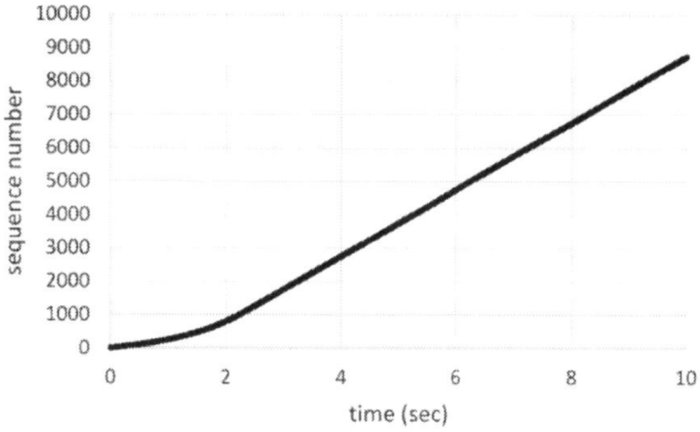

(a) Fine-grained clock

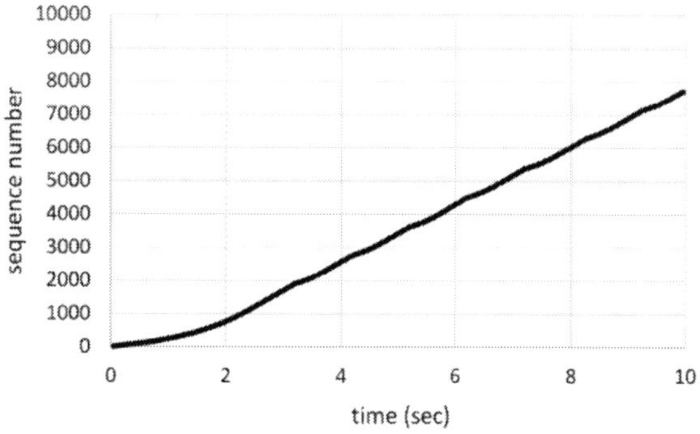

(b) Coarse-grained clock (tick = 50 msec)

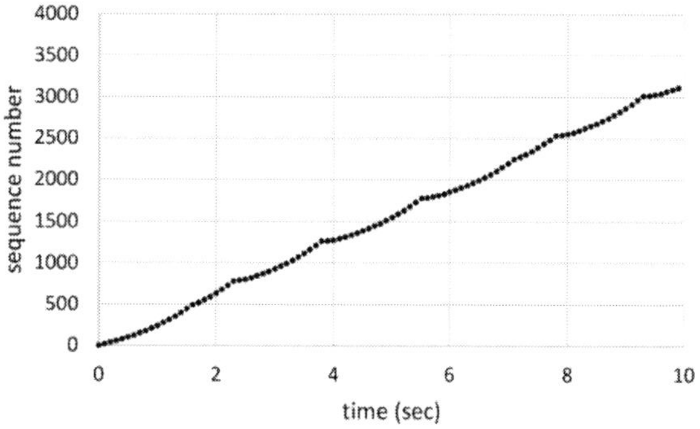

(c) Coarse-grained clock (tick = 100 msec)

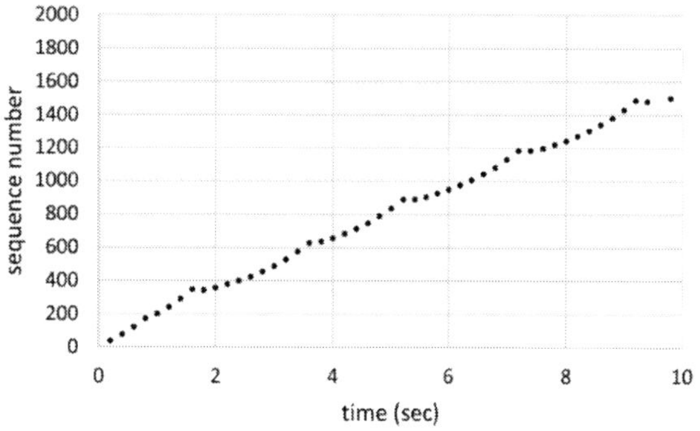

(d) Coarse-grained clock (tick = 200 msec)

Figure 3. Time variation of Interest sequence number.

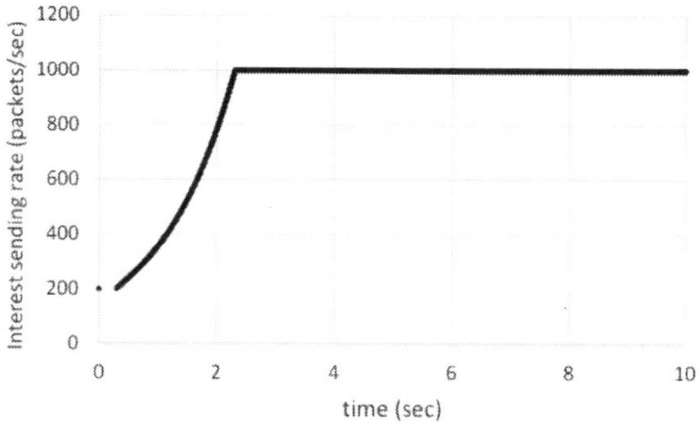

(a) Fine-grained clock

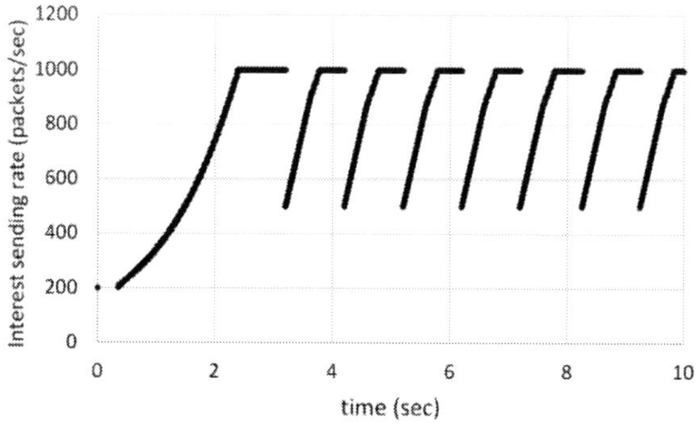

(b) Coarse-grained clock (tick = 50 msec)

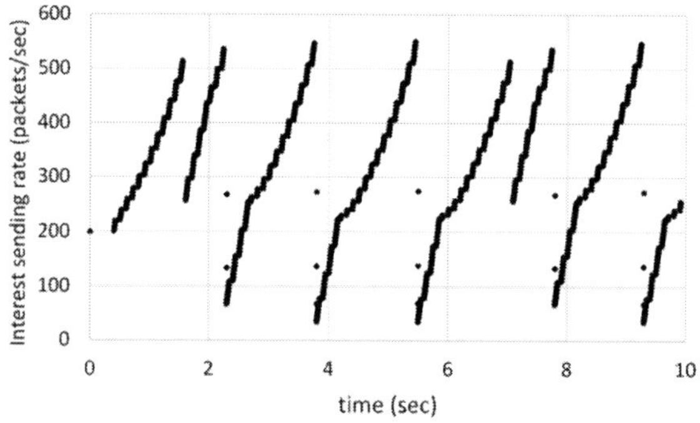

(c) Coarse-grained clock (tick = 100 msec)

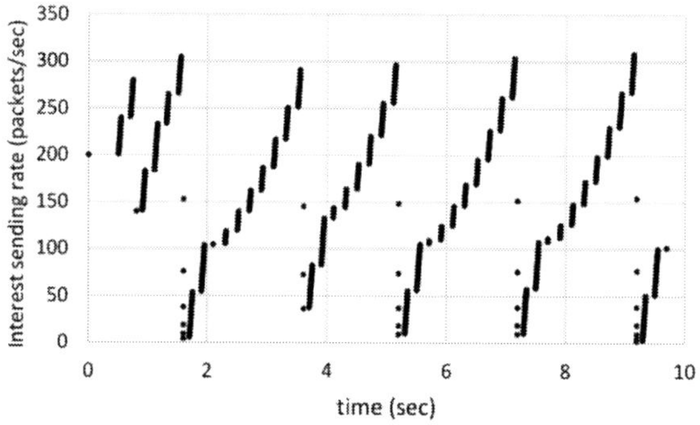

(d) Coarse-grained clock (tick = 200 msec)

Figure 4. Time variation of Interest sending rate

TABLE I. SUMMARY OF RESULTS WITH COARSE-GRAINED CLOCK.

	Original	Tick = 50 msec	Tick = 100 msec	Tick = 200 msec
Data packet throughput (Mbps)	8.75	7.72	3.12	1.50
Number of NACK packets	0	7	20	27

1,000 packets/sec (actually they are transmitted to R1 in a line speed). But in some timing, fifty Interest packets are generated in the situation that there are some packets remaining in the bucket. Then, a NACK packet is generated.

Figures 3 (c) and 4 (c) and Figures 3 (d) and 4 (d) show the results when the clock tick is 100 msec and 200 msec, respectively. In these cases, the increase of the sequence number is suppressed, and the Interest sending rate is limited up to 600 and 300 packets/sec, respectively. This is because the number of Interest packets transmitted back to back is increasing. These results show that, when the clock tick becomes large in the coarse-grained clock system, the rate-based congestion control does not work correctly.

Table I gives a summary of the results. The Data packet throughput is the total content size transferred during an evaluation run divided by ten seconds. In the case of the fine-grained clock (Original in the table), the throughput is 8.75 Mbps and there are no NACK packets transferred. In the case of the coarse-grained clock with 50 msec tick, the Data packet throughput decreases slightly, because the rate goes to 1,000 packets/sec and there are no contiguous NACK receiving. However, the cases with 100 msec tick and 200 msec tick, the number of NACK packets increases and the Data packet throughput decreases largely.

IV. PROPOSAL TO SMOOTHEN INTERST PACKET SENDING

A. *Proposed method*

In the SF mechanism with the coarse-grained clock system described in Section III, we supposed that Interest packets are transmitted only in response to clock ticks. As a result, Interest packets were sent in a burst and this triggered the overflow in a leaky bucket.

Here, we propose an Interest control method that utilizes the Data and NACK packet receiving timing. When a consumer receives a Data or an NACK packet, the receiving processing is triggered by a hardware interrupt mechanism, and it does not give large overhead to computers, different from the software based timeout mechanism. So, the receiving timing is a good chance to proceed the Interest packet sending. So, we have added the following mechanism in the coarse-grained clock system described in Section III.A.(1).

- When a consumer receives a Data or an NACK packet, it processes the received packet and then tries to send the Interest packets stored in the Interest queue.
- This procedure is implemented in the `OnData()` and `OnNack()` methods in the `Consumer` class.

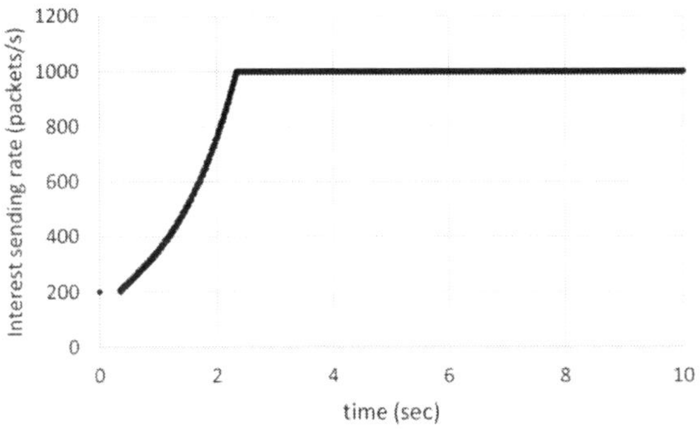

(a) Coarse-grained clock (tick = 50 msec)

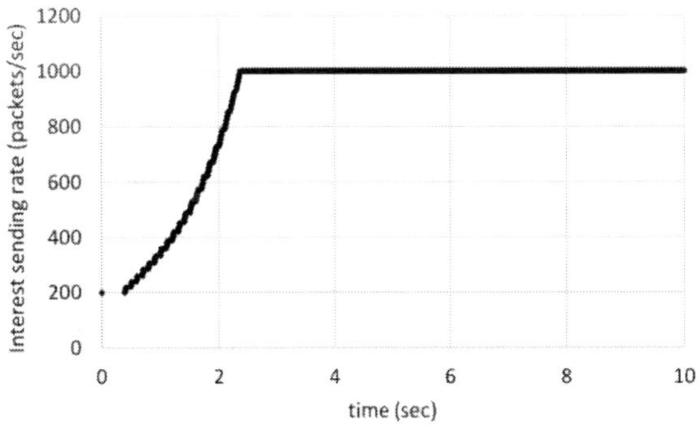

(b) Coarse-grained clock (tick = 100 msec)

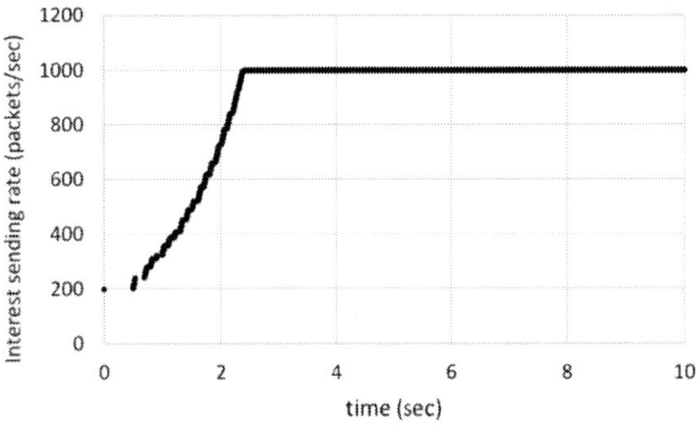

(c) Coarse-grained clock (tick = 200 msec)

Figure 5. Time variation of Interest sending rate in proposed method

B. *Performance evaluation results*

We have conducted the performance evaluation of the proposed method in the same configuration and conditions as the previous section. Figure 5 shows the time variation of the Interest sending rate at the consumer implementing the proposed method.

Different from the results given in Figure 4, all the cases when the clock tick is 50 msec, 100 msec, and 200 msec give the similar results with the fine-grained clock system. That is, the Interest sending rate starts from 200 packets/sec, goes to 1,000 packets/sec straightly, and keeps in this level. This means that there are no NACK packets generated. These

TABLE II. SUMMARY OF RESULTS WITH PROPOSED METHOD.

	Tick = 50 msec	Tick = 100 msec	Tick = 200 msec
Data packet throughput (Mbps)	8.73	8.70	8.69
Number of NACK packets	0	0	0

results mean that the proposed method is effective for smoothening the bursty Interest packet sending caused by the coarse-grained clock system.

Table II shows a summary of the results. There are no NACK packets in all the cases of three clock tick values. The Data throughput are also similar for three cases, and the value is close to that of the fine-grained clock based SF.

V. CONCLUSIONS

This paper described how the coarse-grained clock system influences the NDN rate-based congestion control. Currently, the rate-based congestion control is considered to be effective in NDN. However, the rate-based control over high speed links requires highly precious clock management and this gives a serious processing overhead to off-the-shelf computers. So, we think that commodity based consumers need to use a coarse-grained clock system.

Even if the network did not cause any congestion, the clock ticks 50 msec, 100 msec, and 200 msec generated some NACK packets. Especially, in the cases of 100 msec and 200 msec ticks, the Data throughput decreases largely. These results mean the NDN rate-based congestion control has some problem when it is used with a coarse-grained clock system.

This paper also proposed a scheme to smoothen Interest sending, which allows a queued Interest packets for sending to be transmitted when any Data or NACK packets are received. As the result of simulation evaluation, the proposed method did not generate any NACK packets even if 50 msec, 100 msec, and 200 msec are used as clock ticks.

This paper uses a relatively large tick value, but smaller tick values can be used in actual computers. Besides, this paper uses a simple network configuration with a relatively slow link speed. So, we need to evaluate the performance in a realistic computer / network condition.

REFERENCES

[1] V. Jacobson, et al., "Networking Named Content," Proc. of CoNEXT '09, pp. 1-12, Dec. 2009.

[2] N. Minh, R. Yamamoto, S. Ohzahata, and T. Kato, "A Routing Protocol Proposal for NDN Based Ad Hoc Networks Combining Proactive and Reactive Routing Mechanism," Proc. of IARIA AICT 2017, pp. 80-86, Jun. 2017.

[3] Y. Ren, J. Li, S. Shi, L. Li, G. Wang, and B. Zhang, "Congestion control in named data networking - A survey," Computer Communications, vol. 86, pp. 1-11, Jul. 2016.

[4] A. Afanasyev, et al., "Host-to-Host Congestion Control for TCP," IEEE Commun. Surveys & Tutorials, vol. 12, no. 3, pp. 304-342, 2010.

[5] K. Ramakrishnan, S. Floyd, and D. Black, "The Addition of Explicit Congestion Notification (ECN) to IP," IETF RFC 3168, Sep. 2001.

[6] G. Carofiglio, M. Gallo, and L. Muscariello, "ICP: Design and Evaluation of an Interest Control Protocol for Content-Centric Networking," Proc. of IEEE INFOCOM 2012, pp. 304-309, Mar. 2012.

[7] L. Saino, C. Cocora, and G. Pavlou, "CCTCP: A Scalable Receiver-driven Congestion Control Protocol for Content Centric Networking," Proc. of IEEE ICC 2013, pp. 3775-3780, Jun. 2013.

[8] F. Zhang, Y. Zhang, A. Reznik, H. Liu, C. Qian, and C. Xu, "A Transport Protocol for Content-Centric Networking with Explicit Congestion Control," Proc. of IEEE ICCCN 2014, pp. 1-8, Aug. 2014.

[9] Y. Cheng, A. Afanasyev, I. Moiseenko, B. Zhang, L. Wang, and L. Zhang, "A case for stateful forwarding plane," Computer Communications, vol. 36, no. 7, pp. 779-791, Apr. 2013.

[10] T. Kato and M. Bandai, "Congestion Control Avoiding Excessive Rate Reduction in Named Data Network," Proc. of IEEE CCNC, pp. 1-6, Jan. 2017.

[11] K. Schneider, C. Yi, B. Zhang, and L. Zhang, "A Practical Congestion Control Scheme for Named Data Networking," Proc. of ACM ICN 2016, pp. 21-30, Sep. 2016.

[12] J. Zhang, Q. Wu, Z. Li, M. A. Kaafar, and G. Xie, "A Proactive Transport Mechanism with Explicit Congestion Notification for NDN,"' Proc. of IEEE ICC 2015, pp. 5242-5247, Jun. 2015.

[13] N. Rozhnova and S. Fdida, "An extended Hop-by-Hop Interest shaping mechanism for Content-Centric Networking," Proc. of IEEE GLOBECOM 2014, pp. 1-7, Dec. 2014.

[14] M. Mahdian, S. Arianfar, J. Gibson, and D. Oran, "Multipath-aware ICN Rate-based Congestion Control," Proc. of ACM ICN 2016, pp. 1-10, Sep. 2016.

[15] K. Fall and W. Stevens, "TCP/IP Illustrated, Volume1; The Protocols, Second Edition," Addison-Wesley,

[16] K. Nichols and V. Jacobson, "Controlling Queue Delay," ACM Magazine Queue, vol. 10, issue 5, pp. 1-15, May 2012.

[17] ITU-T, "B-ISDN asynchronous transfer mode functional characteristics," Series I: Integrated Services Digital Nework, Recommendation I.150, Feb. 1999.

[18] Y. Yamamoto, "Estimation of the advanced TCP/IP algorithms for long sistance collaboration," Fusion Engineering and Design, vol. 83, issue 2-3, pp. 516-519, Apr. 2008.

[19] T. Kato and M. Bandai, "A Congestion Control Method for NDN Using Hop-by-hop Window Management," Proc. of IEEE CCNC 2018, pp. 1-6, Jan. 2018.

[20] A. Afanasyev, I. Moiseenko, and L. Zhang, "ndnSIM: NDN simulator for NS-3," NDN, Technical Report NDN-0005, 2012, Oct. 2012.

Scalable Monitoring for Multiple Virtualized Infrastructures for 5G Services

Panagiotis Trakadas, Panagiotis Karkazis, Helen-Catherine Leligou, Theodore Zahariadis, Andreas Papadakis
Synelixis Solutions
Chalkida, Greece
email: {ptrak, pkarkazis, nleligou, zahariad, papadakis}@synelixis.com

Wouter Tavernier, Thomas Soenen, Steven van Rossem
University of Ghent
Ghent, Belgium
email: {wouter.tavernier, thomas.soenen, steven.vanrossem}@ugent.be

Luis Miguel Contreras-Murillo
Telefonica
Spain
email: luismiguel.contrerasmurillo@telefonica.com

Abstract— **This paper presents a high level architecture and functionality details of the monitoring framework that has been implemented and integrated within the SONATA project, in order to support the management of 5G services under the Software Defined Networking / Network Function Virtualization (SDN/NFV) paradigm. The innovative framework, extending the functionality of Prometheus.io, is unique in its support for multiple Points of Presence (PoP), its extensibility using Websockets, and its availability as open-source.**

Keywords-NFV/SDN; Cloud Computing; Monitoring; SDN; NFV; Network Services.

I. Introduction

In the next years, 5G infrastructure will become a ubiquitous, flexible and programmable network that will be in the core of every social, business and cultural process, enabling both economic growth and social prosperity. In order to achieve this goal, the 5G vision poses significant technical challenges that must be fulfilled, including the concept of agile programmability and supporting the introduction of management mechanisms for the efficient instantiation of innovative services across heterogeneous network components, virtualized infrastructures and geographically dispersed cloud environments.

One of the important issues to be addressed in this new era of 5G service management is related to network and service monitoring, demanding for collecting data and metrics on the performance and usage of the resources involved in the lifecycle management of 5G services. However, the already available monitoring tools do not achieve the requirements stemming from the services envisioned in the 5G landscape, since they are in most of the cases: (i) intrusive and heavy-handed for short-lived, lightweight network function instances, (ii) not able to follow the fast pace of management changes enforced by continuous dynamic scheduling, provisioning and auto-scaling, (iii) not covering the requirements of all the involved emerging technologies, including deployments in both hypervisor-based and containerized manner, as well as monitoring data collection from different cloud environments. This paper presents the monitoring framework that has been implemented within the SONATA project, providing an interactive monitoring framework capable of offering real-time data collection, processing and alerting to all involved stakeholders of an SDN/NFV-enabled service platform, i.e., service developers, service platform operators and end-users, under heterogeneous cloud-enabled computing environments.

In Section II, we present the related state of the art, while in Section III the monitoring requirements for 5G services are discussed. Section IV includes the high-level architecture and functionality of our monitoring framework. Section V discusses the scalability of the proposed implementation, while Section VI includes our conclusions and future work.

II. State of the Art

Network monitoring has been an active research topic for more than three decades. Well-established protocols such as Simple Network Management Protocol (SNMP) [1] and Internet Protocol Flow Information Export (IPFIX) [2] are already successfully applied for gathering network metrics through either passive or active measurements. However, network metrics in isolation are not very useful in services-oriented systems; they have to be aggregated and consolidated with service- and resource-related information to produce an integrated picture of the performance of the provided service. Hence, another category of monitoring tools is mostly focusing on computation, storage and memory resources of the infrastructure or the deployed service/application, such as Nagios [3] and Zabbix [4]. One of the most advanced and modern monitoring tools is Prometheus [5] that is an open-source service monitoring system, based on a time series database that implements a highly dimensional data model, where time series are identified by a metric name and a set of key-value pairs. Moreover, Prometheus provides a flexible query language, allowing slicing of collected time series data in order to generate ad-hoc graphs, tables, and alerts. Most importantly, Prometheus provides probes that allow bridging of third-party data into Prometheus in a "pull" fashion, but also supports "push" through an already implemented gateway.

Recently, the concepts of SDN and NFV in combination with the advent of Cloud Computing and containerization of services, has dictated the implementation of monitoring tools in conformance with the respective technologies that will allow the retrieval of SDN-based, per-flow information directly via the Application Programming Interface (API) of the Openflow controller (e.g., OpenDaylight Statistics REST API [6]), the collection of monitoring data within Docker containers via cAdvisor tool [7] as well as the performance monitoring of cloud infrastructures and instantiated services, such as Monasca for OpenStack [8]. Following these trends, the programmability of 5G software network infrastructure will require a flexible and expandable monitoring tool to complement the management of the deployed innovative services, integrating the benefits of the abovementioned tools in a unified framework. During the last years a remarkable effort has been made on the development and integration of such monitoring frameworks under different viewpoints: In [9], the authors introduce a management solution for cloud federation that automates service provisioning and achieves seamless deployment of services across a future internet cloud federation; however, this framework lacks inherent support for NFV deployment. In [10], the challenges of proper NFV monitoring are discussed, focusing on the process of collecting NFV Infrastructure (NFVI) metrics and processing them at Virtualized Infrastructure Management (VIM) level. Finally, in [11], the authors present a monitoring and discovery framework for self-organized network management in virtualized and software defined networks that, is relevant to the management of 5G services under the SDN/NFV paradigm, but lacks proof in terms of scalability.

III. Monitoring Framework Requirements for 5G Services

This section presents the requirements related to monitoring arising from the use case scenarios of SONATA EU-funded project [12], acting as drivers for the monitoring architecture design that has been followed (Table I).

TABLE I. Requirements Fulfilled by the SONATA Monitoring Framework

Req. name	***Description***	***KPIs***
VNF status monitoring	Provide a high level state for each VNF	Provide a dashboard displaying status data
VNF placement and metrics modification during runtime	Allow the user to deploy VNFs at arbitrary points into the network and modify metrics parameters in runtime.	SLA/QoS metrics related to deployment time, cost, etc and interfaces for modification of metrics and thresholds.
Timely alarms for SLA violation	Provide alarms for SLA violations in a timely manner.	Proven performance and scalability of the message bus and websocket creation
VNF real-time monitoring	VNFs will generate in real time information useful for monitoring and response.	Monitoring frequency, time to process alerts.
Quality of service monitoring	Metrics generation and degradation detection of network traffic, should be supported and reported.	Traffic QoS, packet loss, delays.
Monitoring Framework Scalability	Scalable to support multiple and heterogeneous infrastructures and a high traffic load.	Support for multi-PoP and multi-tenancy federated environment.

Although not specifically mentioned in the above-mentioned requirements, it is required that monitoring system must collect data from Virtual Network Functions (VNFs) deployed on virtual machines and containers in different infrastructures. Additionally, in order to facilitate the resource orchestration process, SONATA monitoring system must collect and offer information related to the available resources of the infrastructure, as mandated by VNF placement. Thus, monitoring system must be able to collect data from the underlying infrastructures comprising the SONATA ecosystem. Moreover, the monitoring system must be able to accommodate VNF-specific alerting rules for real-time notifications. Also, the presented SONATA monitoring framework will offer the capability to developers to define service-specific rules, whose violation will inform them in real-time. Finally, there is one requirement related to the Quality of Service that demands special attention with regards to sampling period and monitoring accuracy and another one, directly related to scalability of the SONATA monitoring framework with respect to the Service Platform and respective infrastructures.

IV. High-Level Architecture and Functionality of Monitoring Framework

In a nutshell, the SONATA monitoring framework collects and processes data from several sources, offering the developer the ability to activate metrics and thresholds in order to capture generic or service-specific behaviour. Moreover, the developer can define rules based on metrics gathered from one or more VNFs deployed in one or more NFVIs in order to receive notifications in real time. In general, the developer is able to subscribe to a message queue or he can get the alert notifications by email and/or SMS on his smartphone. Most importantly, monitoring data and alerts are also accessible through an API or directly accessing a websocket URL. The internal architecture of Monitoring Framework is depicted in Figure 1 and explained in the next subsections.

A. Collecting data from several sources

It is of paramount importance to collect monitoring data from as many as possible sources. In the implemented framework, there are four different types of sources for collecting data: 1) *container probe* which runs inside the container-based VNFs to collect data related to their performance, 2) *VM probe* that collects data from Virtual Machines (VMs) hosting VNFs, 3) *OpenFlow probe* which is a Python software that utilizes OpenDayLight API to collect data from the OpenFlow controller, and 4) *OpenStack probe* that has also been developed as a software module (in Python language) that uses OpenStack API to collect data from all OpenStack components.

B. *Push Gateway*

This component is part of the open source Prometheus monitoring solution [5] that has been adopted and extended to cover the needs of SONATA Monitoring Framework. Push Gateway is utilized so that the probes/sources use HTTP POST method to "push" monitoring data to the Push Gateway, while Prometheus server collects the data in a predefined time interval. The advantage of this approach is that in the case of the deployment of a new service, there is no need for the Prometheus monitoring server to search for data related to the newly deployed VNF, but rather collect them from the PushGateway.

C. *Prometheus Monitoring Server*

Prometheus is an open-source service monitoring system, based on time series database that implements a highly dimensional data model. A time series entry is identified by a metric name and a set of key-value pairs. Prometheus has a sophisticated local storage subsystem (LevelDB), which is essentially dealing with data on disk and relies on the disk caches of the operating system for optimal performance. Prometheus server is responsible for collecting the data and communicating with the time-series database for retrieving data upon request.

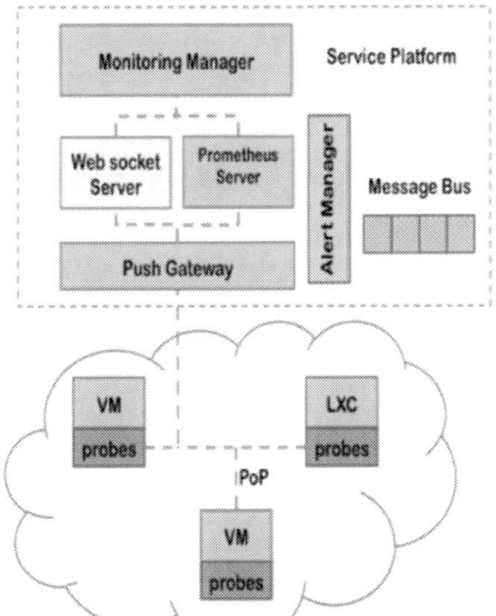

Figure 1: Monitoring Framework high-level architecture.

D. *Monitoring Manager*

The monitoring manager is a Django-based server that offers APIs to the users with respect to the monitoring data of their instantiated 5G services, including: 1) the relation among services, network functions, NFVIs and users, 2) the ability to modify rules and thresholds during service/function runtime, 3) the reconfiguration of Prometheus server, 4) the ability to define the notification methods in case of alert generation, 5) the definition of a new websocket to get data in real-time and many other features.

E. *Alert Manager*

As previously discussed, the Alert Manager is responsible (along with the implementation of a message queuing mechanism, such as RabbitMQ) for sending notifications about firing alerts to the subscribed users. After this notification, the user can take advantage of the API to further investigate the fault or activate a websocket to receive real-time monitoring data.

F. *Websocket server*

The implementation of websockets (Tornado web server) allows the user to collect streaming data from VNFs that have been deployed in the Service Platform. This is highly beneficial to the developers, as they would be able to monitor the performance of a new service in real environment. Prior to the establishment of a new websocket, the user must be aware of the metrics collected per VNF, the VNFs comprising his deployed Network Services and other related information and this information is already provided by the existing Monitoring Manager API framework, as depicted in Figure 2.

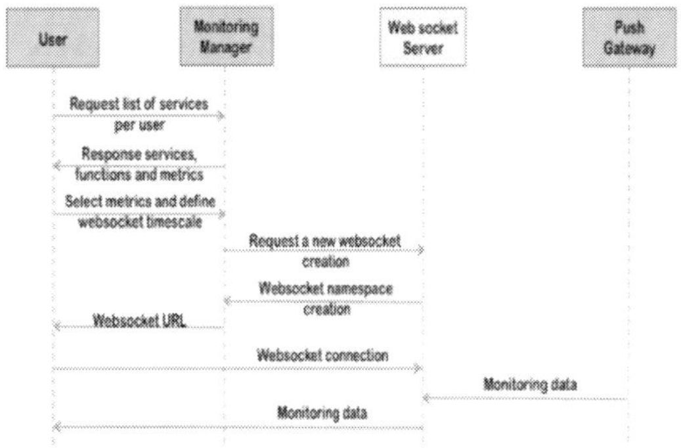

Figure 2: Websocket interactions.

After selecting the VNF and the respective metrics to be sent, the user requests the creation of a new websocket from the Monitoring Manager. After checking the validity of the request, the Monitoring Manager communicates with the Websocket server that creates and sends a new URL for the user to connect to and where metric values are pushed.

V. Scalability and Distributed Architecture

One of the cornerstones of the monitoring framework implementation was to deliver a carrier-grade solution that would fulfill scalability requirements in a multi-PoP environment. As noticed from Figure 3, several components of the Monitoring Framework had to be distributed across the SONATA PoPs. First, each PoP must have its own websocket server to accommodate developers' demands for streaming data, although the management of websockets is handled by the Monitoring Manager instance in a centralized way. Second, Prometheus Monitoring servers follow a distributed (cascaded) architecture. The local Prometheus servers collect and store metric data from the VNFs deployed in the PoP, while only the alerts are sent to the federated Prometheus server for further processing and forwarding to the subscribed users. Moreover, the alerting rules and notifications are based on monitoring data collected in different PoPs and thus the decision must be made on a federation level. Another scalability requirement concerns the large flow of data from the monitoring probes to the Monitoring Server and its respective database that might affect the service performance in extreme cases. In this respect, an architectural decision to address this scalability issue was to support a distributed architecture regarding the monitoring server and its database, working in a cascaded fashion along with proper modifications on component level. In particular, the functionality of the monitoring probe will change so that it will not send data to the monitoring server in cases where the value difference is less than a threshold defined by the developer.

VI. Conclusions and Future Work

The innovative SONATA monitoring framework builds further on state-of-the-art technology including RabbitMQ, Prometheus and Websockets, enabling a multi-PoP framework with extensible and user-friendly monitoring of NFV services involving both containers and Virtual Machines, empowering service management components to dynamically react on triggered monitoring alerts. As a future work, in the context of 5G-TANGO EU-funded project [13], the described Monitoring Framework will be further enhanced by introducing the concept of autonomic management, as described in the respective European Telecommunication Standardization Institute (ETSI) documents [14].

Acknowledgment

This work has been performed in the framework of the SONATA and 5GTANGO projects, funded by the European Commission through the Horizon 2020 and 5G-PPP programmes.

References

[1] J.D. Case, M. Fedor, M. Schoffstall, and J. Davin RFC1157 Simple Network Management Protocol (SNMP), IETF, 1990
[2] B. Claise, Ed., RFC3954, Cisco Systems NetFlow Services Export Version 9, IETF, 2004
[3] Nagios monitoring solution, https://www.nagios.org/ [retrieved: March, 2018]
[4] Zabbix, Enterprise class Open Source Network Monitoring, http://www.zabbix.com/ [retrieved: March 2018]
[5] Prometheus open source monitoring solution, https://prometheus.io/ [retrieved: March 2018]
[6] OpenDaylight Statistics REST API, https://www.opendaylight.org/ [retrieved: March 2018]
[7] cAdvisor, Monitor containers, https://hub.docker.com/r/google/cadvisor/ [retrieved: March 2018]
[8] Monasca OpenStack project, https://wiki.openstack.org/wiki/Monasca [retrieved: March 2018]
[9] Th. Zahariadis, et al., "FI-Lab: Managing Resources and Services in a Cloud Federation supporting Future Internet Applications", 7th IEEE/ACM International Conference on Utility and Cloud Computing (UCC 2014).
[10] G. Gardikis, et al., "An Integrating Framework for Efficient NFV Monitoring", Proceedings of the IEEE NetSoft Conference and Workshops, Seoul, Korea, 6-10 June 2016, pp. 1-5.
[11] A. L. V. Caraguay and L. J. G. Villalba, "Monitoring and Discovery for Self-Organized Network Management in Virtualized and Software Defined Networks", Sensors, 2017, 17, 731, DOI: 10.3390/s17040731.
[12] SONATA project, http://sonata-nfv.eu/ [retrieved: March 2018]
[13] 5GTANGO project, http://5gtango.eu [retrieved: March 2018]
[14] ETSI GS AFI 002, v1.1.1, Autonomic network engineering for the self-managing Future Internet (AFI); Generic Autonomic Network Architecture, 2013.

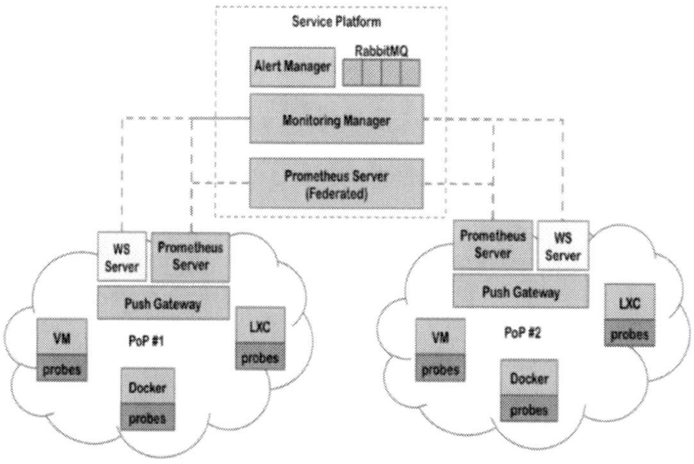

Figure 3: Architecture addressing scalability requirements with respect to the monitoring framework.

Multifactor Biometric Authentication for Cloud Computing

Jihad Qaddour
School of Information Technology
Illinois State University
Normal, Illinois, USA
jqaddou@ilstu.edu

Abstract—**Cloud Computing is a fast-growing technology, which can do everything from running applications to storing data off-site. It means a person can save his work around the globe, retrieve, update, delete and use the data/information stored in the cloud from anywhere in the world at any time. The popularity of cloud in the business world has resulted in its data centers growing at an unprecedented rate. While there are so many benefits, there are always risks involved with sharing resources, which leads to privacy and security concerns. Therefore, usage of Cloud Computing is still not at par with businesses particularly; businesses who have critical data that they cannot afford to lose or have stolen. This paper investigates issues and challenges related to the authentication security of cloud computing. Further, in this paper, a new solution is proposed to enhance user authentication in Cloud Computing using biometrics with multifactor authentication techniques.**

Keywords-Cloud Computing; Security; Security threats; Biometric; Multi-factor authentication.

I. INTRODUCTION

In the modern world, the Internet is growing at an exponential pace. With this pace, many new technologies came into existence and caught the attention of people from different backgrounds, as well as industries. One of the most popular tools is Cloud Computing (CC), which is growing at an unprecedented rate. Cloud Computing is a model for enabling ubiquitous, convenient, on-demand network access to a shared pool of configurable computing resources (i.e., networks, servers, storage, application, and services) that can be rapidly provisioned and released with minimal management efforts or services provider interaction [11][15]. Cloud Computing is a way to store any data, such as images, videos, codes, and sensitive data on a remote location other than the local device. Before Cloud Computing came into existence, people used to save their data on their local drives, where the data was not always accessible. This was one of the main drawbacks, which drove the development of a technology that gives access to data at any place and that can be saved other than on local drives. In addition, CC is a service that is provided by some vendors to users offering options for storing, updating, deletion of data, and developing different applications. Moreover, the data will be stored at the remote location, which gives users an option to retrieve and share data at any time and any place. Every action has a reaction, and similarly, when a new technology comes into existence, it has some benefits as well as drawbacks. It is affected by downtime, security and privacy issues, it is vulnerable to attacks, and it has a limitation of control and security. However, CC also helps in minimizing the infrastructure cost, as it is cheaper than the cost incurred in the infrastructure upgrades. It also eliminates the requirement of upgrading infrastructure related to storage.

In the paper, the focus is on the authentication in Cloud Computing and security issues that may arise or exist during authentication. It is organized into four sections: Section II talks about the Cloud Computing concept, Section III addresses literature review, Section IV talks about the research methodology, and Section IV concludes our work.

II. CLOUD COMPUTING CONCEPT

Cloud Computing has various features and the National Institute of Standards and Technology (NIST) defined the most essential five characteristics of Cloud Computing (CC) [15].

A. Essential characteristics of Cloud Computing

1. Broad network access and shared infrastructure

CC provides access to thin or thick client platforms (for example, mobile phone, laptops, and others) through standard mechanisms. As a part of doing business, cloud providers invest in and build the infrastructure necessary to offer software, platforms or infrastructure as a service to multiple consumers. Capabilities are available through shared networks with multitenant customers. Provider's resources are pooled to serve multiple consumers using a multi-tenant model.

2. On-demand self-service

With on-demand self-service, the cloud consumer will be able to purchase and use cloud services as the need arises. Moreover, a consumer can unilaterally provision computing capabilities, such as server time and network storage, as needed automatically without requiring human interaction with each service provider. To make this possible, a cloud provider must obviously have the infrastructure in place to handle consumers' requests. Most likely, this infrastructure will be virtualized, so different consumers can use the same-pooled hardware.

3. Elastic and scalable

Capabilities can be elastically provisioned and released to scale rapidly outward and inward commensurate with demand. It allows providers to add or remove features, without interruption and, at runtime, to handle the load variation. From a consumer point of view is to have the ability to expand and reduce resources according to their specific service requirement. This service capability provides an elastic and scalable Information technology (IT) resource. Consumers pay for only the IT services they use. Although no IT service is infinitely scalable, the cloud service provides the ability to meet the consumer's IT needs creates the perception that the service is infinitely scalable and increases its value. In the consumption-based pricing model, providers charge the consumer per units consumed. For example, cloud vendors may charge for the service by the hour or gigabytes stored per month.

4. Dynamic and virtualized

The need to leverage the infrastructure across as many consumers as possible typically drives cloud vendors to create a more agile and efficient infrastructure that can move consumer workloads, lower overheads and increase service quality. Many vendors choose server virtualization to create this dynamic infrastructure.

5. Measured Services

CC automatically controls and optimizes resources used by leveraging a metering capability at some level of abstraction appropriate to the type of service [11].

B. Cloud Computing Deployment Models

In addition, researchers have categorized four basic cloud deployment models for delivery purpose and they are as shown in Figure 1 [11]:

a. Public Cloud

Public cloud infrastructure is made available to the public and is owned by organizations selling the cloud service that are responsible for infrastructure, maintenance, controlling the data, and for the operation of CC. Examples of the public cloud include Google App Engine, Microsoft Azure, and Amazon EC2 [11]. All major components are outside the enterprise firewall, located in a multi-tenant infrastructure and access the cloud through a secure IP.

b. Private Clouds

This cloud infrastructure is operated solely by the internal IT of the organization; the organization may choose to manage the CC in-house or contract it to a third party. The computing infrastructure may exist on premises or off premises. Examples of a private cloud include hospitals and universities.

c. Community Cloud

The community cloud shares the characteristics of both the public and private cloud. It has restricted access to the private cloud and shares its resources with many organizations like the public cloud. A good example is a healthcare industry cloud. The infrastructure is a composition of two or more clouds (private and public). Community cloud involves sharing of computing infrastructure between organizations of the same community. For example, all government organizations within the state of California may share computing infrastructure in the cloud to manage data related to citizens residing in California.

d. Hybrid Cloud

The hybrid cloud infrastructure is a composition of two or more clouds (public, private, or community). This is very attractive to smaller businesses for which the security is an important concern. Hybrid Cloud Organizations may host critical applications on private clouds and applications with relatively fewer security concerns on the public cloud. A related term is cloud bursting. In the cloud, bursting, organizations use their own computing infrastructure for normal usage but access the cloud for high/peak load requirements. This ensures that a sudden increase in computing requirements is handled gracefully [4].

C. Cloud Service Models

NIST defined three types of services for the cloud model

a. Software as a Service (SaaS)
b. Platform as a Service (PaaS)
c. Infrastructure as a Service (IaaS)

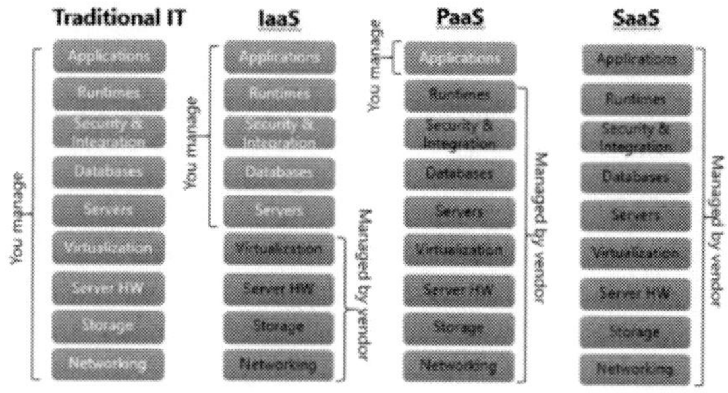

Figure 1. Cloud service model

a. Software as a Service (SaaS)

SaaS is an ever-increasingly popular option for software distribution. The Cloud Provider (CP) provides service to customers in the form of software, specifically application software running on and accessible in the cloud. The applications are accessible from various client devices through simple interfaces such as web browser. Some examples of services are Google Gmail, Microsoft 365, and Cisco WebEx [11].

b. Platform as a Service (PaaS)

PaaS cloud provides service to the customer in the form of a platform on which the customer's application can run. A PaaS cloud provides useful software building blocks and a number of development tools that assist in deploying new applications. In effect, PaaS is an operating system in the cloud. For example. Google PaaS offers to build and host web applications on the Google infrastructure.

c. Infrastructure as a Service (IaaS)

With IaaS, the customer has access to the resources of underlying cloud infrastructure. IaaS cloud provides virtual machines and other abstracted hardware and operating systems. IaaS offers customers processing, storage, networks, and other fundamental computing resources so that the customer can deploy and run arbitrary software. Some examples of IaaS are Amazon Elastic Compute Cloud (Amazon EC2), Microsoft Windows Azure, Google Compute Engine (GCE) [9][11].

III. LITERATURE REVIEW

Cloud Computing overgrows many computing paradigms like grid computing, global computing, and Internet computing in various aspects of on-demand self-service, broad network access and shared infrastructure, elasticity and scalability, guaranteed QoS (Quality of Service), and autonomous system and virtualization [13][14], etc. A few states of the art techniques that contribute to Cloud Computing are:

Wang et al. [1] proposed in their paper a new Cloud Computing model named as a hybrid model with respect to authentication and data security. In that article, a number of methods were discussed in regards to assure data security to protect user data. Authentication for the data based on public key infrastructure, virtualization, and single encryption are some methods discussed in their paper. Hemalatha et al. [2] did a comparative analysis of security issues and encryption techniques in cloud computing. The author of the article discussed the two delivery models for addressing the issues in Cloud Computing and they are cloud classification and encryption mechanisms. In addition, to assure the privacy and security of data over a cloud, authors did a comparative study based on encryption techniques. Xin et al. [3] discussed user authentication and unauthorized user access. They did their research on data security model based on multiple dimensions and proposed a three-layer defense model. In that model, each layer has their own role to perform.

R. Massod et al. [6] did their research on implementing Honey encryption to address brute force attack. A brute force attack is done to get the user password or Personal Identification Number (PIN) by the trial-and-error method. For doing this, an automated software is used which can generate many consecutive guesses. Brute force attack can be of two type. The first is when a security analyst is testing an organization's network security. This type of attack helps the analyst to point the gaps from where any attack for data is possible. The second one is when a criminal uses brute force attack to get encrypted data. The Honey Encryption (HE) technique is used with Secure Repository Manager (SRM) who creates a secure repository at server and client systems. With every attack using the wrong cipher key, HE will yield a fake plain-text or honey messages. This message may seem legitimate but will be incorrect. This way the attackers will have a bunch of fake plain-texts all looking like actual text. So even if the attacker has the actual text they will have to narrow it down from the haystack of false texts.

After implementing honey encryption, it is almost impossible to get any information or data of any user from the server, because of honeypots. Use of honeypots is useful as it generates new words named as honey words that looks like the valid data but difficult to differentiate between the original data and the data with honey words, which is invalid. If the data is of large size, then a large number of chunks are used to secure the data, and if the data is small, then a small number of chunks are used. SRM first encrypts the data before uploading the data to the cloud then performs other functionalities to provide the security and privacy of the encrypted data [4].

Hang et al. [5] proposed a public key encryption method for integrity and authentication issues in cloud computing. While data in transit over an internet, which is a type of unsecured circuit, an unauthorized person, may access the data, which is the main security issue in Cloud Computing services. It is the cloud provider's responsibility to provide the security and integrity of the data to the end user. Therefore, they use a public key to encrypt as well to decryption the data. In a public key encryption method, the only way to set back the data to its original form and make it understandable is to encrypt or decrypt the data with two secret keys (private key and public key). The private key remains with its respective owner as confidential and a public key is available to everyone through a directory or public repository. Private and public keys are related mathematically in a specific way; if the data is encrypted using a public key, it decrypts only with its corresponding private key. On the other hand, if data is encrypted using the private key, then it should only be decrypted by the corresponding public key to make the data intelligible. Public key encryption is implemented in the cloud as:

- The user uses its own private key to encrypt the data.
- Cloud Computing infrastructure units, tools for virtualization, and all other elements in the system have their own keys.
- To perform the authentication, all elements of the system uses private and public key at first place.
- All events occurred in the cloud have their own unique key. Therefore, public key encryption method assures the safe and secure exchange of data over the cloud.
- It is also advisable to the cloud provider that they can design features of the public key infrastructure, which is helpful to improve the security of data over the cloud.
- Data moving in or out should be encrypted or decrypted to assure the security.
- A hardware security model should be used to store the keys and performing decryption and encryption of data to make it intelligible for the intended user and unintelligible for the others.

Akashdeep et al. [16] reviewed the multifactor authentication technique to address the security issues in the

Cloud Computing system that users are facing. They put forward an idea using of at least two separate identifiers for the validation of information instead of using one identifier that is an ID and password, which helps in enhancing security to get an access by introducing numerous barriers for the user. Using this technique will reduce the chances for any hacker to get access to the system by using stolen passwords to have any critical data that he is not intended to retrieve. To assure the safety and security of user data stored in the cloud, use firewalls, multifactor validation, and load balancers to withstand data center infrastructure and security system technique from the hackers and other security threats. Multi-factor authentication technique provides the user with access passwords/keys to gain access to the cloud system. If the user is unable to provide the password or keys correctly, then IDS system will alert about the issue.

He et al. [8] likewise presents new security issues because the information administration and proprietorship are isolated, and the administration is worked on a virtualized stage. In his paper, a novel Dynamic Secure Interconnection (DSI) mechanism is proposed to disengage the distributed computing framework into a few elements of dynamic virtual trust zones with various security approaches actualized for various clients in order to improve security.

There are three different types of components in DSI, namely, DSI clients, DSI server and virtual bridges. The DSI server is the focal controller for taking care of the administration and security approaches. At the point when a VM is introduced, it is associated with the DSI server to enroll and begin to work within the framework. At the point when the VM state changes, e.g. suspend, restart, float or eliminate, it will educate DSI server to redesign the VM state. Therefore, the DSI server keeps up all VM properties what's more, states, for example, the virtual MAC (vMAC) and virtual IP (VIP) locations of VMs, the VM proprietor, the relating virtual scaffold, the ongoing VM state, and so forth.

Likewise, DSI server keeps up the VM correspondence conventions, strategies, and exercises. On the off chance that VMs remain inside the same network, they can converse with each other utilizing vMAC and VIP. On the off chance, that VMs remain in the various nearby system, particularly behind network gadgets, vIP based passages will be set up to associate VMs. In the meantime, suitable activity control approaches will be actualized amid the association bootstrapping stage, for example, encryption calculations, key administration convention, and movement redirection. The DSI clients are a large number of VMs. The properties of each DSI client includes vMAC and vIP addresses, VM state, VM owner, corresponding virtual bridge, host, and its own virtual trust zone ID. Virtual bridges are in charge of performing and implementing the communication protocols and policies. The communication between two DSI clients is performed in a peer-to-peer mode [8].

IV. BIOMETRICS ENHANCED CLOUD SECURITY

Literature survey and reviews point out the researcher's addressed problems related to cloud security and privacy issues. Researchers proposed some solutions regarding the security issues in a Cloud Computing system, which addresses some problems. However, there is still need to do more research in the Cloud Computing area to guarantee security and privacy of end-user data. Usage of Cloud Computing is still not at par with businesses particularly; businesses such as financial institutions which have critical data that they cannot afford to lose or have stolen.

Implementation of biometric features (fingerprint scanning, iris scan) will turn into a helpful tool for protecting the data from threats like identity threat, shared technology issues and many more. The proposed solution with a multifactor biometric feature enhances the security one level ahead than the previous solutions proposed by other researchers. Multifactor authentication is responsible to provide authentication to access with the public and private key provided to the user by the cloud provider. If by chance an unauthorized person gets the keys to access the cloud of another user, without biometric access (unique to a user that cannot be stolen by anyone), a person with bad intentions would not be able to gain access.

The biometric feature is not new in the market. It is used in many organizations for employee registration or attendance, in visa formalities. This biometric feature also serves as a beneficial and unique feature to attract corporations and organizations to convince them to use the cloud system to process and store their data on the cloud system.

The implementation of the proposal of biometrics with multifactor authentication in this paper is unique and different from other researchers.

There have been many developments in the field of biometrics, which means things are more reliable and costs are down. Biometrics offer high-level identification management security operations that have several advantages over traditional means and now they are available to you at lower costs. Currently, the new smartphones and laptops have the feature of scanning fingerprint to unlock phones and applications and taking a picture of the iris. For the systems that lack the feature of biometric scannings, such as older desktops, cheap instruments are available in the market to add. In addition, some major banks have added the option of using fingerprint technology as the login password for the user as it is hard to remember the complex password, which is hard to hack. Biometric log-ins mean a person can be directly connected to a particular action or an event. In other words, biometrics creates a clear, definable audit trail of transactions or activities. This is especially handy in case of security breaches because you know exactly who is responsible for it. As a result, you get true and complete accountability, which cannot be duplicated [17].

In general, there are four biometric types of physical qualities that are utilized or can be utilized as a part of end user verification:

- Unique mark examines (fingerprint scanning), which have been being used for a long time by law implementation and other government organizations and is viewed as a solid, extraordinary identifier.
- Retina or iris checks, which have been utilized to affirm a user's identity by examining the course of action of veins in the retina or examples of shading in the iris.
- Voice acknowledgment, which utilizes a voice print that investigations how a user says a specific word or arrangement of words extraordinary to that person.
- Facial acknowledgment, which utilizes one of kind facial elements to distinguish a person.

The biometrics feature is undoubtedly a more effective method for verification than the more regular methods used for authentication like passwords, smart cards, or a mix of the two. Conceivably, the user would not need to recall secret and complex passwords to get to data. Additionally, passwords have lapse dates that require a new task of passwords and more work for technical employees hired for support. Organizations, enterprises, and medicinal suppliers have found that too often clients forget their passwords, and attempting to explore through a process consisting of multiple steps to get the required data.

Biometric technology also ensures the data security and assures that there will be no manipulation done by any other employee under any circumstances. In addition, it binds the person to be at the place when needed, no other person can take his or her place as the unique physical attribute is used for verification, which cannot be hacked, stolen or copied by others.

V. MULTIFACTOR BIOMETRIC AUTHENTICATION IN CLOUD COMPUTING

The multifactor two-layer authentication is presented as follows:

1. Registration Phase: Client registers with the cloud application by providing all biometric information required for authenticating the users
2. Login Phase: Client uses login form to access the cloud application and its services. This accepts username and password.
3. True Random Number Generator (TRNG) phase: Use TRNG to generate a random number from 1-4
4. Biometric authentication Phase: Once the TRNG number generated, the client will be requested to provide the biometric identity identified by TRNG.
5. Full access phase: once the client provides the biometric identity, it will be compared with the stored user's biometric information. The client will have full access if it is matched, otherwise will be granted basic access, which is accessing not sensitive and valuable data. Figure 3 shows the algorithm steps for successful authentication.

The new proposed methodology is shown in Figure 2.

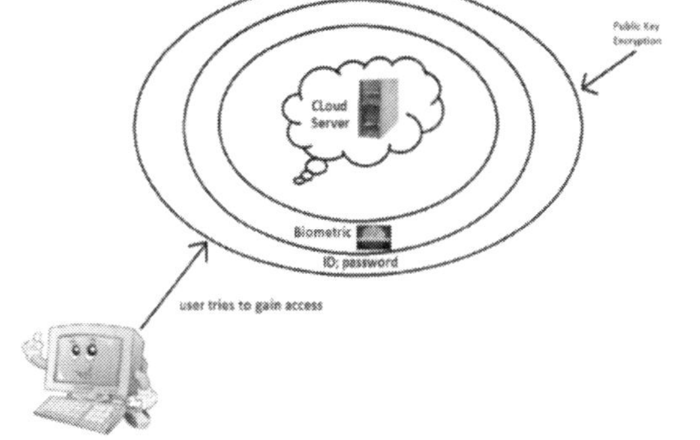

Figure 2. Biometric with multifactor authentication technique

A. *Advantages*

Advantages of this method include that there are two levels of access. The first level is a basic level to access basic data using the regular user id and pw. In the second level, the user has to provide one of his biometric identities based on true random generators to be able to access all sensitive data or to configure his cloud. This method is better suited for customers with more sensitive and valuable data. By using this case, malicious intrusion and brute force attack will become worthless at the very first step, such as the first layer of authentication because biometric identity is unique for everyone. By using biometrics, it would take care of remembering additional passwords or carry extra badges, documents, or ID cards. Moreover, using biometric technology with public key encryption makes the methodology more secure and better protected.

B. *Disadvantages*

The drawback of this method includes that users have to use better equipment, which is capable of providing biometric identities. These technologies are available and affordable.

C. *Algorithm*

The following graph shows the process and algorithm for implementing the multifactor biometric authentication model.

Here is an algorithm that proposes for multifactor biometric authentication implementation with a True Random Number Generator (TRNG) to access the cloud computing.

- Proposed Algorithm

Step 1: Start
Step 2: Register new user with biometric templates Saved Templates = {template1, template2, template3, template4}
Step 3: Registration successful
Step 4: Initiate authentication to Sign In using ID & PW
Step 5: Use a TRNG to generate a random number m
Step 6: Pick the template from 1 to 4, based on m
Step 7: Request the user to input the template identified by TRNG

Step 8: Verify if the user input matches the template in the system
Step 9: If there is a match, the user will have full access to the cloud
Step 10: End

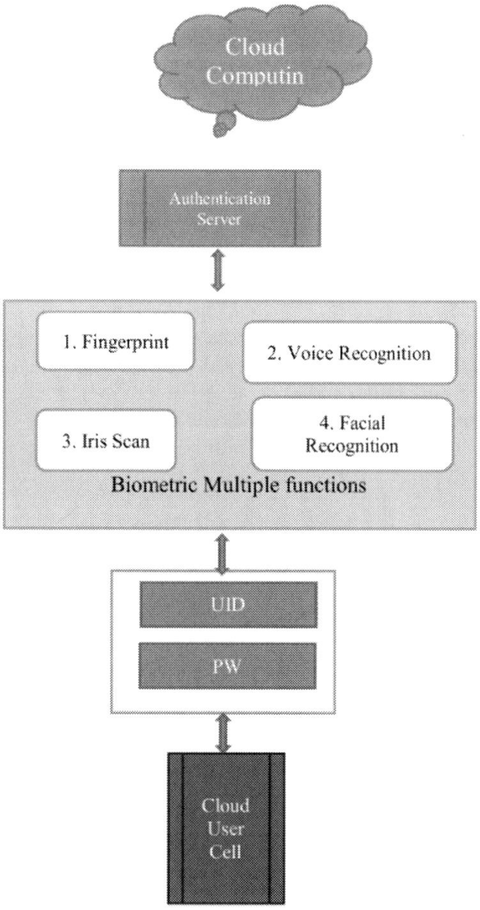

Figure 3. Multifactor biometric authentication

VI. CONCLUSION

We proposed a new multilayer authentication methodology with biometric authentication. The new methodology is introduced using biometric technology with multifactor authentication technique in addition to public key encryption. The model comprises two level authentication. The first level to access the basic data by using the classical user id and pw, but for accessing sensitive data and configuring the cloud, biometric identity is required. This will add an additional layer of security for customer sensitive data and configuration. Therefore, based on the sensitivity of the customer's data, one or two layer's authentications will be required.

Cloud Computing is the technology in the modern era which is widely used by users irrespective of their professions. Cloud is for everyone, which means there is no need to have a specific level of education to be eligible for using the cloud. It eliminates the dependability of data stored at one location that cannot be accessible from anywhere, anytime. With multifactor biometric authentication to the cloud, users can access data from any place at any time, location independent. In addition, it helps in reducing the cost of infrastructure if any upgrade of hardware is required, which has new device purchasing cost, installation cost, maintenance cost.

This methodology helps in avoiding security issues like a malicious intrusion and brute force attack, which are the major threats that need to be addressed first. This methodology works as a catalyst for convincing businesses/ to use the cloud in their organization for the critical data too. By using multifactor biometric authentication, it would take care of remembering more passwords, carry extra badges, documents, or ID cards to access sensitive data.

For future research, with all the available solutions in the cloud, more research is still required to make accessing data automated and transparent to the user. This method is a subject for my second paper and future research including the conversance of cloud NFV and other technologies.

REFERENCES

[1] J. K. Wang and X. Jia, "Data Security and Authentication in hybrid Cloud Computing model," IEEE Global High Tech Congress on Electronics (GHTCE), November 2012, pp. 117-120.

[2] N. Hemalatha, A. Jenis, A. C. Donald, and L. Arockiam, "A Comparative Analysis of Encryption Techniques and Data Security Issues in Cloud Computing," International Journal of Computer Applications, 96 (16), 2014.

[3] Z. Xin, L. Song-qing, and L. Nai-wen, "Research on Cloud Computing data security model based on multi-dimensional," IEEE International Symposium on information technology in medicine and education (ITME), 2012, pp. 897-900.

[4] M. Ahmed and M. A. Hossain, "Cloud Computing and security issues in the cloud, International Journal of Network Security & Its Applications, 6(1), 25, 2014.

[5] F. Hang, and L. Zhao, "Supporting end-user service composition a systematic review of current activities and tools" IEEE International Conference on Web Services (ICWS), June 2015, pp. 479-486.

[6] R. Masood and M. Aslam, "Innovative approach ensuring security and privacy in cloud computing" Pakistan Journal of Science, 68(1) 2016.

[7] A. Juels, and T. Ristenpart, "Honey encryption: Encryption beyond the brute-force barrier," IEEE Security & Privacy, 12(4), 2014, pp. 59-62.

[8] L. He, F. Huang, J. Zhang, B. Liu, C. Chen, Z. Zhang, and W. Lu, "Dynamic secure interconnection for security enhancement in cloud computing," International Journal of Computers Communications & Control, 11(3), 2016, pp. 348-357.

[9] T. H. Noor, Q. Z. Sheng, S. Zeadally, and J. Yu, "Trust management of services in cloud environments: Obstacles and solutions," ACM Computing Surveys (CSUR), 46(1), 12, 2013.

[10] https://www.alertlogic.com/blog/top-5-cloud-security-issues-for-2018//

[11] W. Stallings, "Foundation of Modern Networking SDN, NFV, QoE, IoT, and Cloud," Addison Wesly, 2016.

[12] ITU-T Y.3500, "Cloud computing- overview and vocabulary," August 2014.

[13] L. Wang, J. Tao, M. Kunze, A. C. Castellanos, D. Kramer, and W. Karl, "Scientific cloud computing: early definition and experience," 10th

IEEE Int. Conference on High-Performance Computing and Communications, Dalian, China, Sep. 2008, pp. 825-830, ISBN: 978-0-7695-3352-0.

[14] A. B. Angadi and K. C.Gull, "Security issues with possible solutions in cloud computing- a survey," International Journal of Advanced Research in Computer Engineering & Technology (IJARCET), Volume 2, Issue 2, February 2013, ISSN: 2278 – 1323.

[15] P. Mell and T. Grance, "The NIST definition of cloud computing," http://csrc.nist.gov/publications/nistpubs/800-145/SP800-145.pdf Accessed [12/4/2018]2011.

[16] B. Akashdeep, G. Subrahmanyam, V. Avasthi, and H. Sastry, "Review of solutions for securing end user data over cloud applications," International Journal of Advanced Computer Research, Vol 6 (27), June 2016 pp. 222-229.

[17] http://www.m2sys.com/blog/biometric-hardware/advantages-biometric-identification-management-system/ [Accessed 4-2018]

Allocation and Control of Computing Resources for Real-time Virtual Network Functions

Mauro Marinoni, Tommaso Cucinotta and Luca Abeni

Scuola Superiore Sant'Anna
Pisa, Italy
Email: {name.surname}@santannapisa.it

Carlo Vitucci

Ericsson
Stockholm, Sweden
Email: carlo.vitucci@ericsson.com

***Abstract*—Upcoming 5G mobile networks strongly rely on Software-Defined Networking and Network Function Virtualization that allow exploiting the flexibility in resource allocation provided by the underlying virtualized infrastructures. These paradigms often employ platform abstractions designed for cloud applications which have not to deal with the stringent timing constraints characterizing virtualized network functions. On the other hand, various techniques exist to provide advanced, predictable scheduling of multiple run-time environments, e.g., containers, within virtualized hosts. In order to let high-level resource management layers take advantage of these techniques, this paper proposes to extend network service descriptors and the Virtualization Infrastructure Manager. This enables Network Function Virtualization orchestrators to deploy components exploiting real-time processor scheduling at the hypervisor or host OS level, for enhanced stability of the provided performance.**

***Keywords*–MANO; TOSCA; NFV descriptors; OpenStack, LXC, Sched_Deadline; Linux kernel; Real-Time scheduling.**

I. Introduction

The 5G system architecture has been introduced to provide new services more tailored to specific user needs and Quality of Service (QoS) requirements. These features will allow Telco operators to develop new business cases, able to overcome the current uncertainties that risk compromising their business. In the context of 5G functions, some fundamental requirements have been recognized as of utmost importance for upcoming telecommunication systems [1]:

- the ability to support a wide range of services [2];
- an efficient handling and allocation of resources, through a run-time monitoring and control of resources usage and deployed services;
- the run-time control of the Quality of Service (QoS), including throughput and operational deadlines, so as to comply with a possible Service Level Agreement (SLA).

A feature that is gaining attention in this context is the one of *resource slicing*, the capability of providing strong isolation in resources access, allowing for a precise control of the interferences among different functions/services.

It seems widely recognized that recently proposed Network Function Virtualization (NFV) infrastructures, leveraging on principles of flexible and fully automated infrastructure management typical of cloud environments, enriched with Software-Defined Networking (SDN) techniques employing fully automated and dynamic management and reconfiguration of the network, constitutes the ideal fit for handling the complex requirements of the envisioned upcoming 5G scenarios.

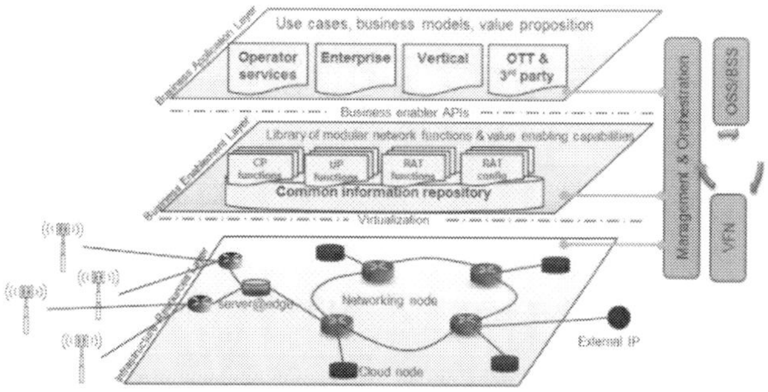

Figure 1. 5G network management proposed by the NGMN Alliance.

To deploy end-to-end SDN-NFV solutions, there is an increasing interest in the use of edge micro-servers. These allow for the provisioning of a virtual, elastic infrastructure that can readily be adapted to time-varying workload patterns. On top of them, network functions can be instantiated and elastically made to grow and shrink, as needed, in a completely automated way, leveraging high-level SDN/NFV function orchestration coupled with appropriate monitoring capabilities. Possible exploitation of these features is the 5G network management approach proposed in [3] by the *Next Generation Mobile Networks* (NGMN) Alliance as shown in Figure 1. It presents an architecture that exploits the structural separation of hardware and software, and the programmability offered by SDN-NFV to support multiple use cases, value creation, and business models.

A. Problem presentation

An efficient management of the underlying physical infrastructure, able to achieve high saturation levels and energy efficiency, calls for time-sharing of the available physical resources (e.g., available CPUs, network links, data stores) across a number of deployed functions, exploiting the unlikely occurrence of synchronous workload peaks for a multitude of functions, often from different vendors/operators, that are co-located on the same physical elements. Increasing the level of sharing of the physical infrastructure introduces unpredictable behavior in the hosted virtualized functions, where the virtualized infrastructures carved upon the physical one suffer from one major drawback: *the impossibility to keep a stable processing/networking performance*, due to the several unpredictable interferences among co-located functions.

Therefore, an uprising trend in NFV infrastructure management, is the one to employ, within the physical NFV infrastructure, proper mechanisms for *resource slicing*, preventing applications to interfere with each other applying strong isolation in resources access and use [4]–[6]. In this context, it is noteworthy to mention that traditional ways to control the stability of the performance exposed by a shared infrastructure, and specifically a cloud infrastructure, include:

1) employing *elasticity loops* able to adapt dynamically the provisioned virtual infrastructure size to the dynamically changing workload;
2) *dedicating individual physical resources* to individual virtual resources, e.g., employing a 1-to-1 mapping among virtual cores of the virtualized infrastructure to physical cores of the underlying physical machines;
3) *dedicating individual physical machines* to individual virtual resources and/or virtual functions, like in a bare-metal provisioning model, where a single function or service is deployed onto a whole physical machine, either encapsulated within a virtual machine, or an OS container, or directly deployed on the bare hardware.

The above mentioned point 1) has the drawback that, albeit on average it is possible to control the provisioned virtual infrastructure capability to match the workload requirements, occasional, unpredictable spikes in a function workload, as well as interfering workloads form other co-hosted/co-located functions, make the instantaneous performance of individual virtualized resources (e.g., single VM/container) highly unstable. The resulting effects can be processing queues temporarily filling up with adverse consequences on the overall end-to-end latency of the realized function/service chain. To avoid such problems, it is possible to couple the technique with the use of dedicated physical cores, as mentioned in point 2) above, where interferences due to time-sharing of multiple functions over the same CPUs are avoided. Still, in a multi-core server as usually used in these contexts, temporal interferences can occur among virtual functions deployed onto different physical cores, as due to their sharing of, and temporary saturation of, such resources as the available memory in the Last Level Cache (LLC), the available transfer bandwidth between the CPUs/LLC and the memory banks in the platform, the available bandwidth on shared network adapters, etc. Therefore, it is sometimes necessary to recur to the use of dedicated whole physical machines, as from point 3) above, to ensure predictable performance of the hosted services.

Unfortunately, employment of the techniques in points 2) and 3) above lead to lower the level of sharing of the infrastructure, decreasing the potential economical advantage arising from the adoption of a flexible on-demand provisioning model, corresponding to a use of the underlying infrastructure that becomes more and more inefficient and power hungry.

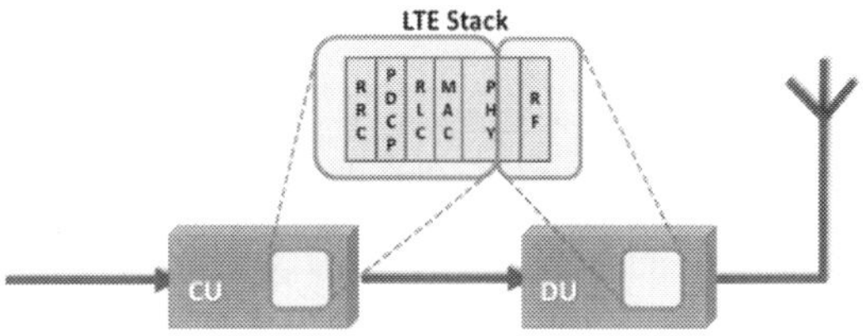

Figure 2. Intra-PHY split (Option 7-1) and placement of the corresponding NFV functions.

In this paper, the point is made that recent advances in scheduling technologies from the realm of soft real-time systems can nowadays be deployed on general-purpose operating systems and hypervisors, allowing for the provisioning of real-time virtualized processing infrastructures whose performance can be controlled at a fine granularity level (see Section III-A). Therefore, it is critical to expose such capabilities at the highest level of the NFV infrastructure management stack, as described by Cucinotta et al. [7]. This approach will improve isolation and predictability of deployed VNFs, with more efficient use of resources and management of the VNF functions more independent of the underlying infrastructure allocation.

B. *Paper organization*

The rest of this paper is organized as follows. Section II describes the Radio Access Networks scenario and outlines how computational resources are handled by NFV orchestrators. Section III describes how to exploit innovative scheduling algorithms to provide CPU reservations across co-hosted Linux containers and presents a proposal regarding the integration of CPU reservations in high-level NFV descriptors. Section IV concludes the paper.

II. BACKGROUND

A. *Virtualized Radio Access Network*

A typical NFV application scenario is the Virtualized Radio Access Network (VRAN), a paradigm that tries to shift computational elements within the networking stack of the access network away from the radio head(s), deploying them in edge micro-server infrastructures. Such a paradigm is also aligned with the increasing need for reducing power consumption in VRAN deployments, which is strongly depending on the radio access network [8], through a wise redistribution of the processing functions. This has the potential to bring tremendous power savings.

This redistribution needs rediscussion of the overall architecture of the network stack, and the optimal split of its components across the hardware elements. The evolved NodeB (eNB) can be divided into two elements: the Central Unit (CU) with a centralized deployed and the Distributed Unit (DU) positioned near the antenna. Regarding the LTE stack, a set of possible functional split solutions are conceivable and still under discussion [9]. Among them, a promising one is the IntraPHY split called Option 7-1 that allows deploying on the DU only the Radio Frequency and part of the Physical layer, while assigning the remaining part of the stack to the CU, as shown in Figure 2. When performing such allocations, it is crucial to consider the timing constraints like the stringent one ($4ms$) imposed on the acknowledgment of packets by the Hybrid ARQ (HARQ) [10] protocol.

The problem of storage and network slicing and isolation has been thoroughly addressed in the literature, primarily driven by data center optimization. For example, Giannone et al. [11] studied the impact of virtualization on the latency in the fronthaul connecting CU and DU for the scenario presented in Figure 2 implemented using OpenAirInterface [12]. Garikipati et al. [13] proposed a new scheduling policy to be applied within a single VNF of a VRAN, but their work deals with dedicated physical resources and the integration with VMs/containers is left as future work. Instead, slicing and temporal isolation at the CPU access level are not yet suitable for RAN purposes and requirements, and the management and orchestration of available SDN-NFV solutions apply simple partitioning strategies only. In this paper, a proposal is presented to bridge the gap between low-level mechanisms for real-time scheduling of VNFs and high-level orchestration layers of a SDN-NFV stack.

Other approaches for dealing with QoS attributes in TOSCA specification can be found, e.g., [14]; however, a comprehensive literature review is out of the scope of this paper.

B. NFV Orchestration

Since NFV involves a consistent number of virtualized resources, its handling demands a significant effort concerning software management, that is named orchestration. Orchestration oversees the required resources from the underlying physical platform for the NFV services. Telco operators apply NFV orchestration to promptly deploy services and Virtual Network Functions (VNFs), exploiting cloud software on COTS hardware platforms.

To address this needs, the European Telecommunications Standards Institute (ETSI) has defined the Network Functions Virtualization MANagement and Orchestration (NFV-MANO) architecture. Inside the MANO architecture is possible to see three main functional blocks: the Virtual Network Function Manager (VNFM), the Virtual Infrastructure Manager (VIM), and the Network Functions Virtualization Orchestrator (NFVO).

The VNFM is in charge of managing the lifecycle of VNFs from creation to termination, dealing with scaling up/down of resources, and handling faults, monitoring, and security.

The VIM manages the NFV Infrastructure (NFVI), including physical resources (e.g., server, storage), virtual resources (e.g., Virtual Machines) and software resources (e.g., hypervisor). In the NFV architecture is possible to have several NFVI, each one handled by a VIM, which is in charge creating/-maintaining/removing VMs, maintaining knowledge on VMs allocation to physical resources, monitoring performance and fault management of all resources in the infrastructure.

NFVO deals with the challenges connected with the management of resources and services in the NFV architecture. It coordinates, authorizes, acquires and discharges NFVI resources within one or more PoPs, interfacing with the VIM instead of directly handling NFVI resources. NFVO interconnects independent VNF functions to provide a coherent end to end service by directly coordinating with the corresponding VNFMs, to avoid talking to every single VNF. Service Orchestration maintains the topology of the service instances.

The TOSCA NFV profile defines a precise NFV data model, allowing to catch in a template all the requirements concerning deployment and operational behaviors. These VNF descriptors are collected in a catalog to make them available for selection, and each one includes three kinds of components (called nodes) that are Virtual Deployment Units (VDU), Connection Points (CP), and Virtual Links (VL). In particular:

- a *Virtual Deployment Unit* describes the features of a virtualized container (e.g., virtual CPUs, memory, disks);
- a *Virtual Link* is a logical connection between VDUs that are deployed dynamically on top of the physical infrastructure. It represents the logical entity to provide connectivity among VNFs;
- *Connection Points* model how Virtual Links connect to Virtual Network Functions and represent the virtual and/or physical interfaces of the VNFs.

Every node can be characterized by type, capabilities, attributes, properties, and requirements, as defined in [15]. When OpenStack [16] is used as Virtual Infrastructure Manager, the descriptor of each VDU node is used to generate a Heat Orchestration Template (HOT) file. The HOT file is supplied to the OpenStack compute service, Nova [17], to express a VNF requirements on the needed virtualized computing platform.

III. Proposed Approach

In what follows, we describe our proposal to employ real-time deadline-based scheduling to temporally isolate VNF in a NFV infrastructure. We highlight the advantages of real-time scheduling for VNFs, and describe how we plan to extend high-level MANO descriptors to support the new scheduling capabilities at the hypervisor layer.

A. CPU reservations for NFV

As presented in Section I, the virtualization of network functions has stringent requirements regarding CPU slicing. In particular, some decoding and demodulation activities that are virtualized by executing them in software (possibly in a VM or a container) must complete within a well-specified time (e.g., the Hybrid ARQ timeout for the acknowledgeof MAC packets), otherwise the connection risks to be interrupted.

Moreover, some of those virtualized functions might be computationally intensive, and risk to starve other services and functions if not properly handled. It is therefore important to properly schedule the virtualized functions and services so that each (virtualized) software component is provided with predictable and well-specified QoS (expressed as the probability to respect a max response-time), and cannot consume more than a given fraction of CPU time. While many modern operating systems provide some way to comply with the second requirement (for example, the Linux kernel provides a *throttling* mechanism), satisfying the first requirement is more difficult, and requires a more theoretically-funded approach. For example, CPU reservations [18] can be used, for which stochastic analysis can be applied to ensure that each component respects its timing requirements [19]. A reservation-based scheduler generally associates 2 scheduling parameters Q and P to each task, and guarantees that the task is allowed to execute for Q time units every P. Q is generally known as maximum budget, or runtime, and P is generally known as reservation period. While these techniques were traditionally implemented in research projects [20]–[22] and not supported by commonly used OSs, the mainline Linux kernel scheduler includes SCHED_DEADLINE [23] today, a CPU reservation mechanism based on EDF [24] [25].

B. Real-time scheduling of single-threaded NFV components

The SCHED_DEADLINE scheduling policy has been shown to be able to provide stable and predictable performance for a number of use-cases [26], including single-threaded NFV functions [19] [27]. For example, whenever submitting a Poissonian traffic to a packet processing server, it is possible to have a precise control on the QoS experienced by the processed packets, when scheduling the processing server under a SCHED_DEADLINE policy. Indeed, the latter allows for granting a budget Q every period of P time units to the functions, regardless of other possible workload deployed onto the same system and specific CPU. Indeed, it has been shown [19] that, under said scheduling parameters, and within reasonable ranges for the choice of the period P (which do not impose an excessive rate of context switches within the platform), a M/M/1 processing function with average arrival rate λ and average processing rate μ behaves approximatively like an equivalent M/M/1 queue with a server having a processing rate $\tilde{\mu}$ reduced to a fraction Q/P of the original one: $\tilde{\mu} = \frac{Q}{P}\mu$. This can be shown by observing the response-times distribution and statistics of such an M/M/1 system.

For example, we ran an experiment on a Freescale LS2085A RDB (ARM8) board, with 8 cores running at 1.8GHz and 16GB of RAM, equipped with a Yocto Linux distribution with a Linux kernel 4.1.8. We deployed a synthetic Poisson workload with parameters mimicking the typical strict requirements of a LTE processing function, where an aggregated input traffic with average rate of $15000pkt/s$ was spread across 8 worker threads, resulting in an input rate at each server queue of $\lambda = 15000/8 = 1875pkt/s$. We tuned our synthetic processing function for an average rate of $\mu = 5300pkt/s$ (sequential processing rate obtained by the single server in isolation on a dedicated CPU). In this scenario, we expected a response-time $99th$ percentile below $2ms$. The latter timing requirement maps in a natural way into the period P to be used for the scheduling reservation, while the budget Q can be decided in function of the expected input workload and desired output QoS. Running a set of experiments with varying budget Q above the minimum stability threshold $Q/P \geq \lambda/\mu \simeq 35.4\%$, we get output response-time distributions whose main statistics are summarized in Figure 3, where the statistics of interest for the scenario are the higher-order percentiles, such as the $p99$.

Theoretical results [19] in this case lead to an (approximated) exponential distribution of the response-times with a cumulative distribution function (CDF) $F_R(\cdot)$ of:

$$F_R(t) = 1 - e^{-\left(\frac{Q}{P}\mu - \lambda\right)t}, \tag{1}$$

where, imposing the condition to respect a percentile of ϕ below the R^* threshold, gives us:

$$\frac{Q}{P} \geq \frac{1}{\mu}\left[\lambda - \frac{ln(1-\phi)}{R^*}\right]. \tag{2}$$

For example, for $\phi = 0.99$ and $R^* = 2ms$, we get $Q/P \geq 78.8\%$, coherently with the obtained experimental

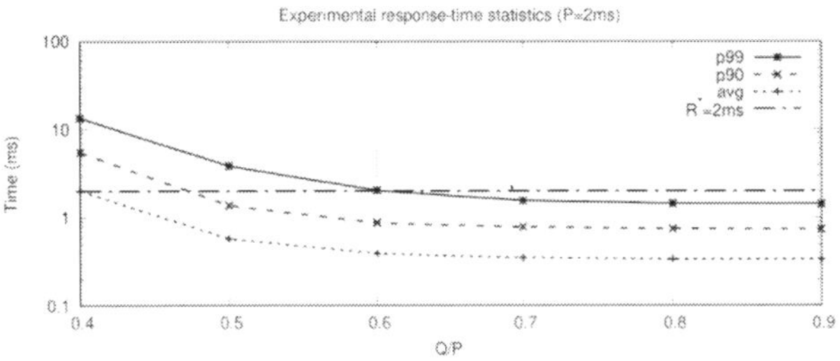

Figure 3. Various statistics on the experimental response-time distribution of a processing M/M/1 system scheduled using SCHED_DEADLINE.

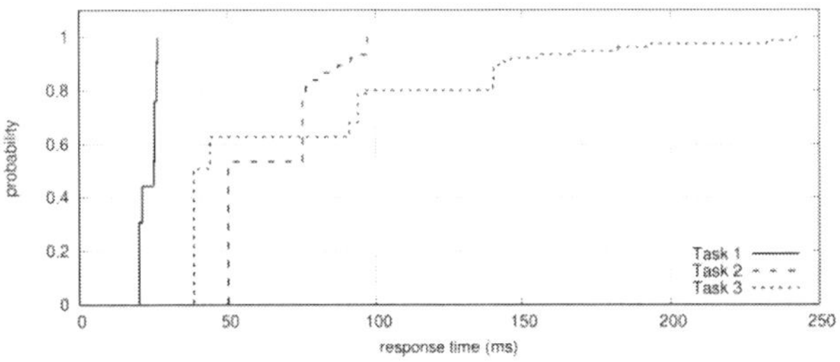

Figure 4. CDF of the response times for three real-time tasks scheduled in a properly dimensioned CPU reservation.

results in Figure 3, where we can see that the $2ms$ response-time percentile requirement is indeed met for $Q/P \geq 0.8$.

C. Real-time scheduling of multi-threaded NFV components

If NFV software components are executed in a KVM-based virtual machine [28], then it is possible to directly schedule the KVM vCPU threads with the SCHED_DEADLINE policy; however, to reduce the virtualization overhead people often tend to use container-based solutions (also known as "OS virtualization"), such as lxc [29] on Linux. In this case, the SCHED_DEADLINE policy cannot be directly used, because the same CPU reservation must be used to schedule multiple tasks (all the processes and threads in the container). Hence, a *hierarchical extension* for SCHED_DEADLINE has been developed, allowing to create two-levels scheduling hierarchies:

- at the root level, a CPU reservation (implemented as a SCHED_DEADLINE scheduling entities) schedules the various containers (basically, lxc VMs);
- at the second level (inside the container), a fixed priority scheduler (based on SCHED_FIFO or SCHED_RR) schedules the real-time tasks inside the container.

This solution allows to assign a *runtime* Q and a *period* P to a set of tasks scheduled with fixed priorities, guaranteeing that the tasks will never consume a fraction of the CPU time larger than Q/P, but also allowing to provide performance guarantees to the tasks. Such guarantees can be provided by using hierarchical real-time analysis [30].

As an example, three periodic real-time tasks $(15ms, 70ms)$, $(33ms, 150ms)$ and $(27ms, 250ms)$ (where (C_i, P_i) indicates a task with execution time C_i and period P_i) have been scheduled with fixed priorities (assigned according to Rate Monotonic [24]) inside an lxc container.

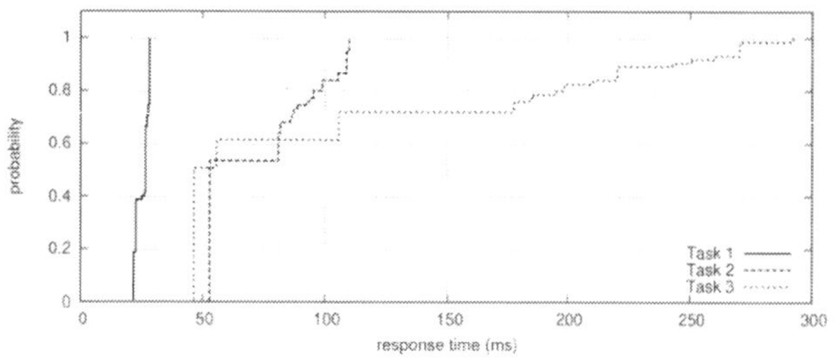

Figure 5. CDF of the response times for three real-time tasks scheduled in a smaller CPU reservation.

When the container is associated to a runtime $Q = 10ms$ and a period $P = 100ms$ and one single CPU core, the container does not consume more than 10% of the core time, showing that the implemented scheduling algorithm provides temporal protection (even if the three tasks require $15/70 + 33/150 + 27/250 = 54.23\%$ of the CPU time). When the runtime and the period are changed according to hierarchical real-time analysis so that the three tasks have response times smaller than their periods, the measured response times are distributed as indicated in Figure 4. As it can be noticed, all the temporal constraints (response time smaller than period) are respected, consistently with the theory; hence the scheduler works correctly.

The implemented algorithm supports multiple CPUs / cores and allows to provide performance guarantee to software modules scheduled with a global fixed priority algorithm [31]. It uses the Linux "control groups" software interface, and is hence usable to serve lxc-based VMs. Basically, the configuration for an lxc VM is extended with two additional attributes indicating the runtime Q and the period P assigned to the real-time tasks running inside the VM. These two low-level parameters are exported to Nova, and OpenStack has to be modified to properly map high-level descriptions into them. A first step in this direction is represented by RT-OpenStack [32], but more work is still needed.

It is also important to properly dimension the two parameters Q and P: while hierarchical schedulability analysis provides the theory needed to exactly control all the response times, this kind of analysis can result in an over-allocation of system resources and a more relaxed approach can be used as shown in Section III-B. For example, returning to the previous example the runtime and period dimensioned according to hierarchical scheduling analysis are $Q = 10ms$ and $P = 15ms$; if the runtime assigned to the lxc container is decreased to $Q = 9ms$, then the distribution of the response times changes as shown in Figure 5. This is consistent with the fact that a runtime $Q = 9ms$ does not guarantee that all the response times of all the tasks are smaller than the period, but shows how changing the scheduling parameters allow to control the response times.

D. *MANO descriptors and real-time reservations*

Standard MANO descriptors from the TOSCA specification allow one to specify processing requirements of a VDU to be deployed, in the form of properties within the `nfv_compute` descriptor, which is of type `tosca.datatypes.compute_properties`. This type

```
topology_template:
  node_templates:
    VDU1:
      type: tosca.nodes.nfv.VDU.Tacker
      capabilities:
        nfv_compute:
          properties:
            disk_size: 10 GB
            mem_size: 2048 MB
            num_cpus: 2
            cpu_allocation:
              cpu_policy: reservation
              cpu_runtime: 60 ms
              cpu_period: 100 ms
```

Figure 6. Proposed VDU template

allows for the specification of such properties as `num_cpus`, `mem_size`, `cpu_allocation`. The latter is a map allowing the specification of:

- `socket_count`, `core_count`, `thread_count`: additional details on the desired topology of the needed computational elements;
- `cpu_affinity`: differentiates between virtual cores pinned down onto dedicated physical cores, or left free to migrate among shared physical cores;
- `thread_allocation`: specifies how to map virtual cores onto hyper-threads of the underlying physical host.

We are working on extending the `cpu_allocation` map of type `tosca...CPUAllocation`, adding additional properties that allow for the specification of our scheduling parameters, namely a `cpu_runtime` and a `cpu_period`, used to instantiate a resource reservation within the underlying hypervisor (or host OS, in the case of Linux+KVM) scheduler.

A sample VDU template showing our proposed syntax is visible in Figure 6, where we are requiring the use of an underlying container with 2 cores, scheduled under a real-time reservation of $60ms$ every $100ms$.

In case heterogeneous processing physical machines are available within the infrastructure, we plan to use a processing requirement specification (the runtime value) in terms of some generic architecture-independent unit, for example expressed in terms of *CPU capacity* [33], a metric used in the Linux kernel scheduler in the context of heterogeneous platforms, e.g., big.LITTLE^{TM} ones.

An implementation of the proposed mechanism, based on Tacker with an OpenStack binding as VIM, exploiting our hierarchical variant of the SCHED_DEADLINE real-time scheduler for Linux, is under way at the moment.

IV. CONCLUSIONS

The current standard for NFV orchestrators manifests limitations in the context of the challenging scenarios posed by VRAN. This paper has shown that the level of detail in describing computational resources is not sufficient to efficiently allocate them while providing strong real-time processing guarantees. To address this issue, an extension to the NFV descriptor has been proposed to exploit experimental reservation capabilities available in a hypervisor CPU scheduler. This solution enables the seamless integration of current infrastructures with dedicated nodes able to deal with timing requirements of specific NFV components.

ACKNOWLEDGMENT

This work was partially funded by Ericsson and has been partially supported by the RETINA Eurostars Project E10171.

REFERENCES

[1] C. Vitucci and A. Larsson, "Flexible 5G Edge Server for Multi Industry Service Network," International Journal on Advances in Networks and Services, vol. 10, no. 3-4, 2017, pp. 55–65, ISSN: 1942-2644.

[2] ITU-R, "IMT vision - framework and overall objectives of the future of IMT for 2020 and beyond," International Telecommunication Union, Recommendation I.2083-0, September 2015.

[3] NGMN Alliance, "NGMN 5G White Paper," Tech. Rep., February 2015.

[4] R. Ravindran, A. Chakraborti, S. O. Amin, A. Azgin, and G. Wang, "5G-ICN: Delivering ICN Services over 5G Using Network Slicing," Comm. Mag., vol. 55, no. 5, May 2017, pp. 101–107.

[5] X. Foukas, G. Patounas, A. Elmokashfi, and M. K. Marina, "Network Slicing in 5G: Survey and Challenges," IEEE Communications Magazine, vol. 55, no. 5, May 2017, pp. 94–100.

[6] J. Ordonez-Lucena, P. Ameigeiras, D. Lopez, J. J. Ramos-Munoz, J. Lorca, and J. Folgueira, "Network Slicing for 5G with SDN/NFV: Concepts, Architectures, and Challenges," IEEE Communications Magazine, vol. 55, no. 5, May 2017, pp. 80–87.

[7] T. Cucinotta, L. Abeni, M. Marinoni, and C. Vitucci, "The importance of being OS-aware in performance aspects of Cloud Computing research," in Proceedings of the 8th International Conference on Cloud Computing and Services Science, March 2018, pp. 626–633.

[8] SCTE, "SCTE analysis of available Energy 2020 participating MSO data," Brochure, 2016. [Online]. Available: http://www.telespazio.it/docs/brodoc/GCC_eng.pdf

[9] "3rd Generation Partnership Project; Technical Specification Group Radio Access Network; Study on New Radio Access Technology; Radio Access Architecture and Interfaces (Release 14) – 3GPP TR 38.801 V1.0.0," 3GPP Organizational Partners, Tech. Rep., December 2016.

[10] "3rd Generation Partnership Project; Transport requirement for CU-DU functional splits options; R3-161813 (document for discussion)," in 3GPP TSG RAN WG3 Meeting 93, August 2016.

[11] F. Giannone, H. Gupta, D. Manicone, K. Kondepu, A. Franklin, P. Castoldi, and L. Valcarenghi, "Impact of RAN Virtualization on Fronthaul Latency Budget: An Experimental Evaluation," in Proceedings of the Workshop on 5G Test-Beds and Trials Learnings from implementing 5G (5G-Testbed), December 2017, pp. 1–5.

[12] N. Nikaein, M. K. Marina, S. Manickam, A. Dawson, R. Knopp, and C. Bonnet, "OpenAirInterface: A Flexible Platform for 5G Research," SIGCOMM Comput. Commun. Rev., vol. 44, no. 5, October 2014, pp. 33–38.

[13] K. C. Garikipati, K. Fawaz, and K. G. Shin, "Rt-opex: Flexible scheduling for cloud-ran processing," in Proceedings of the 12th International on Conference on Emerging Networking EXperiments and Technologies, ser. CoNEXT '16. New York, NY, USA: ACM, 2016, pp. 267–280.

[14] A. Brogi and J. Soldani, Matching Cloud Services with TOSCA. Berlin, Heidelberg: Springer Berlin Heidelberg, 2013, pp. 218–232.

[15] OASIS, "TOSCA Simple Profile for Network Functions Virtualization (NFV) Version 1.0," Tech. Rep., May 2017. [Online]. Available: http://docs.oasis-open.org/tosca/tosca-nfv/v1.0/csd04/tosca-nfv-v1.0-csd04.pdf

[16] O. Sefraoui, M. Aissaoui, and M. Eleuldj, "OpenStack: toward an open-source solution for cloud computing," International Journal of Computer Applications, vol. 55, no. 3, October 2012, pp. 38–42.

[17] "Nova," visited on March 12, 2018. [Online]. Available: https://www.openstack.org/software/releases/ocata/components/nova

[18] C. W. Mercer, S. Savage, and H. Tokuda, "Processor Capacity Reserves: Operating Systems Support for Multimedia Applications," in Proceedings of the IEEE International Conference on Multimedia Computing and Systems, May 1994, pp. 90–99.

[19] T. Cucinotta, M. Marinoni, A. Melani, A. Parri, and C. Vitucci, "Temporal Isolation Among LTE/5G Network Functions by Real-time Scheduling," in Proceedings of the 7th International Conference on Cloud Computing and Services Science, April 2017, pp. 368–375.

[20] S. Xi, J. Wilson, C. Lu, and C. Gill, "RT-Xen: Towards real-time hypervisor scheduling in Xen," in 2011 Proceedings of the Ninth ACM International Conference on Embedded Software (EMSOFT), October 2011, pp. 39–48.

[21] T. Cucinotta, G. Anastasi, and L. Abeni, "Respecting Temporal Constraints in Virtualised Services," in 33rd Annual IEEE International Computer Software and Applications Conference, vol. 2, July 2009, pp. 73–78.

[22] F. Checconi, T. Cucinotta, D. Faggioli, and G. Lipari, "Hierarchical Multiprocessor CPU Reservations for the Linux Kernel," in Proceedings of the 5th International Workshop on Operating Systems Platforms for Embedded Real-Time Applications (OSPERT 2009), June 2009, pp. 1–8.

[23] J. Lelli, C. Scordino, L. Abeni, and D. Faggioli, "Deadline scheduling in the Linux kernel," Software: Practice and Experience, vol. 46, no. 6, 2016, pp. 821–839.

[24] C. L. Liu and J. Layland, "Scheduling alghorithms for multiprogramming in a hard real-time environment," Journal of the ACM, vol. 20, no. 1, January 1973.

[25] L. Abeni and G. Buttazzo, "Integrating multimedia applications in hard real-time systems," in Proceedings of the IEEE Real-Time Systems Symposium, Madrid, Spain, December 1998, pp. 4–13.

[26] J. Lelli, D. Faggioli, T. Cucinotta, and G. Lipari, "An experimental comparison of different real-time schedulers on multicore systems," Journal of System Software, vol. 85, no. 10, Oct. 2012, pp. 2405–2416.

[27] C. Vitucci, J. Lelli, A. Parri, and M. Marinoni, "A Linux-based Virtualized Solution Providing Computing Quality of Service to SDN-NFV Telecommunication Applications," in Proceedings of the 16th Real Time Linux Workshop (RTLWS 2014), Dusseldorf, Germany, October 2014, pp. 1–9.

[28] "Kernel-based Virtual Machine (KVM)," visited on March 12, 2018. [Online]. Available: http://www.linux-kvm.org

[29] "Linux Containers (lxc)," visited on March 12, 2018. [Online]. Available: http://www.linuxcontainers.org/lxc

[30] R. I. Davis and A. Burns, "Hierarchical fixed priority pre-emptive scheduling," in 26th IEEE International Real-Time Systems Symposium (RTSS'05), December 2005, pp. 10 pp.–398.

[31] E. Bini, M. Bertogna, and S. Baruah, "Virtual multiprocessor platforms: Specification and use," in 2009 30th IEEE Real-Time Systems Symposium, December 2009, pp. 437–446.

[32] S. Xi, C. Li, C. Lu, C. D. Gill, M. Xu, L. T. X. Phan, I. Lee, and O. Sokolsky, "RT-Open Stack: CPU Resource Management for Real-Time Cloud Computing," in 2015 IEEE 8th International Conference on Cloud Computing, June 2015, pp. 179–186.

[33] M. Rasmussen, "Energy cost model for energy-aware scheduling." [Online]. Available: https://lkml.org/lkml/2015/7/7/754

Adaptive Life-cycle Based on Traffic Prediction on ONOS Controller

Seungbeom Song, Jaiyong Lee
School of Electrical and Electronic Engineering
Yonsei University
e-mail: {glistar, jyl}@yonsei.ac.kr

Abstract— **Smart device and Internet of Things (IoT) require high Quality of Service (QoS). A centralized network emerged as the most suitable alternative network and it is expected to be the leading future network. At this moment, the most popular centralized network is Software Defined Network (SDN) which can be separated into control plane and data plane in terms of software. SDN reduces complexity in distributed networking and manages network resources easily. Due to these advantages, SDN is undergoing a drastic increase in networking deployment. However, despite these merits, SDN still has problems with congestion. The congestion problem with inevitable performance decrease affects the QoS of the end users. In our study, we propose ALTP based on the Open Network Operating System (ONOS) controller to provide high QoS to users through adaptive monitoring and forwarding. For implementing the traffic estimating subsystem in SDN controller, we used Time Series Analysis (TSA). We got the meaningful benefit of performance while increasing overhead slightly by implementing the adaptive control of ALTP system.**

Keywords- SDN; QoS; ONOS; Adaptive Life-cycle

I. INTRODUCTION

In the last few years, with the great increase in the smart device's distribution rate, various communication networks have been constructed and managed globally. Moreover, various kinds of services, leading real-time services, such as video streaming, are provided using these networks. About these communication services, users require high Quality of Service, which guarantees high throughput reliability. Network providers satisfy these demands and guarantee continuous and high throughput or control the network QoS parameters such as throughput, delay, jitter, bitrate and so on. But, in today's legacy network at the congestion situation, throughput decline is occurring rapidly. By reducing the window size through congestion control in each end host [1], it is controlled a little bit. However, it is impossible to quickly recognize the whole network state and respond to unstable situations. Because of these points, the legacy network structure has the limitation to guarantee consistent high rate throughput required by present users. To solve this limitation, the network infrastructure should handle the traffic in a more flexible way.

SDN developed by Berkeley and Stanford University is a relatively new paradigm. SDN proposed a solution of Open Shortest Path First (OSPF)'s limitation through centralized management hierarchy. At the same time, in contrast to traditional IP networks, it provides a separate data plane and control plane of the network [2]. In SDN, network control such as routing table is processed on the controller. It sends instructions to the data plane. It reduces duplicate and unnecessary calculation. It suggests complete control of the network at the controller. SDN infrastructures have a major advantage from the abundant availability of computing resources in the control plane layer which is typically hosted on high-performance commodity servers [6], reduce the complexity of distributed configuration and ease the network management tasks programmability [5]. Due to these advantages, the 5G network architecture is proposed based on SDN. However, the current controller lacks a system implementation that takes advantage of the benefits of the central control. It only consists of the existing method based on software. For example, topology-based methods such as cloud distributed routing on Quagga [6] are used instead of SDN-specific routing. Also, although it provides reactive forwarding, link connectivity only reacts based on periodic link level discovery protocols or link events. This is a non-reactive control that reflects network conditions.

In this paper, we focus on the Open Network Operating System Controller system which assures high quality using Adaptive Life-cycle of data plane based on Traffic Prediction (ALTP) in SDN environment.

The paper is organized as follows. Section II gives an overview of SDN and ONOS [3] controller. Section III introduces reasons for the need for adaptive life-cycle control in network congestion. Section IV highlights significant related work. Section V describes the proposed ALTP ONOS system. Section VI analyzes the results achieved with ALTP. We conclude and outline future work in Section VII.

II. BACKGROUND

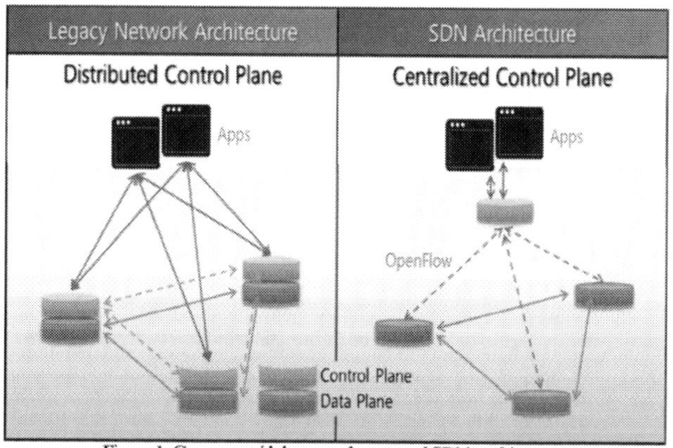

Figure 1. Compare with between legacy and SDN architecture.

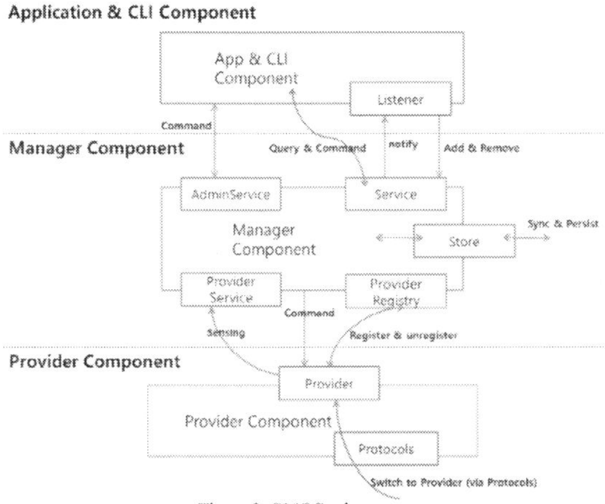

Figure 2. ONOS subsystem structure.

A. *SDN Overview*

SDN [7], developed by Berkeley and Stanford University in 2008, is a new paradigm for controlling and managing networks [8]. Unlike other centralized networks such as OSPF, SDN has a unique concept, which is the separation of network control and data plane, as shown Figure 1. Network management functions based on software are centralized. SDN can help more scalable vendors independently. This means providers need not consider expensive vendor-specific devices and protocols when expanding the network, and easily recognize the whole network's state [7]. In the network configuration, these ease the network management tasks and control forwarding rules of the whole switch more efficiently [5]. For this reason, SDN lets network managers configure, manage, store, and optimize management parameters directly as basic operations [6]. Overall, SDN can become intelligent, responsive, and programmable [7].

B. ONOS subsystem structure and OpenFlow specification

The ONOS subsystem of the control plane is composed of several elements shown in Figure 2. The provider component is the interface with data plane. The provider communicates with the data plane through south-bound protocols such as OpenFlow [7]. The manager component is the main body of the controller. It is composed of manager, service, store, and registry. The manager is the core, which operates to combine all components of manager body. The service interface has functions, which help to use methods to other components and through calling. It can receive another component's sensing or query data. Store saves methods which need to utilize and determine to synchronize or persist manager component's methods. The register interacts with the provider. The application component is network service function such as forwarding service, firewall and so on. By using the service of the manager component, applications can be more flexible. Any application has its own listener which helps receive control signaling and use the service parameter. In the overall control plane, the provider communicates with several switches, and the manager processes stats to command query and the application operates network functions.

III. Congestion and High Quality-Service in SDN

The dissatisfaction with high quality service is the delay caused by link congestion. If congestion occurred in the network, the end host's window size is decreased through congestion control whereby the average delay is high in the traditional network. Furthermore, link congestion brings QoS degradation through the re-routing process handled by traffic engineering at the point of network management, which can bring a delay also. In this aspect, for high quality service, it is important to improve the re-routing process speed for the average delay when congestion occurred and to avoid congestion. In ONOS system, re-routing happens when the flow-table and topology are refreshed or when the switches links status is changed. Therefore, network status table, flow table, meter table and topology table should be refreshed to implement new QoS operations. In other words, updating the meter table fast and flow entry is very important for fast QoS operation. However, this frequently updating come from message communication in controller and switch in SDN environment. So, for more accurate and faster management, the controller must communicate with the switch frequently. This process triggers an increase in messages and leads to link congestion between controller and switch. Hence, the tradeoff between controller management messages and control plane resource usages will be considered.

To solve this problem, we propose the ONOS system using a method to predict the traffic variation for increasing the updating life-cycle more only on congestion switch candidates. But, though we recognize the traffic trend, it was hard to manipulate because traffic is varied too much irregularly. However, if we predict traffic a few later times in SDN environment, controlling congestion can be proactive in advanced. We suggest TSA [10] to solve this problem. TSA is one of the mathematical methods to find the trend of data flow. In this paper, we do not deal with TSA. If we find a proper trend and suggest a suitable model, forecasting future traffic models could be predicted. In other words, TSA is one of the proper methods for this study because it uses recent data and can predict instantly.

IV. Related Work

There are numerous research studies of predicting flow's fluctuation. Bozakov et al. [5] studied how to estimate the autocorrelation of network flow from monitoring data. To gather data, they use random sampling, i.e., random inter-query times. As a consequence, this trial could increase the quality of the whole network successfully without exceeding the control plane overhead issue. And there were develop a system for traffic matrix estimation using the sampling of OpenFlow counters [11]. But these studies just focused on reducing message overhead without specific network function of controller's query message. Fast recovery after a node or link failure is very important in any routing protocol. In the legacy network, the authors of [12] discussed node recovery efficiency using Lagrange multipliers and suggested 'pop-routing' which is applied in OSPF. But this approach runs only legacy environment, not a centralized network, and focused on making the recovery faster and reliable. Therefore, this new routing policy cannot help to reduce the link's own congestion phase. There was an approach of SDN's polling command and query, namely [13], where they used a polling scheme and changed dramatically based on real-time traffic in the whole network. But, the fast response of traffic change is a very important issue and real-time based scheme cannot fulfill in burst traffic due to the bottleneck effect. There was a suggestion of adaptive scheme in SDN environment. Authors of [14] studied the avoidance of congestion in SDN by re-routing when link utilization is more than 70%. Authors of [15] studied for control idle flow timeout using several time interval data. That operated like a Round Trip Time (RTT) in Transmission Control Protocol (TCP), but compared with RTT, they don't use weight function and just used raw arrival rate. Despite the fact that the study does not consider link bandwidth and congestion, the concept of adjusting interval, using special network function, is meaningful enough.

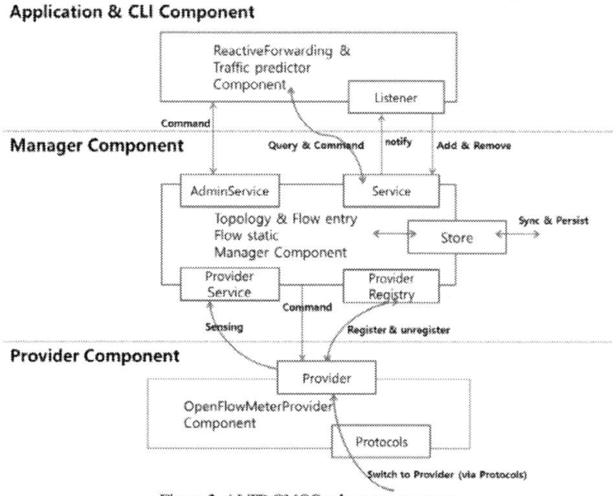

Figure 3. ALTP ONOS subsystem structure

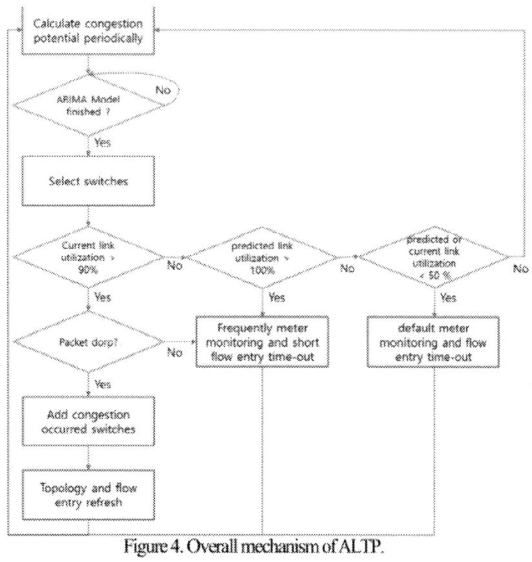

Figure 4. Overall mechanism of ALTP.

V. Implementation

For improving the present SDN environment, we propose the new ONOS subsystem structure satisfying high quality service. This system's characteristic can be roughly categorized into two genres. First, we have the Traffic prediction using Time-Series Analysis, and second we have a more rapid response to congestion by the re-configuring life cycle of the network topology for Adaptive Life-cycle based on Traffic Prediction (ALTP) mechanism.

A. ALTP ONOS Subsystem Design Concept

Rapid responding to congestion is essential for satisfying high QoS. In this paper, two measures are suggested for rapid responding to congestion. The first is the fast re-routing when congestion occurred, and second is applying QoS to each flow when link condition is varied by congestion, and consequently reducing delay as much as possible.

B. Design Requirement

Two measures stated above, the accuracy of meter entry showing link status and flow entry in charge of routing are needed on SDN controller management. These can be executed by the frequent update of those two entries. However, the frequent update occurs inevitably message overhead between switch and controller. To improve this overhead problem in meter entry updating, updating must be executed selectively in the switches which have congested link or predicted link congestion. Also, flow entry time-out updating must be executed selectively when congestion occurred or high probability of congestion is expected.

As a result, the ALTP ONOS subsystem requires two functions, like below.

1) The Function recognizing switches and links where a risk of congestion is high or congestion occurred.

2) The Function applying for adaptive meter entry and flow entry to selected switches and links, which makes message overhead become the least.

C. ALTP ONOS Subsystem Sturcture

We assume that no packet loss occurs at links and do not assume link down. Packet loss occurs only in case of congestion. Also, increasing message overhead between controller and switches only reduces controller's handling time by control plane congestion, but no control packet loss occurs between controller and switch. In this structure, shown in Figure 3, we modified the manager component and services to get the information about switches and links where congestion occurred or predicted the probability of congestion is high. In addition, to manipulate updating frequency of entry, the provider component has modified MeterStatCollector and the application component has modified ReactiveForwarding.

1) Overall Mechanism of ALTP ONOS Subsystem

The diagram which is shown in Figure 4 simply schematizes the mechanism proposed ALTP ONOS subsystem structure. First, for the flow path which the service requiring high service level agreement used, the ALTP ONOS subsystem calculates congestion potential using TSA for all switches using network status database updated by periodic polling messages. Congestion potential refers to the bandwidth utilization of the link interface mentioned in [14]. The utilization of the link interface is defined as currently used bit rate per ports divided by the maximum bit rate per ports. It selects the switch wherein congestion occurred or congestion risk is high. Congestion occurred means link utilization is over 90% or packet drop has occurred. In this case, topology graph except that interface is requested immediately. In the case of a single path for that service, diverting other flow using the same link is derived by setting the weight of the link high. The flow entry is immediately refreshed. High congestion risk means that predicted link utilization exceeds 100% by TSA in the path meter polling. In this case, it sets the meter pilling interval and flow entry timeout to half. This is to compensate for imperfect predicted value. The system reacts more quickly in congestion situations by using more control messages. The setting parameters are changed to default after the predicted utilization of link is 50% or less in a sequence of the system. It is also applied when current link utilization is 50% or less. Then, adjust flow entry updating speed according to the flow that passes pertinent switches. Similarly, by adjusting meter entry updating speed for pertinent switches, responding to the congestion can be faster.

2) Flowchart of interactions between Subsystems

Figure 5 presents the flowchart showing how subsystems provide the adaptive updating rate of flow entry and meter entry to switches by using exchanged data between subsystems. Table I represents which data is exchanged between subsystems and what is this data's meaning. DeviceService provides port state information of all existing ports of topology to TrafficPredictor. Next, TrafficPredictor expects the potential of congestion phase of each port by using TSA and transfers the list of ports which has expected to be congested to LinkService in the mechanism of ALTP ONOS Subsystems.

LinkService returns the list of links which is connected to received port list information and is already congested. This means that LinkService returns the list of links which is expected to be congested or is already congested and transfers this list to ReactiveForwarding and DeviceService. ReactiveForwarding adjusts the life-cycle of flow entry. DeviceService, by using the information of the list of links, returns the list of devices which has the congestion-expected link or has congested link and transfer it to MeterStatsCollector. MeterStatsCollector, by using this information, adjust the updating rate of meter entry and monitoring rule.

For ALTP ONOS subsystem we proposed, we added and modified five classes in ONOS system, as follows.

Traffic predictor (Added): Traffic predictor is newly added device service function, which is involved in Manager Component. The autoregressive integrated moving average (ARIMA) of TSA models [16] is used and predicts the traffic transition. Traffic predictor collects all the amount of present traffic-bandwidth usage calculated in [14] from each port of each switch in current topology. According to this collected data, it predicts if the congestion will occur or not in that port. At this moment, for accurate prediction of traffic bandwidth usage amount, at least past 50 usage amount data is needed. So, the predicted value will not be returned before accumulate 50 data and only return present traffic bandwidth. Using predicted value, traffic predictor returns the list of ports that have a high probability of congestion, and it transmits the info to the LinkService and DeviceService.

LinkService (Modified): In modified LinkService, the transmitted port list which has high congestion probability from the Traffic Predictor is used. If any link is connected to the congested port interface, it decides predicted congestion link or has congestion now for all links in topology now. We get the list of links that have congestion or has a high probability of congestion.

DeviceService (Modified): Modified DeviceService recognizes devices expected congestion for all links. We can get the list of switches expected to be congested and already congested.

ReactiveForwarding (Modified): In modified ReactiveForwarding, when the congestion occurrs, ONOS controller processes the re-routing by using this class. When we want to make this re-routing time faster, we should update the flow entry, which sets the path of each flow faster. So, by getting the links which are the member of flow's path, SDN controller decides the potential of congestion of links of that path using the proposed system. This also means deciding the possibility of re-routing. If the path is expected to be re-routed, it should increase the updating rate of flow entry for reacting faster to this situation. This can be executed by reducing flow timeout of flow entry.

MeterStatsCollector (Modified): In modified MeterStatCollector, when the congestion and re-routing occurrs, the new path is set and the link state that the flow uses as the path is changed. Therefore, it is necessary to provide changed QoS to each flow by updating the meter entry faster. Therefore, by increasing the updating rate of meter entry for switches that are expected to be congested or are already congested, we should provide changed QoS as fast as possible. By doing this, ALTP ONOS controller can react to congestion phase faster.

TABLE I. THE MESSAGE DESCRIPTION OF ALTP

	Data	Description
1	Port statistics	For every period, compute whole port statistics
2	Port list	Attain and transfer port list which expected to be congested through port statistics
3	Link list	Transfer link list which expected to be congested through the port list
4	Device list	Transfer device list which expected to be congested through the port list
5	Monitoring rule	Command adjusted meter entry polling interval to selected switch
6	Forwarding rule	Command adjusted flow timeout to every flow which passes the selected switch

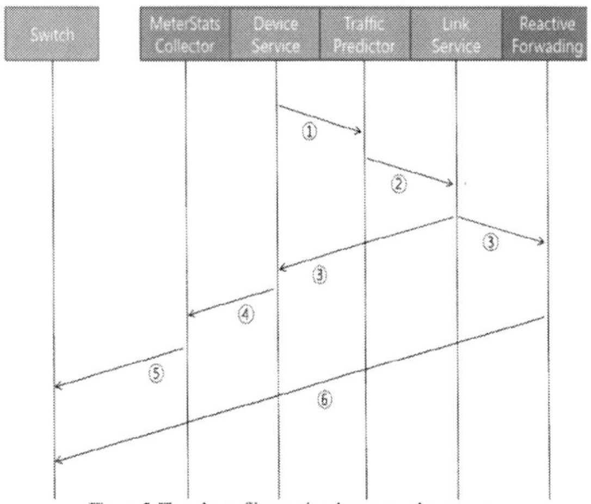

Figure 5. Flowchart of interactions between sub systems

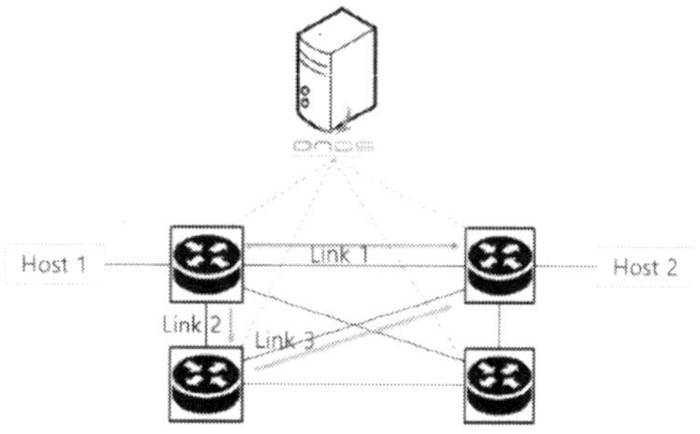

Figure 6. Topology setting for simulation

VI. RESULTS AND DISCUSSION

Here we describe the analysis of the result of the experiment showing how much ONOS controller's performance is improved when ALTP ONOS controller we suggested is used. We use the ALTP ONOS controller based on ONOS version 1.5.2 with OpenFlow version 1.3. To verify the fast reaction of ALTP ONOS controller for congestion, we set the simple topology as experiment environment shown in Figure 6.

We generate the traffic from host 1 to host 2 in Poisson's distribution which has average 2Mbps velocity while link1 has 1Mbps bandwidth. This is for deliberate congestion occurrence. Link2 and link3 on the re-routing path have 10Mbps bandwidth, respectively. By setting like this, when the routing path is changed, which means ALTP changes the life-cycle time interval of flow entry and meter entry form 10 seconds (default life-cycle time interval) to 5 seconds when congestion is expected, we can observe how much delay is improved by faster updating meter entry. Because in case of meter entry that is applied by prior routing path, it cannot guarantee 2Mbps to each flow. However, after the meter entry update, it can guarantee 2Mbps to each flow, so the delay would be considerably improved. In other words, ALTP ONOS controller can provide High-QoS by reacting faster in case of congestion occurrence.

In Table II, by increasing the Life-cycle interval of selected switches' entries, two important factors that have a dominant effect on high QoS are considerably improved. However, this result is reasonable because it is ached by increasing message overhead between controller and switches.

However, when we compare the results of the cases which increasing updating rate is applied to selected switches or not, we can find that the performance we can achieve by increasing adaptive message is much bigger. Table II indicates the performance and message overhead in three cases. The first case is applying the default life-cycle rate in the traditional ONOS controller. The second case is applying the faster life-cycle rate to selected switches in ALTP ONOS controller. The last one is applying the faster updating rate to all switches in the traditional ONOS controller.

We achieve better performance of updating entries more frequently for all switches (not selective). However, the messages are increased too, which lead to an overhead of control plane. This indicates that ALTP ONOS controller has better performance compared to the traditional ONOS controller by increasing message overhead as small as possible.

TABLE II. RESULT DATA WITH ADPTIVE LIFE-CYCLE RATE

(Life-cycle interval) updating rate	Default (10) Life-cycle (non-selective)	ALTP (5or10) Life-cycle (adaptive)	Double (5) Life-cycle (non-selective)
The average number of message in control plane	3766	4114	4775
Message Increase rate	-	9.2%	26.7%
Average Flow Delay(s)	2.5356	2.1011	2.03976
Average Packet drop rate	10.24%	8.03%	7.76%
Average Re-routing Convergence time(ms)	51.598	43.969	42.844

VII. CONCLUSION AND FUTURE WORK

In this paper, to provide high QoS in IoT services, we design ALTP ONOS controller which predicts or recognizes congestion phase and executes a fast response to congestion phase. The method for congestion phase estimation is performed by TSA. Moreover, the method for fast response to congestion phase is updating flow and meter entry more frequently. In the experiment, it is verified that traffic prediction by using ARIMA model in TSA is sufficiently reliable. By using these methods, the components such as traffic delay, throughput, and drop rate which have a dominant effect on high QoS are improved. This result indicates that the suggested methods perform fast response in congestion phase. Also, adjusting entries process is performed only on selected devices. So, we can minimize message overhead increment between controller and switch due to frequent entry update.

The proposed ALTP ONOS controller induced performance improvement successfully. However, in case of ARIMA model used in ALTP, it is strong for trend analysis but weak for burst analysis. So, to perform burst analysis more accurately, an additional prediction model would be beneficial for further performance improvement. Long-term analysis can be one of the alternatives, and it is possible to predict burst potential by accumulating data for various time periods. Therefore, adjustment of flexible monitoring rule is possible. Deep-learning can be helpful for trend analysis by accumulating data.

In brief, the suggested method in this paper is capable of managing congestion with minimized message overhead.

ACKNOWLEDGMENT

This research was supported by the MSIT (Ministry of Science and ICT), Korea, under the ITRC (Information Technology Research Center) support program (IITP-2018-2017-0-01633) supervised by the IITP (Institute for Information & communications Technology Promotion)

REFERENCES

[1] Network working group, "TCP Congestion Control", Purdue University, 2009.

[2] A. l-Najjar, S. Layeghy, M. Portmann, "Pushing SDN to the End-Host, Network Load Balancing using OpenFlow", IEEE 13th International Workshop on Managing Ubiquitous Communications and Services, pp. 1-6, 2016.

[3] U. Krishnaswamy et al., "ONOS: An open source distributed SDN OS," 2013. [Online]. Available: http://www.slideshare.net/umeshkrishnaswamy/open-networkoperating-system

[4] Z. Bozakov, A. Rizk, D. Bhat and M. Zink, "Measurement-based Flow Characterization in Centrally Controlled Networks", IEEE INFOCOM 2016, pp. 1-9, 2016.

[5] H. Kim and N. Feamster, "Improving network management with software defined networking", IEEE Communications Magazine, pp.114–119, Feb. 2013.

[6] M. R. Nascimento, C. E. Rothenberg, M. R. Salvador and M. F. Magalhães, "Quagflow: partnering quagga with openflow", In ACM SIGCOMM Computer Communication Review ,Vol. 40, No. 4, pp. 441-442, 2010.

[7] Software-Defined Networking (SDN) Definition, ONF (Open Networking Foundation), Available: https://www.opennetworking.org/sdn-resources/sdn-definition/

[8] A. l-Najjar, S. Layeghy and M. Portmann, "Pushing SDN to the End-Host, Network Load Balancing using OpenFlow", IEEE 13th International Workshop on Managing Ubiquitous Communications and Services, pp. 1-6, 2016.

[9] Software Defined Networking, TechCentral, Available: http://www.techcentral.ie/software-defined-networking/

[10] Hamilton, J. D. (1994). Time series analysis (Vol. 2). Princeton: Princeton University Press.

[11] A. Tootoonchian, M. Ghobadi, Y. Ganjali, "OpenTM: Traffic matrix estimator for openflow networks", University of Toronto, p.201–210, 2010.

[12] L. Maccari, and R. L. Cigno, "Messages for Faster Route Convergence Pop-Routing: Centrality-based Tuning of Control", IEEE INFOCOM 2016, p.694, 2016.

[13] Z. Su, T. Wang, Y. Xia and M. Hamdi, "FlowCover: Low-cost Flow Monitoring Scheme in Software Defined Networks", In IEEE Global Communications Conference 2014 (GLOBECOM 2014), pp. 1956-1961, 2014

[14] S. Song, J. Lee, K. Son, H. Jung and J. Lee, "A congestion avoidance algorithm in SDN environment", IEEE 30st Intnternational Conference on in Information Networking (ICOIN 2016), pp. 420-423, 2016.

[15] L. Xie, Z. Zhao, Y. Zhou, G. Wang, Q. Ying and H. Zhang, "An Adaptive Scheme for Data Forwarding in Software Defined Network", IEEE. 2014 Sixth International Conference on Wireless Communications and Signal Processing (WCSP), pp. 1-5.

[16] S. Basu, A. Mukherjee and S. Klivansky, "Time series models for internet traffic", In IEEE INFOCOM'96, pp. 611-620, 1996.

APPENDIX

Traffic predictor (Added)

```
Public boolean TrafficPredictor(port, currentspeed, maxspeed)
  Make list of fifty current speed samples. If the list is not set, return
currentspeed;
  Expected speed = getArima(current speed list);
  If (expected speed > max speed)
    Return true; Return false; }
Public List<Port> getCongestionExpectedPort(){
  For(about all existing ports in topology);
    Get current speed, maxspeed, port number from each port statistics using
DeviceService's getPortstatistics;
    If(TrafficPredictor(port,currentspeed,maxspeed) == true)
      Return the list of ports;}
```

LinkService (Modified)

```
Public Iterable<Link> getInActiveLinks(){
  Return list of links its state is inactive; }
Public boolean RecognizeLinkisCongested(Link link){
  If (link is connected to getCongestionExpectedPort()'s port list)
    Return true;
  Else{ Return false; }
Public Iterable<Link> getCongestionExpectedLinks(){
  for(all existing links){
        if(RecognizeLinkisCongested(link)==true);
          return link list which is connected to congested port;}
Public Iterable<Link> getAllCongestionLinks(){
  Return list of links which is already congested + lists of links which is
expected to be congested;}
```

DeviceService (Modified)

```
Public Iterable<Device> getAllCongestionDevices(){
  Return list of devices which has congested link + list of devices expected
to be congested;}
Public Iterable<Device> getCongestionDevices(){
  For(all existing devices)
    If( RecognizeDeviceCongestion(deviceId)==true){
     Return list of devices;}
Public Iterable<Device> getCongestionExpectedDevices(){
     For(all existing devices)
    If (RecognizeDeviceisExpectedCongestion (deviceId)==true){
     Return list of devices;}
Public boolean RecognizeDeviceisExpectedCongestion(DeviceId deviceId){
  For(all links of this device)
    If ( RecognizeLinkisCongested(links)==true)
     Return true; Break; return false; }
Public boolean RecognizeDeviceCongestion(DeviceId deviceId){
     For(all links of this device)
    If ( link state is inactive
     Return true;
     Break; return false; }
```

ReactiveForwarding (Modified)

```
Flow Time out = DEFAULT_TIMEOUT;
phase or already has congestion
For(all links which are members of selected path){
  If( link is in getAllCongestionLinks){
   FlowTimeout = DEFAULT_TIMEOUT / 2;}}
InstallRule;
```

MeterStatsCollector (Modified)

```
Public void run(Timeout timeout){
  adaptvieInterval = DEFAULT;
if(this device is in getAllCongestionDevices){
  adaptiveInterval = DEFAULT / 2;}
timeout.getTimer().newTimeout(adaptiveInterval); }
```

Network Function Virtualization Experiments using SONATA Framework

Andra Țapu, Cosmin Conțu, Eugen Borcoci
University POLITEHNICA of Bucharest – UPB
Bucharest, Romania
Emails: andratapu@elcom.pub.ro, cosmin.contu@elcom.pub.ro, eugen.borcoci@elcom.pub.ro

Abstract — **Network Function Virtualization (NFV) represents a novel and strong technology to support the development of flexible and customizable virtual networks in multi-tenant and multi-domain environment. Open issues still exist for architectural, interoperability, design and also related to implementation and experimental aspects. This paper presents two experiments in which a virtual firewall and a graph of virtual routers have been integrated in two different topologies and have been tested using SONATA framework.**

Keywords — Network Function Virtualization; Software Defined Networking; Cloud computing; SONATA; Containernet; Docker.

I. Introduction

Network Functions Virtualization (NFV) is an emerging powerful concept, as well as a technology. It aims to solve some of the current telecommunication world limitations, problems and challenges, like large number of proprietary hardware appliances dedicated to specific services, lack of flexibility and dynamicity, low interoperability, high capital and operational expenditures: capital expenditure (CAPEX), operational expenditure (OPEX), energy consumption and installation space issues [1][2]. NFV decouples the hardware appliances from the network functions that are running over them, by using generic hardware (servers, storage and switches) and running the network functions over virtual machines installed on this generic equipment.

Based on virtualization, NFV allows faster development and deployment (compared to traditional approach) of services composed of network functions that can be implemented in virtualized way. Different virtualized network functions can be deployed or moved using the same infrastructure, created, modified and deleted without needing to physically visit a site to change the hardware supporting those network functions.

The CAPEX and OPEX can be reduced, due to software development (taking advantage of the growing IT industry). Energy consumption reduction is also possible, if a clever power management and migration plan for the virtual machines (VM) is designed.

Software Defined Networking (SDN) [3] is a complementary technology to NFV. The main concept of separating the control plane from the data plane creates high flexibility, programmability and network technology abstraction. This approach offers powerful capabilities for the management and control functions. While independent of each other, SDN and NFV can cooperate in order to construct powerful and flexible systems in cloud computing and networking areas.

According to ETSI [4][5], the NFV architecture is divided into four main functional blocks: *Network Function Virtualization Infrastructure (NFVI)* which contains the physical resources and their abstraction (virtual resources constructed by a virtualization layer); *Virtual Network Functions* (VNF) which defines different functions that can be composed in services; *Management and Orchestration* (MANO) which provides the orchestration and the lifecycle management of the network functions and infrastructure; *Operations and Business Support Systems* (OSS/BSS).

Numerous studies, realizations, projects, proofs of concepts, demos are currently developed in NFV, SDN areas [6][7]. There are still open issues which exist for such technologies and these are related to architectural aspects, to use cases, service creation and composition, manageability, virtualization methods, performance obtained in dynamic and mobile environment, scalability, implementation aspects and selection of the software technologies applicable, multi-domain features, security.

In terms of *Development and Operations* (DevOps), [8] several problems are recognized to exist, like: SDN/NFV infrastructures are not yet stable; Virtual Network Functions (VNFs) are not sufficiently interoperable with orchestrators; multi-vendor environments are not certified; the number of services for which the SDN/NFV framework brings very strong benefits in marketplaces is not yet so large; SDN/NFV combination is difficult and does not offer easy E2E multi-site support; frequently, there is a need for some additional development; key features like network slicing are not yet completely clarified; auto VNF scalability, SP recursiveness, VNF intelligent placements, security, etc., are other open research issues.

Therefore more extensive experiments with SDN/NFV frameworks are necessary to further clarify different development aspects.

The EU H2020 project *Service Programming and Orchestration for Virtualized Software Networks* (SONATA) [9] is a relevant example and offers a framework allowing DevOps oriented to SDN/NFV area.

The main purpose of this paper is to develop experiments based on SONATA framework in order to understand the capabilities of the framework, to test its scalability for using it to develop and test some custom VNFs.

The paper is organized as follows. Section II is an overview of related work. Section III shortly presents the architecture of SONATA framework. Section IV contains the results of the experiments done with SONATA framework and all the steps taken. Section V presents conclusions and future work.

II. RELATED WORK

This section shortly presents a selective view on some related work dedicated to service development and orchestration in virtualized networks and its relation to SONATA architecture, when applicable. It is split in brief overview firstly on EU-funded collaborative projects, opensource solutions and commercial solution provided.

UNIFY [10] (*EU-funded Collaborative Projects*) architecture is similar to those of ETSI-MANO and *Open Networking Foundation* (ONF)-SDN. Its objective is to reduce operational costs by removing the need for costly onsite hardware upgrades, taking advantage of SDN and NFV. Across the infrastructure one can develop networking, storage and computing components, through a service abstraction model. The UNIFY global orchestrator consists of algorithms used for optimization of elementary service components across the infrastructure. The project exposes the fact that all the resource orchestration related functionalities existing in a distributed way in the MANO SONATA framework, can be logically centralized, when there is an abstraction combination of compute, network and storage resources.

Even if the main idea of a recursive service platform is specific both for UNIFY and SONATA, the implementation is different. First, the recursiveness in UNIFY is obtained as a repeatable orchestration layer for each infrastructure design, while within SONATA is implemented as a repeated deployment of a complete SONATA platform. Another difference is related to the service specific functionality: in UNIFY it is added by developer inside a Control Network Function (NF), as a dedicated part of the Service Graph, running in the infrastructure; in SONATA the service functionality is obtained using plugins in the service platform which means that it is mandatory not to be on the same infrastructure where the Virtual Network Function (VNF) is running.

OpenStack [11] is an *open source project*, mainly written in Python, that provides an *Infrastructure as-a-Service* solution through a variety of loosely coupled services. Each service offers an API that facilitates the integration. Due to its variety of components, the current version of the OpenStack not only provides a pure *Virtual Infrastructure Manager* (VIM) implementation, but spans various parts of the ETSI-NFV architecture. OpenStack is made up of many different moving parts. Because of its open nature, additional components can be joined to OpenStack in order to meet specific needs. *OpenStack Keystone* [12], for instance, offers authentication and authorization not only to the VIM part, but it can be integrated to other services as well. *OpenStack Ceilometer* [13] provides a pluggable monitoring infrastructure that consolidates various monitoring information from various sources and makes the available to OpenStack users and other services. *OpenStack Tacker* [14] aims at the management and orchestration functionality described by ETSI-NFV.

The overall architecture relies on message buses to interconnect the various OpenStack components. To this end, OpenStack uses the *Advanced Message Queuing Protocol* (AMQP) [15] as messaging technology and an AMQP broker, namely either RabbitMQ [16] or Qpid [17], sits between any two components and allows them to communicate in a loosely coupled fashion. More precisely, OpenStack components use *Remote Procedure Calls* (RPCs) to communicate to one another. The OpenStack architecture has been proven to be scalable and flexible. Therefore, it could act as a blueprint for the SONATA architecture.

From SONATA's perspective, OpenStack is used as being supportive and complementary. For the SONATA developers there is the need to have access to a running OpenStack installation to use the capabilities of a VIM for running services from the Service Platform.

Another option for service developers when it comes to SONATA is the SONATA's emulation platform to locally prototype and test complete network service chains in realistic end-to-end scenarios. The emulator of SONATA supports OpenStack-like API endpoints to allow carrier-grade MANO stacks (SONATA, Open Source MANO) to control the emulated VIMs.

To raise their NFV holding, commercial vendors have started to market solutions for the orchestration layer. Even if they created their own NFV context, the first generation of NFV Orchestrator (NFVO) is based off ETSI MANO specifications. But there are also several orchestration solutions developed by established network vendors to further expand a larger NFV ecosystem [18].

From SONATA's perspective, the NFV orchestration concept meets the commercial solutions from the following points: to the complete VNF and network service lifecycles, including onboarding, test and validation, scaling, assurance and maintenance. Vendor marketing material and white papers present their upcoming products as holistic solutions for both service and network orchestration, compatible with current ETSI MANO specifications.

These orchestration solutions are commonly part of a fully integrated NFV management platform, including NFVO, VNFM, NFVI and extended services such as enhanced monitoring and analytics. For example, IBM's SmartCloud Orchestrator can be integrated with its counterpart solutions, SmartCloud Monitoring and IBM Netcool Network Management System, providing an end-to-end offering.

III. SONATA FRAMEWORK

In order to make this paper self-contained, this section very shortly presents the SONATA framework architecture [19] along with its objectives, use cases and features.

SONATA main goal is to develop a NFV framework that provides to third party developers a programming model, a suite of tool for virtualized services integrated with an orchestration system. SONATA allows to achieve a reduced time-to-market of networked services, to optimize and reduce the costs of network services (NS) deployment.

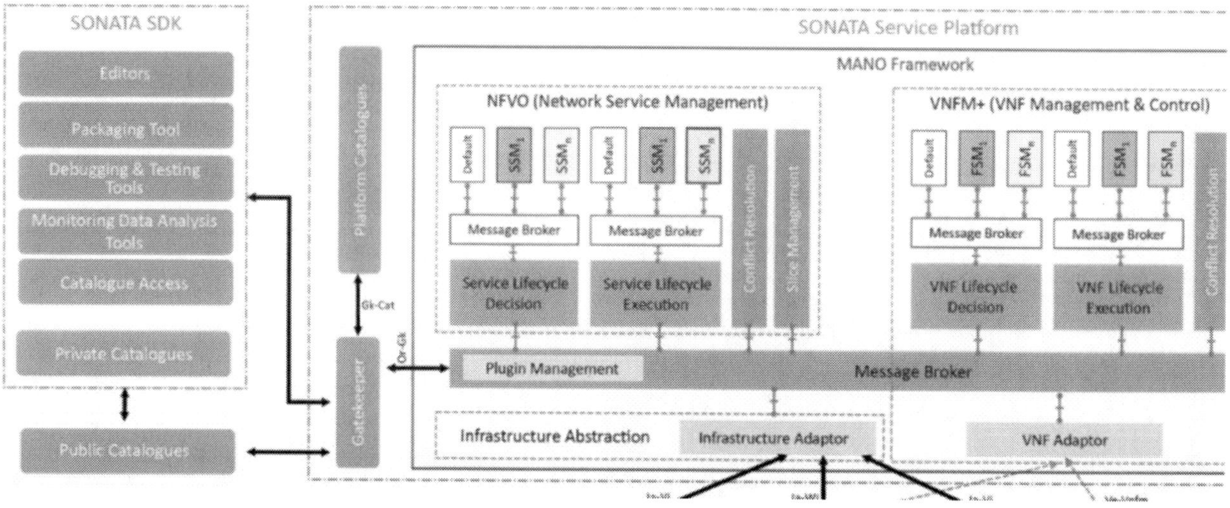

Figure 1. SONATA Framework [19].

The general architecture of SONATA framework, as it can be seen in Figure 1, contains the following components: Software Development Kit (SDK), the Service Platform (SP) and different catalogues in which one can find different system artefacts.

The SDK helps the third-party developers to create complex services composed of multiple VNFs, with a set of software tools and also supports service providers to deploy and manage their created NSs on multiple SONATA SPs.

The Service Platform (SP) is responsible for management and control of network functions and services. It is a modular and customizable environment in which the platform operators can create specific platforms appropriate for their business model, by replacing components of MANO plugins. This environment is also flexible from service developers' perspective which can customize their own services through *Function Specific Managers* (FSMs)/*Service specific managers* (SSMs). Service platform is a component where the users are created and authorized, NS and function descriptors are validated and stored.

The Catalogues consist of network function and services information like code, executables, configuration data and other requirements. These catalogues are divided into private, service platform and public catalogues.

SONATA runs directly on the top of an infrastructure which may belong to the service platform operator or to a third-party operator. To assure the communication between SP and infrastructure, the Virtual Infrastructure Managers (VIMs) are used (example: OpenStack) whose role is to abstract the infrastructure resources.

IV. EXPERIMENTS WITH SONATA

This section presents NFV experiments whose purpose is to test the functionality of different VNFs in various topologies using SONATA framework.

These topologies are represented as custom emulated networks which use Docker [20] containers as compute instances to run VNFs. Moreover, these experiments are developed around SONATA framework and using some specific tools as:

a) Virtual Machine (VM) : the experiments are running on a VM of 80GB storage on a 64 -bit Ubuntu distribution ready to use which has been downloaded from SONATA repository [18]

b) Containernet [21]*:* it is a ramification of Mininet network emulator which allows to create network topologies using Docker containers.

c) Opensource utilities: to create and test the VNFs needed in the proposed topologies, the following collection of utilities has been used: "*iptables*"[22], "*iproute*", "*bridge-utils*", "*traceroute*", "*inetutils-ping*".

d) SONATA emulator (son-emu): this is a part of SONATA SDK and it is based on MeDICINE emulation platform. MeDICINE is intented for service developers who can create network service chains and then test them in realistic emulated environments.

A. *Virtual Firewall Experiment*

a) *Main objectives:* create a virtual firewall which has the purpose to block the traffic between two hosts.

b) Topology: the topology explained in Figure 2 contains data centers (DC) in terms of point of presence (PoP) which can be defined as specific emulated hardware by installing docker images which contain the VNFs. In this experiment three DCs have been used as following:

- Two hosts (dc1 and dc2)
- Firewall (dc3)

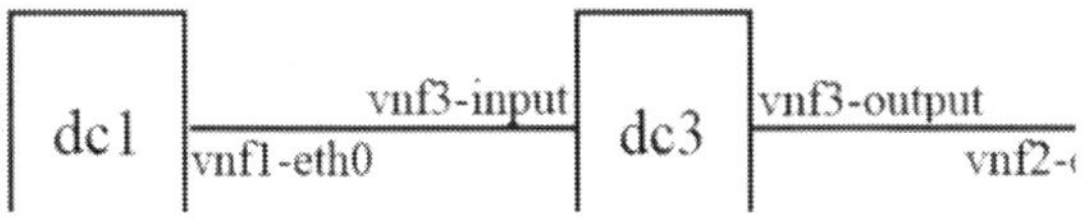

Figure 2. vFw Experiment Topology

The subnet 10.0.0.0/8 has been used together with the "bridge-utils" utility on dc3 to make the communication between dc1 and dc2 possible. Utility "iptables" has been used to create the "DROP" rule for the traffic which is forwarded by dc3.

c) *Tests and results:* first step was to deploy the topology and then instantiate and start the VNFs on each DC as can be seen in Figure 3:

```
root@demo:/home/sonata# son-emu-cli compute list
+--------------+-------------+-------------------+------------------+
| Datacenter   | Container   | Image             | Interface list   |
+==============+=============+===================+==================+
| dc2          | vnf2        | ubuntu:trusty     | vnf2-eth0        |
+--------------+-------------+-------------------+------------------+
| dc3          | vnf3        | vfw-iptables-img  | input,output     |
+--------------+-------------+-------------------+------------------+
| dc1          | vnf1        | ubuntu:trusty     | vnf1-eth0        |
+--------------+-------------+-------------------+------------------+
```

Figure 3. vFw Experiment compute list

Further, the "DROP" rule has been added for vnf3 and the connectivity between the two hosts (vnf1 with 10.0.0.7 on interface vnf1-eth0 and vnf2 with 10.0.0.5 on interface eth2) has been tested.

If the "DROP" rule is removed, it can be seen in Figure 4 that the two hosts can communicate with each other:

```
containernet> vnf3 iptables -D FORWARD -j DROP
containernet> vnf1 ping -c3 vnf2
PING 10.0.0.5 (10.0.0.5) 56(84) bytes of data.
64 bytes from 10.0.0.5: icmp_seq=1 ttl=64 time=61.7 ms
64 bytes from 10.0.0.5: icmp_seq=2 ttl=64 time=62.0 ms
64 bytes from 10.0.0.5: icmp_seq=3 ttl=64 time=62.0 ms

--- 10.0.0.5 ping statistics ---
3 packets transmitted, 3 received, 0% packet loss, time 2002ms
rtt min/avg/max/mdev = 61.781/61.947/62.045/0.118 ms
```

Figure 4. vFw Experiment ping without "DROP" rule

When "DROP" rule is added then the whole traffic between the 2 hosts does not exist anymore. This rule is exposed in Figure 5:

```
containernet> vnf3 iptables -A FORWARD -j DROP
containernet> vnf1 ping -c3 vnf2
PING 10.0.0.5 (10.0.0.5) 56(84) bytes of data.
--- 10.0.0.5 ping statistics ---
3 packets transmitted, 0 received, 100% packet loss, time 2025ms
```

Figure 5. vFw Experiment ping with "DROP" rule

B. *Virtual Routers Graph Experiment*

a) *Main objectives:* create a small network of virtual routers which will forward traffic through a network graph between three hosts from three different subnets.

b) Topology (Figure 6): it consists of six DCs using two different docker images, one for the virtual routers and another for virtual hosts.

- Three hosts (dc1, dc2 and dc3)
- Three routers (dc4, dc5 and dc6)

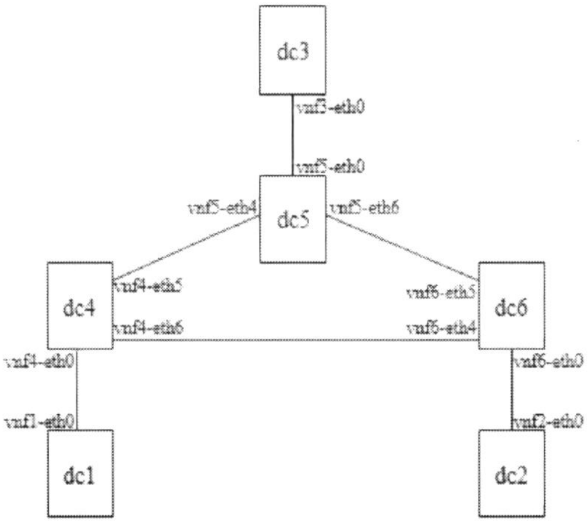

Figure 6. vRouters Graph Experiment Topology

Routing tables (containing static routes) have been made for the entire topology using "iproute" utility. The hosts are assigned within the subnets 11.0.0.0/8, 12.0.0.0/8, 13.0.0.0/8 and the subnets between routers are 10.0.0.0/8 (dc4-dc5), 20.0.0.0/8 (dc5-dc6) and 30.0.0.0/8 (dc4-dc6).

c) *Tests and results:* after deploying the topology, the VNFs were instantiated and started on each DC and the links between them were also added as ilustrated in Figure 7:

```
root@demo:/home/sonata# son-emu-cli compute list
+--------------+-------------+-------------------+------------------------------------
--------+
| Datacenter   | Container   | Image             | Interface list
        |
+==============+=============+===================+====================================
========+
| dc6          | vnf6        | vnat-iptables-img | vnf6-eth0,vnf6-eth5,vnf6-eth4
.s1-eth5 |
+--------------+-------------+-------------------+------------------------------------
--------+
| dc4          | vnf4        | vnat-iptables-img | vnf4-eth0,vnf4-eth5,vnf4-eth6
.s1-eth5 |
+--------------+-------------+-------------------+------------------------------------
--------+
| dc5          | vnf5        | vnat-iptables-img | vnf5-eth0,vnf5-eth4,vnf5-eth6
.s1-eth6 |
+--------------+-------------+-------------------+------------------------------------
--------+
| dc2          | vnf2        | vhost-iptables-img | vnf2-eth0
        |
+--------------+-------------+-------------------+------------------------------------
--------+
| dc3          | vnf3        | vhost-iptables-img | vnf3-eth0
        |
+--------------+-------------+-------------------+------------------------------------
--------+
| dc1          | vnf1        | vhost-iptables-img | vnf1-eth0
        |
+--------------+-------------+-------------------+------------------------------------
```

Figure 7. vRouters Graph Experiment compute list

Another way to visualize, as in Figure 8, and monitor the state of the topology and output of *son-emu-cli* is through web-based emulator dashboard:

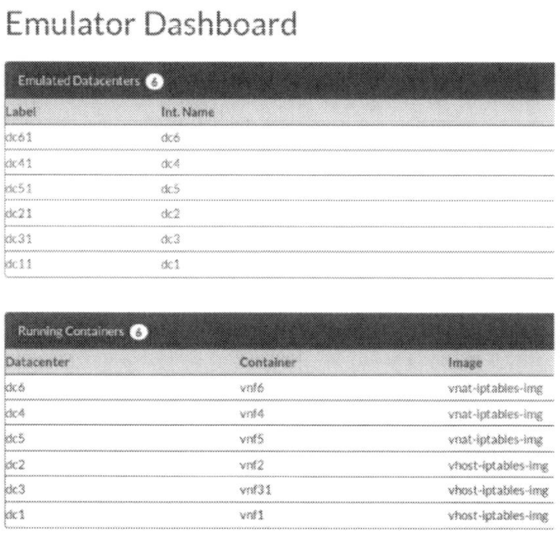
Emulator Dashboard

Emulated Datacenters 6	
Label	Int. Name
dc61	dc6
dc41	dc4
dc51	dc5
dc21	dc2
dc31	dc3
dc11	dc1

Running Containers 6		
Datacenter	Container	Image
dc6	vnf6	vnat-iptables-img
dc4	vnf4	vnat-iptables-img
dc5	vnf5	vnat-iptables-img
dc2	vnf2	vhost-iptables-img
dc3	vnf31	vhost-iptables-img
dc1	vnf1	vhost-iptables-img

Figure 8. vRouter Graph Experiment emulator dashboard (partial view)

For dc4 vRouter there are two routes with different generic metrics: the route via interface vnf4-eth5 has metric 20 and via vnf4-eth6 has metric 10. (same settings were made respectively on dc6 since static routing is in place). A shortest path route selection is supposed.

To verify the functionality of the experiment, a traceroute between dc1 and dc2 hosts has been made and it can be seen in Figure 9 that the traffic has been forwarded through the route with the lowest metric (10):

```
containernet> vnf1 traceroute vnf2
traceroute to 12.0.0.1 (12.0.0.1), 30 hops max, 60 byte packets
1  11.0.0.2 (11.0.0.2)  20.589 ms  20.560 ms  20.552 ms
2  30.0.0.2 (30.0.0.2)  82.123 ms  82.116 ms  82.109 ms
3  12.0.0.1 (12.0.0.1)  123.580 ms  123.574 ms  123.569 ms
```

Figure 9. vRouters Graph Experiment traceroute metric 10

If the interface vnf6-eth4 is down and the link between dc4 and dc6 is stopped, it can be observed in Figure 10 that traffic will be forwarded through the route with metric 20 (the only one now remained) when a traceroute between dc1 and dc2 is made again:

```
containernet> vnf6 ifconfig vnf6-eth4 down
containernet> vnf1 traceroute vnf2
traceroute to 12.0.0.1 (12.0.0.1), 30 hops max, 60 byte packets
1  11.0.0.2 (11.0.0.2)  22.001 ms  22.025 ms  22.028 ms
2  10.0.0.2 (10.0.0.2)  43.172 ms  43.165 ms  43.157 ms
3  20.0.0.1 (20.0.0.1)  84.176 ms  84.168 ms  84.160 ms
4  12.0.0.1 (12.0.0.1)  125.179 ms  125.171 ms  125.163 ms
```

Figure 10. vRouters Graph Experiment traceroute metric 20

Although the above experiments are rather simple, they illustrate a complete successful sequence of steps to define, instantiate and then run VNF-based topologies on the complex SONATA framework. Modification of the operational parameters are also demonstrated.

V. Conclusions and Future Work

This paper presented two NFV experiments using SONATA SDK framework in which it was tested the functionality of two VNFs: a virtual firewall which blocks and filters the traffic between two endpoints and a graph of virtual routers configured to be able to route traffic according to metrics in a static routing configuration.

For the development of these experiments, SONATA architecture has been chosen for multiple reasons: complexity framework, appropriate platform to develop VNFs and to test, explore and emulate virtual networks and topologies.

Beyond the results of these two experiments presented in section IV, there can be proved also the fact that SONATA can:

- offer an open source simulation environment which can be transformed as well into a production environment for the developers who have the need of it
- be a flexible and dynamic test platform and a good support in NFV area
- be able to reduce costs by removing the need of dedicated hardware

As future work, several other experiments will be done using more complex topologies for testing the scalability of SONATA framework. Other area of experiments development is intended to use the emulator within the SONATA NFV eco system to create multiple chained VNFs and descriptors grouped as "network service packages" which will be deployed and uploaded on the SONATA NFV platform and emulator.

Following this direction, after the completion of the proposed future experiments and getting a deeper knowledge of SONATA framework capabilities, the final scope would be to develop and test new VNFs.

References

[1] NFV White paper: "Network Functions Virtualisation, An Introduction, Benefits, Enablers, Challenges & Call for Action. Issue 1". Available from: https://portal.etsi.org/NFV/NFV_White_Paper.pdf [retrieved: February, 2018].

[2] R. Mijumbi et al., "Network function virtualization: State-of-the-art and research challenges", IEEE Commun. Surveys Tuts., vol. 18, no. 1, pp. 236-262, 1st Quart. 2016.

[3] B. N. Astuto, M. Mendonca, X. N. Nguyen, K. Obraczka, and T. Turletti, "A Survey of Software-Defined Networking: Past, Present, and Future of Programmable Networks", Communications Surveys and Tutorials, IEEE Communications Society, (IEEE), 2014, 16 (3), pp. 1617 – 1634.

[4] NFV White paper: "Network Functions Virtualisation (NFV) ,Network Operator Perspectives on Industry Progress. Issue 1".Available from: https://portal.etsi.org/NFV/NFV_White_Paper2.pdf [retrieved: February, 2018].

[5] ETSI GS NFV 002: "Network Functions Virtualisation (NFV); Architectural Framework". Available from: http://www.etsi.org/deliver/etsi_gs/NFV/001_099/002/01.02.01_60/gs_NFV002v010201p.pdf [retrieved: February, 2018].

[6] S. Van Rossem et al, "Deploying elastic routing capability in an sdn/nfv-enabled environment", 2015 IEEE Conference on

Network Function Virtualization and Software Defined Network, pp. 22-24, 2015.

[7] ETSI Plugtests Report: "1st ETSI NFV Plugtests, Madrid, Spain, 23rd January–3rd February". Available from: https://portal.etsi.org/Portals/0/TBpages/CTI/Docs/1st_ETSI_NFV_Plugtests_Report_v1.0.0.pdf [retrieved: February, 2018].

[8] J.Martrat, "SONATA approach towards DevOps in 5G Networks", SDN World Congress, 2017, Hague. Available from: http://sonata-nfv.eu/content/sonata-approach-towards-devops-5g-networks-0 [retrieved: February, 2018].

[9] S. Dräxler, H. Karl, M. Peuster, H. R. Kouchaksaraei, M. Bredel, J. Lessmann, T. Soenen, W. Tavernier, S. Mendel-Brin, and G. Xilouris, "Sonata: Service programming and orchestration for virtualized software networks," in 2017 IEEE International Conference on Communications Workshops (ICC Workshops), May 2017, pp. 973–978

[10] Mario Kind et al. "Deliverable 2.2: Final Architecture". Available from: https://www.fp7-unify.eu/files/fp7-unify-eu-docs/Results/Deliverables/UNIFY%20Deliverable%202.2%20Final%20Architecture.pdf [retrieved: February, 2018].

[11] The OpenStack Project. OpenStack: The Open Source Cloud Operating System. Available from: http://www.openstack.org/ [retrieved: February, 2018].

[12] The OpenStack Project. Openstack keystone developer. Available from: http://www.openstack.org/developer/keystone [retrieved: February, 2018].

[13] The OpenStack Project. Openstack ceilometer developer. Available from: http://docs.openstack.org/developer/ceilometer [retrieved: February, 2018].

[14] The OpenStack Project. Openstack tacker: An open nfv orchestrator on top of openstack. Available from: https://wiki.openstack.org/wiki/Tacker [retrieved: February, 2018].

[15] OASIS. Advanced messaging queuing protocol. Available from: https://www.amqp.org/ [retrieved: February, 2018].

[16] Pivotal Software. RabbitMq - Messaging. Available from: https://www.rabbitmq.com [retrieved: February, 2018].

[17] Apache Software Foundation. Qpid.Available from: https://qpid.apache.org/ [retrieved: February, 2018].

[18] Containernet and SONATA Emulator Demo. Available from: https://github.com/sonata-nfv/son-tutorials/tree/master/upb-containernet-emulator-summerschool-demo [retrieved: February, 2018].

[19] SONATA. D2.2 Architecture Design.Available from: http://sonata-nfv.eu/sites/default/files/sonata/public/content-files/pages/SONATA_D2.2_Architecture_and_Design.pdf [retrieved: February, 2018].

[20] Docker - Build, Ship, and Run Any App, Anywhere. Available from: https://www.docker.com/ [retrieved: February, 2018].

[21] Containernet. Available from: https://containernet.github.io/ [retrieved: February, 2018].

[22] The netfilter.org "iptables" project.Available from: http://netfilter.org/projects/iptables/ [retrieved: February, 2018].

[23] M. Peuster, H. Karl, and S. v. Rossem: "MeDICINE: Rapid Prototyping of Production-Ready Network Services in Multi-PoP Environments". IEEE Conference on Network Function Virtualization and Software Defined Networks (NFV-SDN), Palo Alto, CA, USA, pp. 148-153. doi: 10.1109/NFV-SDN.2016.7919490. (2016)

Implementation Problems Facing Network Function Virtualization and Solutions

Krishna Gandhi
School of Information Technology
Illinois State University
Normal, IL, USA
e-mail: kgandh1@ilstu.edu

Jihad Qaddour
School of Information Technology
Illinois State University
Normal, IL, USA
e-mail: jqaddou@ilstu.edu

Abstract- **Network administrators prefer the Network Function Virtualization (NFV) concept as it is cost-efficient and easy to maintain. However, the new technologies based on this concept might lead to security threats, such as denial of service attacks, availability attacks, exploitation, malware injection, or other undiscovered threats. Network Functions Virtualization represents a very large paradigm shift in the development and the deployment of network services. Many research works on NFV address the virtual concept. It can be a cloud or a virtual private server. The security is the most important thing since the virtual environment can also be compromised by cyber-attacks. The paper focuses on the problems facing NFV implementation and offers ways of navigating through the main security related problems stated above.**

Keywords-Network Function Virtualization (NFV); Virtual Network Function (VNF); Cloud Security Alliance (CSA); Software-Defined Networking (SDN).

I. INTRODUCTION

The evolution of cloud computing has led to an increase in cyberattacks targeted towards individuals, corporations or any vulnerable entity within the cloud system. The increase in the attacks forces bodies such as the Cloud Security Alliance (CSA) to convene and deliberate on the best ways to secure the systems, making them impervious to cyber attacks. One area facing the blow of cyber attacks is the network function virtualization. In computing, the term virtualization can be applied to storage devices, operating systems, hardware platforms, computer network resources and much more. The evolution of technology allows the virtualization of nearly all computer software and hardware. Basically, nearly all network functions can be virtualized. In this article, we explore virtualization in network functions. Moreover, there will be mentions of Software-Defined Networks (SDN), which alter the network function behaviors and allow dynamic changes in the configurations of a network [1]. Network function virtualization, commonly referred to as NFV, is a concept recently introduced with numerous goals, like reducing overall cost, ease of management, scalability, and also reducing the proprietary hardware required during the launch or operation of network services [2]. If the concept is implemented successfully, most of the network services will launch and operate virtually decoupling the functions of dedicated hardware devices in a network, such as firewalls, routers, and load balancers.

The concept relies on a hypervisor that controls the network functions making it easier to run them on the standard X86 servers. The implementation of the NFV makes the network administrators work easier by eliminating the need for dedicated hardware devices when building a service chain, thus reducing the operating expenses (OPEX) and capital expenses (CAPEX) since the services will run on a virtual machine. Moreover, NFV gives the network administrators agility and flexibility when troubleshooting errors in the system or when performing the routine maintenance. SDN and NFV are different, yet complementary techniques applicable by network administrators: the NFV infrastructure allows SDN to run, enabling it to forward data packets to and from network devices, while the control functions run on a Virtual Machine (VM) [3]. The implementation of NFV creates various challenges and complexities in the security controls of networks.

According to Amogh et al. [4], the CSA addresses some problems that exist when implementing NFV, regardless of the benefits it conveys such as cost reduction, agility, and flexibility. There are six problems evident according to the authors, and they include (1) scalability of available resources, (2) stateful versus stateless inspection, (3) service insertion, (4) hypervisor dependencies, (5) dynamic workloads, and (6) elastic network boundaries. The six problems revolve around the security of network function virtualization and if each of them is not addressed individually, the incompleteness of configurations, lack of integrity and lack of clearness defining security policies can lead to attacks like denial-of-service. In NFV implemented environments, stateful inspection of data-flow in the network requires asymmetric flows which allow seeing every data packet in transit, granting access controls to NFV, and stateless inspection fails to see all the data packets in transit making it difficult to grant access controls to NFV. The problem brings about security issues since the NFV does not know or have access to the data packets in transit. Service insertion into the NFV relies on overlay models that fail to coexist across the vendor boundaries, allowing the implementation of NFV to be vulnerable to the security breach. Insertion of services in NFV requires existing layered services in the hypervisor, causing it to be difficult to deal with asymmetries in the network, which arise from their creation by redundant network devices and paths. To ensure security is top-notch, vendors must all agree on standards addressing security issues. The implementation of NFV makes the understanding of the underlying architecture difficult for the vendors, leading to the production of different hypervisors for different systems. It is imperative for the vendors to come in unison to ensure the security vulnerabilities are non-existent such as, patching vulnerable code that risks security breaches. Recent changes in network topology make it difficult for traditional security methods to evolve as per the current demand; additionally, traditional methods are static compared to NFV, which is dynamic and agile in its capabilities. Unlike the traditional methods, NFV has no defined boundaries; its capabilities can expand as far as the network administrators can fathom. Traditional methods are bound by cable lengths, location and much more, creating a definite boundary. The lack of clear boundaries puts the network systems at risk in matters pertaining to security.

In the paper, the focus is on the security issues that may arise or exist during or after the implementation of NFV. The paper is organized into four sections: Section II discusses literature review, Section III presents a comparative study, Section IV performs an analysis and discussion, Section V describes the proposed solution, while Section VI concludes the paper and suggests possible future developments.

II. LITERATURE REVIEW

According to research, NFV is a major milestone in the networking and telecommunications sector. Stringent laws govern the administration of NFV enabling the availability, security, and superb performance of the concept. NFV revolutionizes the telecommunications and construction networks by reducing the costs incurred purchasing new gadgets or hardware and increasing the automation of systems. Some challenges of NFV implementation include the reliability of additional software, the effective key escrow for the functions of the hosted network, reduced isolation of the functions in a network, and fate-sharing resulting from multi-tenancy [5].

According to the article by Yang and Fung [6], *a survey on security in network functions virtualization*. The authors acknowledge NFV as an emerging innovation that focusses on the removal of hardware equipment responsible for various network functions. The removal of the hardware equipment gives room for the implementation of virtual machines running on cloud computing infrastructure that takes on the tasks tasked with the hardware equipment. As a result, there is a reduction in the energy consumption and equipment costs. Additionally, the authors acknowledge that the rate of innovation poses risks for the NFV and they focus their paper on the emerging security challenges and issues. Yang and Fung present various techniques for overcoming the challenges by offering security products and solutions to tackle the rising insecurities. They explore future works applicable to the security issues accompanying NFV implementation after conducting a survey on NFV security use cases. The paper is in line with what our research entails and therefore is a chief resource in our work. The use of various research methods gives insight on the directions we should take while tackling the topic. The authors suggest that the main contribution of NFV is the realization of software-based NFs such as virtual gateways and firewalls, unlike the traditional methods where hardware appliances were key to the realization of networking.

The paper addresses most of our research and offers research methodologies used in the conclusion of the findings. Moreover, the paper focusses on the security issues revolving around the implementation of NFV in the modern systems and offers various ways of mitigating past the security issues. The information is crucial to our research as it gives us a guideline on how the paper should be and what it should address unlike other related research papers published by different authors. Yang and Fung conducted a survey similar to what the paper will use to gain credible data on the issue of security in the network function virtualization implementation.

According to Raina et al. [7], the implementation of NFV has resulted in the adoption of advanced security measures to curb the rise in security vulnerabilities resulting from the amalgamation of the traditional methods and NFV. Virtualization addresses some of the deployed network security functions focused on reducing the vulnerabilities arising from the adoption of NFV [7]. The security measures focus on malware protection, access control, denial-of-service protection, access and identity management, intrusion prevention and detection, and cryptography. Malicious computer experts target systems with poor security measures in the hope of accessing valuable information that they may use to their gain or conduct fraudulent activities. For example, a bank scenario where the bank has recently adopted the use of NFV with little or no security measures may compromise the personal information of its clients. Malicious people may try to secure crucial data linked to the customers' accounts and transfer huge amounts of funds to their accounts making the bank vulnerable to litigations, customer distrust, or closure. The data presented is credible to some extent since most the stated challenges are still a challenge to date. The paper addresses the problems and challenges related to the paper thus it is a vital reference material.

According to Han, Gopalakrishnan, Ji, and Lee [8], the introduction of NFV was to reduce the time taken to market novel services and improve the flexibility of the provision of the network system. NFV aids in the decoupling of software implementations from underlying dedicated hardware. In the article, the authors explain the architectural framework and requirements of NFV and later discuss the challenges experienced and the available opportunities for innovation. In relation to the topic, we will look into the challenges of NFV. The authors clearly state that network administrators ought to be careful when implementing NFV in existing systems to ensure security features are unaffected. Elements such as hypervisors and orchestrators pose a security threat to the network system when wrongly implemented and lead to a rise in the intrusion. An increase in intrusion forces the system to concentrate on intrusion prevention mechanisms, which lead to an overload of the intrusion detection systems. However, when correctly implemented, NFV makes work easier for all concerned parties and allows the possibilities of virtualized firewalls creation and domain protection thus increasing the security of the network system. Virtualizing network resources poses risks since applications and services rely on the virtual machine to complete commands, for instance, when a service is bugged and requires certain resources from the virtual machine, it can easily infect the core of operations thus increasing the spread of the bug or virus within the network.

According to T. Qasim [9], research on NFV machine learning the huge population communication services is leading to the heavy loaded signaling system. It uses Signaling System No 7 (SS7). SS7 was protected due control owned by state-owned telecommunication operators. SS7 and network function virtualization have introduced many new security challenges. There can be some vulnerability in a virtualized environment. There should be many methods that mitigate machine learning techniques from gathering network traffic [9]. The research done by A. Kalliola and S. Lal developed security orchestration in NFV environment and is crucial. It represents Distributed Denial of Services attacks and other cyber-attacks. The most important finding is that it can mitigate future variation of attacks. These are all done by machine learning orchestrating virtualized network functions around the affected components to isolate those components and redirect, capture and filter the traffic for further analysis. This would allow maintaining a high quality of service to given network functions [10].

Network Function Virtualization security is a vast area of concern in many forms. Most of the NFV researches done with an example are scenarios, especially research conducted for Distributed DoS attack mitigation [9]. It implements an SDN enable network in the OpenStack environment and demonstrates and explains the effectiveness with various kinds of attacks [Figure 1]. The mitigation architecture was designed and implemented for the cloud environment. It used underlying software-defined network elements for attack mitigation and view of traffic.

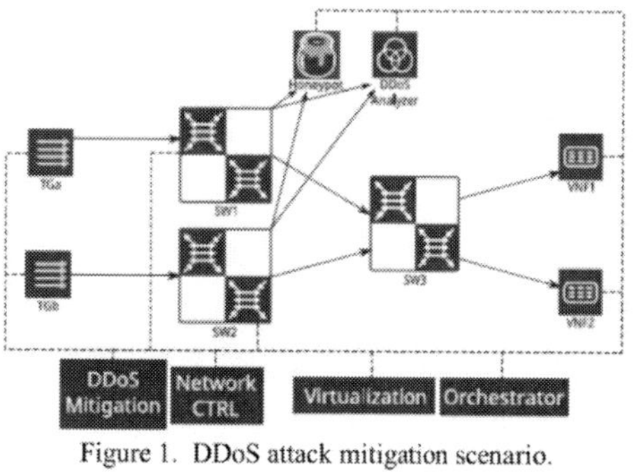

Figure 1. DDoS attack mitigation scenario.

SS7 network vulnerability detection of NFV using machine learning [10] also uses proper simulation to present the many attacks. Machine learning techniques are proposed as a detection mechanism. The experimental setup has implemented to provide proof of concept [Figure 2]. SS7 traffic is generated in a properly setup virtual environment. DoS and man in the middle attacks are launched on the network.

There are many advantages if it presents in a virtual environment because real devices do not get the actual effect of the attacks. Using automation software such OpenStack provides real benefits to visualize the real attack.

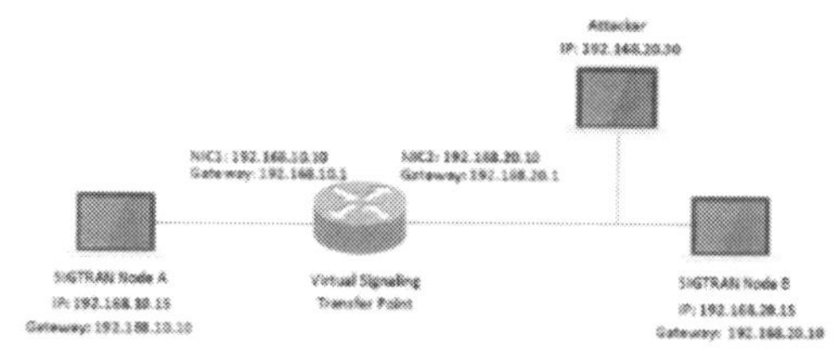

Figure 2. Simulation Setup.

According to F. Reynaud et al. [16], the network functions come to resolve many network several issues which come with the growth of the infrastructure, as power consumption, difficulties to manage the environment, elevated costs, low dynamism and scalability and misconfiguration proneness. To break those paradigms the virtualization and softwarization emerged. European Telecommunications Standard Institute (ETSI) created it to simplify the management and reduce costs of networking hardware as well since before it the companies have to buy one or more equipment for each network function. The clearest advantage of using it is the reduction of costs, but it has also many advantages as a facility on the network management using a centralized programmable controller. It reduces the complexity of management and allows more flexible and fewer errors on network configuration. However, there are some problems related to attack vulnerabilities when using the standard. One of them is DDoS, which brings many problems as opened ports and direct denial of services running since the resources are not really unlimited. The traffic can be identified, but it needs a 3rd party resource to work. Another Man in the Middle attack which is possible when a proper authentication mechanism does not exist is a case of an attack that will fatally put the NFV down.

The last attack we refer to here is the Network Visibility Poisoning, an attack that may come from several security breaches as Host Location Hijacking, Link Fabrication Attacks or insufficient protection from the northbound applications. There is another 3rd application which can work side by side with NFV and helps it to check the integrity of the packets.

According to T. Dimitrakos [17], NFV brings even more advantages to the users such as the increase of time to market and services fast deployment, the scalability of services that can be up or down rapidly as required. Based on the document [17], the standard makes the virtualized infrastructure go along with the market challenges delivering good features, fast, reliable and easier than traditional solutions. One of the main quotations of T. Dimitrakos [17] is if the NFV standard can maintain traceability to threats, challenges and customers, standards and compliance requirements. Since we are very near to the big expansion of Internet of Things (IoT), the NFV must come as an interesting solution for decentralized environments and networks, since it can be deployed inside or together with the virtual machine and its components.

Some of the NFV challenges according to him are that it would be very hard to put high-end security functions, the intelligent management of the specific traffic designated to Virtual Network Functions. Another challenge is that, since the SDN (controller) must intercept, steer and mirror traffic for security inspection since it is asynchronous, maybe the NFV function cannot work properly.

T. Thanh et al. [18] built a specification called MANO, which consists in automatization of known NFV that makes it more reliable when in use. MANO seeks to automate the learning of NFV model and resolve many security problems. The simple security framework consists of Security Planning, Security Enforcement, and Secure Monitoring, and every part of this schema feeds the other, making a stronger and faster security solution for NFV. The Security Enforcement and Monitoring work together mitigating the risks and feeding the Security Planning layer for better updates and deployments. They had some success making a two-sided management system, which could work with Access Control and Decision-making lists, using OpenBaton, a toolkit that implements a current ETSI NFV MANO. They provided virtual infrastructure and monitored it using ZABBIX. They had great results using it with the developed application and there were gains on Embed Security Functions, a security protection that can be embedded automatically and transparently to a virtual infrastructure. Security Management Lifecycle Support, which makes the security policy, adapts itself to application lifecycle and Dynamic Security Incident Response that adapts in case of DoS attack or other unforeseen events (Zero-Day Threats).

The article does not address all the challenges we identified arising from the implementation of NFV. However, the paper gives a comparative study of the work done so far and also gives the direction on the future works possible from the implementation of network function virtualization.

III. COMPARATIVE STUDY

A comparative study is presented in TABLE 1. The table is showing different security problems in NFV and the solution proposed as a summary.

TABLE I. COMPARATIVE STUDY IN NFV SECURITY

Year	Security Problems in NFV	Solutions	Challenges
2017	Security Adaptability of NFV environment [18]	A toolkit named OpenBaton was used which consists in identifying network threats, generating security policies and makeing an active monitoring of network packets, adapting the rules according to the properties of packets on the ports monitored.	Build a Hypervisor using this feature embedded and transparent, it could be expensive and take some time to be made.
2015	Network visibility poisoning of NFV standard	Two 3rd solutions can be used within NFV standard to solve this problem. One of those is Rosemary [19] that is an SDN controller that resolves the lack of access control and authentication for the applications responsible for the Link Deletion attack by employing a sandbox approach (App Zone). Another solution is TopoGuard [20] that uses Topology Update Checker to verify the legitimacy of a host migration, the integrity/origin of an LLDP packet and switch the port property once detecting a topology update	The complexity of implementing the two 3rd party applications must be a problem since no Hypervisor is using it.
2016	Side Channel Attacks to the VM frequency [16]	To defend against this attack it is required to eliminate or reduce the signal information generated by the channel or introduce some kind of noise to the channel.	Some organizations already have this functionality embedded into their systems. The only challenge is to find the most efficient system in the market.
2009	Denial of Services at forwarding plane level [16]	The feature FlowVisor [21] reads the traffic in slices, it learns and read the packets over the network and receive an update from the network controller and applies the new rules to a specific slice of the network. This feature can prevent the Denial of Services from affecting the whole environment since it can block the traffic at a small part of the packet or sequence.	When receiving a DoS attack it is hard to differentiate between the attack packets and normal packets.
2018	Signaling System 7 attacks in NFV [9]	SIGTRAN protocol and MTPSec, IPSec and an enhanced firewall combined with the intrusion detection feature are the proposed solutions to identify and mitigate the SS7 attacks.	The solutions for signaling system 7 attack are quite expensive and not easy to implement in the VM environment making it impracticable.
2017	Access Control Management in NFV[18]	ETSI NFV MANO specifications can automatically update the system policies, making the access control stronger and self-managed into the systems.	This is based on theoretical logic and did not process in actual NFV environment.

III. ANALISYS AND DISCUSSION

Based on the comparative study performed, we found that SS7 attack in NFV is the biggest security challenge because it is the newest released attack. Due to solution implementation cost and configuration complexity, the solution for SS7 becomes impracticable. This also has four big breaches divided into User Information, Eavesdropping, Financial Thievery and Misuse of Service. Considering SS7 is a silent attack, it can leak multiple information and protocols, for example, Logical Application Part (CAP). When a Man-in-the-Middle attack is launched on the SS7 layer, the attacker intercepts the traffic and makes the router busy in processing inconsistent packets while it sends the attack packets to the full traffic. This action may steal data in various levels of communication since it can capture network packets and application layer packets as well.

IV. PROPOSED SOLUTION

NFV can be improved in many ways. One of them, which we consider most important, is putting encryption of the traffic across the NFV environment will protect it against many threats such as SS7. Our proposed solution is embedded integration of Hypervisors with IPS and IDS systems. Since they can monitor the network and auto create policies to defend the environment, this can be the best solutions for newer attacks as signaling systems 7. Another point is that with the data created by IPS and IDS systems, the researchers will have the capability to understand and improve security quickly and efficiently.

V. CONCLUSION AND FUTURE WORK

The NFV findings reveal that the concept is widely accepted by various individuals mainly due to its reduction in cost and dedicated hardware. However, NFV faces or gives rise to various security concerns as it is open to some security breaches and it is not capable to avoid a DDoS attack, for example. Organizations that use NFV systems can have better performance than those using the traditional computer networking systems. Since NFV is vulnerable to a dangerous attack such as SS7, it is highly recommended that the network specialist ensure to have a good firewall combining IPS and IDS features, since we do not have an embedded hypervisor OS yet. Also, there is a huge growth of IoT devices globally. Solutions such as NFV will often need to make new equipment connected to the Internet viable, so the investment in upgrades is needed, especially thinking about threats and concerns, for example, SS7 attack over NFV, since SS7 is one of the biggest security challenges for NFV environment since it exploits the vulnerability of the communication infrastructure.

To implement the proposed solutions it is required a dedicated research to improve the NFV capabilities and integrate with the market security solutions as Deep Packets Inspection and Intrusion Detection Systems so we can implement a fully embedded virtual network solution. We will also be customizing an OpenStack OS that uses its own native IPS when the NFV feature is enabled, so it can grant only genuine packets and users to access the systems behind it, making it more reliable and robust.

The focus will also be on the protocols such as SIGTRAN and MTPSec which can make it easier for the NFV host to identify the threat and take some action to avoid the breach. The IPSec protocol will also be used, so its capacity to ensure the origin and destination details inside the packet can be a good option to ensure the environment security.

In the future, the above features and protocols can be tested inside the NFV environment to validate the functionality and protect against the SS7 breach.

REFERENCES

[1] M. Odini, "NFV Testing. IEEE Software Defined Networks," pp. 24 November 2016.

[2] R. Mijumbi, J. Serrat, J. Gorricho, N. Bouten, F. De Turck, and R. Boutaba. "Network Function Virtualization: State-of-the-Art and Research Challenges," IEEE Communications Surveys and Tutorials, pp. 236-262, 2016.

[3] E. Duarte and M. Hiltunen. "Workshop on Dependability Issues on SDN and NFV (DISN)," 2015 45Th Annual IEEE/IFIP International Conference On Dependable Systems And Networks, 2015.

[4] N. Amogh, A. Gelman, and M. Ulema. "IEEE SDN/NFV Standardization - IEEE Software Defined Networks," sdn.ieee.org, pp.1-5, 24 November 2016.

[5] D. Bernardo and B. Chua. "Introduction and Analysis of SDN and NFV Security Architecture (SN-SECA)," 2015 IEEE 29Th International Conference On Advanced Information Networking And Applications, 2015.

[6] W. Yang and C. Fung, "A survey on security in network function virtualization," IEEE Netsoft Conference And Workshops (Netsoft), pp.1-5, 2016.

[7] K. Raina, S. Chaudhry, A. Milenkoski, B. Jaeger, M. Harris, and S. Chasiri. et al. "Security Position Paper Network Function Virtualization," Cloud Security Alliance, pp.5-26, 2016.

[8] B. Han, V. Gopalakrishnan.,L. Ji, and S. Lee. "Network Functions Virtualization: Challenges and Opportunities for Innovation," pp.93-96, 2016.

[9] T. Qasim, M. H. Durand, A. Khan, F. Nazir and T. Qasim."Detection of signaling system 7 attacks in NFV using machine learning," IEEE 15th international bhurban conference on applied sciences & technology, 2018.

[10] A. Kalliola, S. Lal, K. Ahola, I. Oliver, and Y. Miche. "Testbed for security orchestration in an NFV environment," IEEE Conference on Network Function Virtualization and Software Defined Networks, 2017.

[11] C. L Hwang and K. Yoon. "Multiple attribute decision making: methods and applications a state-of-the-art case," Vol. 186, Springer Science & Business Media, pp.25-48, 2012.

[12] A. Tong. "An Inside Look at Winning SDN and NFV Case Studies (1st ed.)," pp.2-18, 2016.

[13] J. Buchmann. "Introduction to cryptography," Springer Science and Business Media, pp. 1-5, 2013

[14] J. Katz and Y. Lindell. "Introduction to modern cryptography," CRC Press, pp.2-4, 2014

[15] C. Buyukkoc. "SDN Initiative Creates Subcommittee to Address SDN, NFV Fragmentation-IEEE Software Defined Networks" Sdn.ieee.org, pp.1-4, 24 November 2016

[16] Reynaud, François, François-Xavier Aguessy, Olivier Bettan, Mathieu Bouet, and Vania Conan. "Attacks against network functions virtualization and software-defined networking:

state-of-the-art." In *NetSoft Conference and Workshops (NetSoft), 2016 IEEE*, pp. 471-476. IEEE, 2016

[17] T. Dimitrakos, "Security Challenges and Guidance for Protecting NFV on Cloud IaaS," 2014.

[18] T. Thanh, S. Covaci, M. Corici, and T. Magedanz. Fraunhofer Institute FOKUS, 2 Technical University Berlin Germany,"Access Control Management and Orchestration in NFV Environment."

[19] S. Hong, L. Xu, H. Wang, and G. Gu, "Poisoning Network Visibility in Software-Defined Networks: New Attacks and Countermeasures," NDSS'15, Feb. 2015.

[20] S. Shin et al. , "Rosemary: A Robust, Secure, and High-performance Network Operating System," CCS'14, Nov. 2014. Milenkoski, A., Jaeger, B., Raina, K., Harris, M., Chaudhry, S., Chair, S., ... & Liu, W. (2016). Security position paper network function virtualization. *Cloud Security Alliance-Virtualization Working Group*.

[21] R. Sherwood, G. Gibb, K.-K. Yap, G. Appenzeller, M. Casado, N. McKeown, and G. Parulkar, "FlowVisor: A Network Virtualization Layer," OpenFlow Switch Consortium, Tech. Rep, Oct.